The WordNet in Indian Languages

Niladri Sekhar Dash · Pushpak Bhattacharyya
Jyoti D. Pawar
Editors

The WordNet in Indian Languages

Springer

Editors
Niladri Sekhar Dash
Linguistic Research Unit
Indian Statistical Institute
Kolkata, West Bengal
India

Jyoti D. Pawar
Department of Computer Science
and Technology
Goa University
Taleigao, Goa
India

Pushpak Bhattacharyya
Department of Computer Science
and Engineering
Indian Institute of Technology-Bombay
Mumbai
India

ISBN 978-981-10-1907-4 ISBN 978-981-10-1909-8 (eBook)
DOI 10.1007/978-981-10-1909-8

Library of Congress Control Number: 2016943855

Printed on acid-free paper

This Springer imprint is published by Springer Nature
The registered company is Springer Science+Business Media Singapore Pte Ltd.

Preface

IndoWordNet: A Rainbow in the Indian Lexical Panorama

1. The Mission

The IndoWordNet is a consortium-mode multilingual project that was to develop WordNets for seven Indian languages, namely (in alphabetical order) Bangla, Gujarati, Kashmiri, Konkani, Odia, Punjabi, and Urdu. It is funded by the Department of Electronics Information Technology (DeitY), Ministry of Communication & Information Technology (MCIT), Govt. of India, and is executed by a consortium of nine academic institutions of India, namely the Goa University, Goa (the Consortium Leader); Indian Institute of Technology Bombay, Mumbai; Indian Statistical Institute, Kolkata; Dharmasinh Desai University, Nadiad; University of Kashmir, Srinagar; University of Hyderabad, Hyderabad; Punjabi University, Patiala; Thapar University, Patiala; and Jawaharlal Nehru University, New Delhi. The final deliverable of the project is the integrated WordNet (http://www.cfilt.iitb.ac.in/indowordnet) consisting of minimum of 30 000 linked synsets for each of the seven languages included in the project (Table 1).

The work on development of WordNet for Indian languages started in 2000 when the Natural Languages Processing group from the Center for the Indian Language Technology, Department of Computer Science and Engineering of the Indian Institute of Technology, Bombay (IIT-B), initiated an effort for developing the Hindi WordNet (http://www.cfilt.iitb.ac.in). This digital resource was made publicly available in 2006 under the GNU (http://www.cfilt.iitb.ac.in/wordnet/webhwn). It was generated with the financial support from the Technology Development for the Indian Languages (TDIL) (http://tdil.mit.gov.in/) project of the Ministry of Communication and Information Technology (MCIT), Govt. of India, and the Ministry of Human Resources Development (MHRD), Govt. of India. It was the first WordNet among the Indian languages, and the methods and strategies adopted for developing this WordNet was almost the same as that of the Princeton WordNet for English. (http://wordnet.princeton.edu/). The WordNet for other Indian languages (e.g., Indradhanush WordNet and Dravidian

Table 1 Synset generation statistics of IndoWordNet Consortium as on June 2015

S.N.	Name of Institute	Nouns	Adjectives	Verbs	Adverbs	Total
1.	Goa University (Konkani)	22,985	5644	2983	450	32,062
2.	Indian Institute of Technology Bombay (Hindi)	28,312	6090	3108	461	37,971
3.	University of Kashmir (Kashmiri)	21,041	5365	2660	400	29,466
4.	University of Hyderabad (Odia)	27,216	5273	2418	377	35,284
5.	Punjabi University and Thapar University (Punjabi)	21,573	5830	2836	443	30,682
6.	Jawaharlal Nehru University (Urdu)	21,595	5787	2800	443	30,625
7.	Indian Statistical Institute (Bangla)	27,281	5815	2804	445	36,345
8.	Dharmsinh Desai University (Gujarati)	24,896	5828	2805	445	33,974

WordNet) followed the same course of action initiated for the Hindi WordNet. A large nationwide project for building WordNets for the Indian languages was conceptualized as the IndoWordNet, which was conceived under the active guidance obtained from the WordNet Team of the IIT-B, Mumbai. The IndoWordNet, in principle, is a linked lexical knowledgebase of WordNets of 18 scheduled languages of India (in alphabetical order): Assamese, Bangla, Bodo, Gujarati, Hindi, Kannada, Kashmiri, Konkani, Malayalam, Manipuri, Marathi, Nepali, Odia, Punjabi, Sanskrit, Tamil, Telugu, and Urdu. The Indradhanush WordNet Consortium is one of the core members of the IndoWordNet Project.

2. The Learning Experience

Every research work is a journey from the known to unknown through the terrains of trials and errors with a sanguine scope for learning and knowledge gathering. Our Indradhanush project is no exception. The experience which we have gathered and the knowledge which we have gained from this consortium project may be summed up as follows.

While creating culture-specific synsets (CSS) for each member language of the WordNet, we have came across many unfamiliar concepts and ideas, which are not only unique to a particular language or a culture, but are also instrumental in the generation of new information on and insights into the multilayered fabric of human life and living. For instance, the term '*bhairavjap*' in Gujarati refers to the act of embracing death by jumping from the top of a high mountain—as a part of self-sacrificing *yajna* or prayer to the almighty which is practised by a specific religious group. Such a unique practice of the specific religious community of Gujarat is rarely known to other speech and cultural communities in India.

The border languages or adjacent languages share many cultural concepts and ideas, which are the outcomes of close cultural interactions between the communities due to their geographical proximities. For instance, many concepts in Konkani, which are also found in Marathi and Kannada, are hardly observed in other language communities. Similar situations are observed for Bangla and Odia, Kashmiri and Punjabi, or Bodo and Assamese, even though some of these languages are not always genealogically linked. It would be right in assuming the existence of such cultural meeting points between Odia and Telugu due to their geographical closeness, even though they belong to two different language families of India.

While working on CSS, we realized that there is an urgent need of pictorial representation of items and objects that are claimed to be unique to a particular culture or community. Although it is not always possible to give a picture or an image for an abstract idea or an elaborate function carried out by the members of a culture or language, it is always sensible to have images and pictures for concrete items and objects, so that people of other languages and cultures may either identify similar items and objects in their culture to record cultural and linguistic solidarity or create the new concepts properly. For instance, in Konkani, we came across a new term ‘pilot,’ which refers to a ‘machine-pulled rickshaw that is normally used as a carrier of goods and commodities in the state.’ Although it seemed to be a unique idea at the initial stage, the actual picture of the vehicle helped others to confirm that it is not a new concept, since a similar type of vehicle is also found in other cultures and language communities. For instance, look at the pictures given below:

Since it is presumed that the present WordNets will not only serve the online lexical queries of end users, but also be used for machine translation across Indian languages (as well as between English and Indian languages), it is rational that CSS should have their legitimate places in the synset database of the member languages so that cross-lingual translation and information sharing are not blocked. For instance, the concept of '*bihu*,' which is a unique cultural event of Assamese speech community, may be incorporated in the CSS of Assamese with elaborate audio-visual information and reference so that the people of other language communities can access the concept, and, if required, are able to translate (manually or automatically) the concept in their respective languages in an appropriate manner. Similar treatment may be extended to the concept of '*baishakhi*' in Punjabi, '*pongal*' in Tamil, '*onam*' in Malayalam, '*raja*' in Odia, or '*bhaadu*' in Bangla.

Sense marking of words in corpus of Indian languages does help increase the coverage of the concepts in WordNets as well as enhance their quality and utility potential of the resource. It is indeed practiced on a trial basis to see whether the senses that are recorded and presented against each synset listed in the WordNet are at all inclusive of the senses that are found to be assigned to the terms when these are actually used in language texts. Some preliminary surveys have shown that many of the senses of the synsets are not captured in the WordNets. Conversely, many of the senses that are stored in a WordNet are not always found in the corpus texts. This implies that the knowledge base as well as the senses assigned to the synsets needs to be verified, validated, and updated against the data and information retrieved from the corpora of Indian language texts.

While marking senses of words in newspaper texts, we find that newspaper texts of corpora of present-day Indian languages contain many named entities, transliterated words, item names, function words, abbreviations, acrostic words, etc., which are not incorporated in the WordNets. This raises a serious theoretical question in regard to the list of synsets included in the WordNet: Should we keep only universally approved (i.e., present across all languages) nouns, verbs, adjectives, and adverbs or should we include rare words in all parts-of-speech as well as terms of specialized domains, areas, and fields? Also the question of including non-Indian proper names and foreign names as well as non-Indian words in the synset list is a crucial issue that deserves serious attention and careful deliberation.

The making of Indradhanush WordNet is actually a long learning process of discovering India through the meanders of language diversity as well as understanding India through the terrains of cultural difference. Even if there are registered and acknowledged diversions in Indian languages and culture, the Indradhanush WordNet has taught us to imbibe the skill to bring all Indian languages under one umbrella and accommodate all conceptual diversities within a single frame of a synset. Moreover, it has taught us to develop unique ways to work in a consortium environment, where multiple teams from different institutes across the nation can work in an integrated manner to develop the resources and solve the challenges. The teleconferences among the member teams helped us realize the impact of collective team work with shared responsibilities—a unique feeling that incorporated solidarity among the members of a collective effort.

Finally, the creation of WordNet resource and WordNet home pages has given us ample opportunity and valuable experience to be creative while working. We had to be scientific in approach and artistic in attitude; informative in data and innovative in explanation; and analytic in interpretation and methodical in presentation. We had to club together both information and imagination in an innovative manner so that a lifeless and monochromatic concept becomes lively and colorful in the audio–video format of the home page.

3. Development of Tools and Utilities

Member teams of the Indradhanush WordNet have worked together to identify the problems relating to the development of the system and the resource. In the process of addressing these problems, some of the more experienced and expert members have been assigned the tasks for developing required tools and other devices:

(a) Synset Categorization Tool is developed by IIT-Bombay to choose common linkable synsets across all languages by classifying them as Universal, Pan-Indian, Language Specific, etc.
(b) Synset Creation Tool is developed by IIT-Bombay. It is an offline interface to create target language synsets by using Hindi language synsets as source data.
(c) Sense Marker Tool is developed by IIT-Bombay to track the amount of synset coverage of a WordNet in the newspaper corpus of respective Indian languages.
(d) Generic Stemmer for Indian Languages is developed by IIT-Bombay to find out possible stems of a given inflected/suffixed word used in newspaper corpus.
(e) WordNet Linkage Tool is developed by IIT-Bombay to link up Hindi WordNet with the English WordNet. The tool uses 13 different heuristics to automatically identify top 5 English synsets for a given Hindi synset.
(f) Word Sense Disambiguation Tool is developed by IIT-Bombay. It provides single access point to 9 different state-of-the-art word sense disambiguation algorithms.
(g) WordNet Content Management System (CMS) [v1.0, v2.0] is developed by Goa University. It allows creation of WordNet Web sites with versatile user interface and desired functionalities in a very short time for many Indian languages.
(h) CSS Manger Tool (v1.0) is developed by Goa University. It is a centralized Web-based tool that assists in creation of Concept-Specific Synsets (CSS) as well as manages their linkages to the WordNet of other Indian Languages. It can also be used for validation of synsets in the WordNets.
(i) Sense Marking Statistic Finder Utility Tool is developed by Goa University. It assists to find coverage statistics of the sense-marked corpus.
(j) Synset Merger Utility is developed by Goa University. It merges different synset files into one single file for synchronized access.

4. Development of Web Sites and Digital Resources

One of the primary goals of the project was to design and develop separate Web sites for the WordNet of each of the languages included in the Indradhanush project. It was a part of the primary deliverables of the project which could be directly accessed by the users as an open source resource for Indian people—the mission for which the TDIL and the DeitY, as well as the MCIT, Govt. of India, are committed to. It is a happy moment for the entire consortium to declare with some satisfaction that the all language groups have successfully developed separate WordNet home pages which are operational and globally accessible. The IP addresses of each of the WordNet Web sites are given below for general reference and access.

- Indradhanush WordNet Consortium: http://indradhanush.unigoa.ac.in/
- Bangla WordNet: http://www.isical.ac.in/~lru/wordnetnew/
- Gujarati WordNet: http://www.cfilt.iitb.ac.in/gujarati/
- Kashmiri WordNet: http://indradhanush.unigoa.ac.in/kashmiriwordnet/
- Konkani WordNet: http://konkaniwordnet.unigoa.ac.in/
- Odia WordNet: http://indradhanush.unigoa.ac.in/odiawordnet/
- Punjabi WordNet: http://punjabiwordnet.com/
- Urdu WordNet: http://indradhanush.unigoa.ac.in/urduwordnet/
- IndoWordNet Database v1.0, v2.0, v3.0—by Goa University: Relational database structure to store WordNet data and relationships.
- http://indradhanush.unigoa.ac.in/public/downloadTools/download Tools.php
- IndoWordNet API—v1.0, v2.0, v3.0—by Goa University: IndoWordNet Application Programming Interface (IWAPI) helps in providing access to the WordNet resources independent of the underlying storage technology.
- http://indradhanush.unigoa.ac.in/public/downloadTools/downloadTools
- http://www.tdil-dc.in/indowordnet/

A close look into each of the WordNet Web sites clearly shows how life, culture, custom, and history of each language is distinctly reflected in the Web site even though each Web site is developed following the same structure and composition of the Hindi WordNet Webpage. Another vital component of these Web sites is the option of feedback from the WordNet users—based on which each Webpage desires to update its content, upgrade its composition, and improve its application. In fact, future growth and application relevance of these Web sites heavily depend on how the end users utilize these resources and how these online portals are able to serve various linguistic and extralinguistic requirements of the people of the country.

5. Milestones Achieved

Several milestones have been reached in the course of the project:

- We have developed one of the largest lexical databases in digital form for seven Indian languages. The uniqueness of the lexical stock is that it is not just a compilation of lexical items in some order or other; rather, it is repository where lexical items are systematically classified based on certain predefined parameters, such as part-of-speech and lexical type.
- The lexical resource is the first of its kind in Indian languages. It is a useful free lexical resource available to general people. It is a great learning experience for a learner to find conceptually equivalent words—for a synset of his/her query—from seven Indian languages.
- It is an important part for building machine translation system across Indian languages and English. By ensuring the interlinking of synsets among the Indian languages and also with English, we can provide the basic means of translation of words.

- People who want to learn a new Indian language can use this resource effectively access logs and feedbacks bear testimony to this.
- The resource is enabler of word sense disambiguation (supervised and unsupervised) research in Indian languages. This leads to the development of state-of-the-art WSD mechanisms leading to international publications.
- It has been possible to develop standard sense-marked (annotated) corpora in Indian newspaper texts, which are useful both for WordNet and for semantic role labeling, for example, in Universal Networking Language (UNL).
- Cross-lingual Information Retrieval (CLIR) systems use linked WordNets query translation.
- Similarity computation has been possible due to WordNets.
- The bilingual and multilingual dictionaries that are in the state of compilation from the WordNet are useful for manual as well as statistical machine translation.
- Urdu is the official language of Jammu and Kashmir. Even then, there is no online Kashmiri–Urdu dictionary. The present WordNet may be used as an online Kashmiri–Urdu dictionary as well. Furthermore, it can be used as Kashmiri–English dictionary with more than thirty thousand entries.
- In fact due to the linked nature of WordNets, it has been possible to create bilingual mappings for 18 languages (18 × 17 pairs) which are freely downloadable for research purposes (http://www.cfilt.iitb.ac.in/Downloads.html).
- This project has succeeded in establishing a unique synergy between computer scientists and linguists. This cross-fertilization of disciplines, on one hand, has helped linguists understand the nature and complexities of computation, and on the other hand, has helped computer scientists, realizes the intricacies of the way natural languages operate.

6. Technological Spin-Offs

IndoWordNet has emerged as a digital lexical knowledge base of 18 different Indian languages. This resource is used in many NLP projects related to Indian languages, such as ILILMT (Indian Language to Indian Language Machine Translation), CLIA (Cross-lingual Information Access), and Indian language sentiment analysis.

Multilingualism presents a major challenge for developing a semantic Web in a multilingual country such as India, where information spread across Indian languages needs utmost care for its processing and synchronization. Since millions of people like to access relevant content in their own native tongues, it is required to form a framework or an interface which can provide scopes for information sharing and reuse across the Indian languages. In order to achieve this goal, it is important to make WordNet resources available across the Indian languages through a common representation format so that people can share data across the languages.

An offshoot of the IndoWordNet project is the semantic Web porting of Indian language WordNets. The worldwide semantic Web project aims to achieve complete interoperability and linkage of Web data (linguistic linked open data or LLOD). The steps toward this aim are (i) converting WordNets of different Indian languages into RDF format and (ii) creating resources and tools that can be used to develop semantic Web application for Indian languages. Major stages and outcomes of the project are as follows:

- Conversion of the existing IndoWordNet database to RDF (resource description language) format.
- Development of mechanism to use IndoWordNet for Multilingual semantic search.
- Development of IndoWordNet applications which can help larger population in various tasks such as computer-assisted language learning and multilingual dictionary.
- Enrichment of IndoWordNet through gamification.
- Cognitive Study of lexical and relational semantics using eye-tracking mechanism.

7. The Present Volume

This volume contains 11 research papers presented in the 2nd National Workshop of Indradhanush WordNet held at Goa University, Goa, from August 8 to August 10, 2011. Also, it includes two papers related to Tamil and Malayalam WordNets—two major components of the Dravidian WordNet which in turn is a part of the IndoWordNet.

While some papers raise theoretical questions in regard to concept definition and encapsulation in the form of WordNet synsets, majority of papers provide details of the problems faced by the researchers during the process of generating conceptually equivalent synsets in their respective languages. The problems encountered during finding equivalent of Hindi synsets and example sentences in their respective languages are discussed by quite a few authors.

In majority of the cases, the authors have not only identified the problem areas which demand serious investigation into the texture and information embedded within a synset and its elaboration, but they have also have provided some solutions to overcome these problems.

We visualize all those interested in WordNets of Indian languages to be the target users of this volume. The included papers are neither highly technical in approach, nor rigorously critical in data analysis, nor elusively intellectual in presentation of content. The book, therefore, may be used as a reference book on Indian language WordNets by one and all. It can be specifically useful for those who are working in WSD in Indian languages. It can be used by teachers who use WordNets to teach Indian languages. Moreover, language researchers, linguists, grammarians, morphologists, and language technologists, who are working in different areas of descriptive, applied, and computational linguistics, can benefit from this volume. In essence, the anthology is a valuable reading for NLP scholars, linguists, lexicographers, and language teachers.

We shall consider our efforts successful if people find this volume useful for their respective needs.

Kolkata, India — Niladri Sekhar Dash
Mumbai, India — Pushpak Bhattacharyya
Taleigao, India — Jyoti D. Pawar

Contents

Editors and Contributors

Editors

Niladri Sekhar Dash Ph.D. is an associate professor, Linguistic Research Unit, Indian Statistical Institute, Kolkata. He is also the Editor-in-Chief, *Journal of Advanced Linguistic Studies*, principal investigator of the Indian Languages Corpora Initiative-Bengali and the Digital Bangla Pronunciation Dictionary. His main areas of research are corpus linguistics, natural language processing, computational, lexicography, machine translation, WordNet design and development, lexical semantics, computer-assisted language teaching, digital language resource development, language documentation and digitization, etc.

Pushpak Bhattacharyya Ph.D. is the director of Indian Institute of Technology Patna. Previously, he was Vijay and Sita Vashee Chair Professor, Department of Computer Science and Engineering, Indian Institute of Technology Bombay, Mumbai; consortium leader of the Indradhanush WordNet in Indian languages; associate editor, *ACM Transaction on Asian Language Information Processing*; leader of multi-institute consortia projects on Indian language WordNets, Indian language search engine, and machine translation. Professor Bhattacharyya has been a visiting professor at Stanford University (2004), University of Grenoble (2005, 2009, and 2011), and distinguished lecturer at the University of Houston (2012). His research areas are natural language processing, machine learning, cross-lingual IR, information extraction, WordNet design and development, etc.

Jyoti D. Pawar is an associate professor, Department of Computer Science and Technology, Goa University, Goa. She is co-consortium leader of the Indradhanush WordNet in Indian languages. Her research areas are natural language processing (NLP), data mining, data structures, etc.

Contributors

Farooq Ahmad Department of Linguistics, University of Kashmir, Srinagar, India

S. Arulmozi Centre for Applied Linguistics and Translation Studies, University of Hyderabad, Hyderabad, Telangana, India

Brijesh S. Bhatt Department of Computer Engineering, Faculty of Technology, Dharmsinh Desai University, Nadiad, Gujrat, India

Pushpak Bhattacharyya Department of Computer Science and Engineering, Center for Indian Language Technology, Indian Institute of Technology Bombay, Mumbai, India

C.K. Bhensdadia Department of Computer Engineering, Faculty of Technology, Dharmsinh Desai University, Nadiad, Gujrat, India

Sudha Bhingardive Department of Computer Science and Engineering, Indian Institute of Technology Bombay, Mumbai, India

Bhimasena Bhol Centre for Applied Linguistics and Translation Studies, University of Hyderabad, Hyderabad, India

Dinesh Chauhan Department of Computer Engineering, Faculty of Technology, Dharmsinh Desai University, Nadiad, Gujrat, India

Niladri Sekhar Dash Linguistic Research Unit, Indian Statistical Institute, Kolkata, India

Shilpa N. Desai Konkani WordNet Team, Goa University, Panaji, India

Mansoor Farooq Department of Linguistics, University of Kashmir, Srinagar, India

Muneera Hakim Department of Linguistics, University of Kashmir, Srinagar, India

Mazhar Mehdi Hussain Centre of Indian Languages, Jawaharlal Nehru University, New Delhi, India

Salil Rajeev Joshi Department of Computer Science and Engineering, Indian Institute of Technology Bombay, Mumbai, India

Aadil Amin Kak Department of Linguistics, University of Kashmir, Srinagar, India

Ramdas N. Karmali Konkani WordNet Team, Goa University, Panaji, India

Laxmi Kashyap Department of Computer Science and Engineering, Indian Institute of Technology Bombay, Mumbai, India

M.C. Kesava Murty Dravidian University, Kuppam, India

Malhar Kulkarni Department of Humanities and Social Sciences, Indian Institute of Technology Bombay, Mumbai, India

Parteek Kumar Department of Computer Science and Engineering, Thapar University, Patiala, India

Ramesh C. Malik Centre for Applied Linguistics and Translation Studies, University of Hyderabad, Hyderabad, India

Nazima Mehdi Department of Linguistics, University of Kashmir, Srinagar, India

Panchanan Mohanty Centre for Applied Linguistics and Translation Studies, University of Hyderabad, Hyderabad, India

Kirit Patel Department of Computer Engineering, Faculty of Technology, Dharmsinh Desai University, Nadiad, Gujrat, India

Jyoti D. Pawar Konkani WordNet Team, Goa University, Panaji, India

Lata Popale Department of Computer Science and Engineering, IIT Bombay, Mumbai, India

Rizwanur Rahman Centre of Indian Languages, Jawaharlal Nehru University, New Delhi, India

S. Rajendran Department of Computational Engineering and Networking, Amrita Vishwa Vidyapeetham, Coimbatore, Tamil Nadu, India

R.K. Sharma Department of Computer Science and Engineering, Thapar University, Patiala, India

K.P. Soman Department of Computational Engineering and Networking, Amrita Vishwa Vidyapeetham, Coimbatore, Tamil Nadu, India

Shantaram W. Walawalikar Konkani WordNet Team, Goa University, Panaji, India

Chapter 1
IndoWordNet

Pushpak Bhattacharyya

Abstract India is a multilingual country where machine translation and cross-lingual search are highly relevant problems. These problems require large resources—such as WordNets and lexicons—of high quality and coverage. WordNets are lexical structures composed of synsets and semantic relations. Synsets are sets of synonyms. They are linked by semantic relations such as hypernymy (is-a), meronymy (part-of), and troponymy (manner-of). IndoWordNet is a linked structure of WordNets of major Indian languages from Indo-Aryan, Dravidian, and Sino-Tibetan families. These WordNets have been created by following the expansion approach from Hindi WordNet which was made available free for research in 2006. Since then, a number of Indian languages have been creating their WordNets. In this paper, we discuss the methodology, coverage, important considerations, and multifarious benefits of IndoWordNet. Case studies are provided for Marathi, Sanskrit, Bodo, and Telugu, to bring out the basic methodology of and challenges involved in the expansion approach. The guidelines the lexicographers follow for WordNet construction are enumerated. The difference between IndoWordNet and EuroWordNet also is discussed.

Keywords WordNet · Concept · Community · Merge · Expansion · Coverage · Minimality · Hindi

1.1 Introduction

WordNets have emerged as crucial resources for natural language processing (NLP). WordNets are lexical structures composed of synsets and semantic

---

P. Bhattacharyya (✉)
Department of Computer Science and Engineering, Indian Institute of Technology-Bombay, Mumbai, India
e-mail: pb@cse.iitb.ac.in

N.S. Dash et al. (eds.), *The WordNet in Indian Languages*,
DOI 10.1007/978-981-10-1909-8_1

relations (Fellbaum 1998). Synsets are sets of synonyms. They are linked by semantic relations such as hypernymy (is-a), meronymy (part-of), and troponymy (manner-of). The first WordNet in the world was built for English at Princeton University.[1] and then followed WordNets for European Languages: EuroWordNet[2] (Vossen 1998). Since 2000, WordNets for a number of Indian languages are getting built, led by the Hindi WordNet[3] (Narayan et al. 2001) effort at Indian Institute of Technology Bombay[4] (IITB).

In WordNet creation, the focus shifts from words to concepts. For example, surya (Sun), prithvi (Earth), jal, paanii (Water), etc., are very common concepts. After selecting a concept, all the words standing for that concept are stored as the set of synonymous words.

In what follows we first describe the general methodology used in WordNet construction in Sect. 1.2. The points made therein are substantiated through a case study of Hindi and Marathi WordNets construction in Sect. 1.3. Section 1.4 describes the process details of IndoWordNet construction. Section 1.5 describes the experiences of a few Indian languages in expanding from Hindi WordNet. Section 1.6 enumerates some guiding principles of IndoWordNet construction. Section 1.7 describes difference between IndoWordNet (IWN) and EuroWordNet (EWN). Section 1.8 concludes the paper and points to future directions.

1.2 General Methodology for WordNet Creation

The foundation of WordNet construction is relational semantics (Cruse 1986). Words and concepts can be looked upon as forming entries in a structure called the **lexical matrix**. Table 1.1 illustrates this. In the lexical matrix, rows represent word meanings and columns the forms. For example, in Table 1.1, the column F2 shows different meanings of bank, i.e. the polysemy of bank, while the rows M1 and M2 show different synonyms of bank.

It is clear from the presence of other words in the same row (e.g. depend in M1 and embankment in M2) what these meanings or senses are. This is the principle of relational semantics. Words when put together in a common set disambiguate each other. Such sets are known as synsets.

There are three principles the synset construction process must adhere to. **Minimality** principle insists on capturing that minimal set of the words in the synset which uniquely identifies the concept. For example, {*family, house*} uniquely identifies a concept (e.g. '*he is from the house of the King of Jaipur*'). **Coverage** principle then stresses on the completion of the synset, i.e. capturing all the words

[1]http://www.wordnet.princeton.edu.

[2]http://www.illc.uva.nl/EuroWordNet/.

[3]http://www.cfilt.iitb.ac.in/wordnet/webhwn.

[4]http://www.iitb.ac.in.

Table 1.1 Lexical matrix showing the word bank

Word meanings ↓	Word forms →			
	F_1	F_2	F_3	F_k
M_1	Depend	Bank	Rely	
M_2		Bank		Embankment
M_3				
...		Bank		
M_n				

that stand for the concept expressed by the synset (e.g. {*family, house, household, ménage*} *completes the synset*). Within the synset, the words should be ordered according their frequency in the corpus. **Replaceability** demands that the most common words in the synset, i.e. words towards the beginning of the synset, should be able to replace one another in the example sentence associated with the synset.

WordNets are constructed by following either the *merge approach* or the *expansion approach* (Vossen 1998). In the former—which can be said to be WordNet construction from *first principles*—exhaustive sense, repository of each word is first recorded. Then, the lexicographers construct a synset for each sense, obeying the above three principles. In the expansion approach, the synsets of the WordNet of a given source language LS are provided. Each synset is carefully studied for its meaning. Then, the words of the target language LT representing that meaning are collected and put together in a set in frequency order.

1.2.1 Comparing Merge and Expansion Approaches to WordNet Building

Both the merge and expansion approaches have their advantages and disadvantages. In the former, there is no *distracting influence* of another language, which happens when the lexicographer encounters culture- and region-specific concepts of the source language. The quality of the WordNet is good, provided the synset maker is well versed with the nuances of the language. But the process is typically slow. In the latter approach, the whole WordNet making process is well guided in the sense of following the synsets of the source language. Also it has the advantage of being able to borrow the semantic relations of the given WordNWet. This saves an enormous amount of time. However, the lexicographer oftentimes is distracted by synsets standing for highly culture- and region-specific concepts. Also common is the problem of not finding the target language's *'own concepts'*.

One finds the predominance of the expansion approach in the WordNet building community. Many concepts are common across languages. Creating synsets for these *universal concepts* should be the first step in the construction of any WordNet. If a language has already done this job, it makes sense to leverage from this work. This fact and the fact of being able to borrow the semantic relations from the source language tilt the balance in favour of the expansion approach. If the source and target languages happen to have strong kinship relationship, the expansion approach becomes all the more attractive, since distracting influences of culture- and region-specific concepts are minimal in this case.

In the next section, we present a case study to elucidate the above ideas.

1.3 A Case Study: Creation of Hindi WordNet (HWN) and Marathi WordNet (MWN)

We follow Chakrabarty et al. (2007) in this section. We have, for long, been engaged in building lexical resources for Indian languages with focus on Hindi and Marathi (http://www.cfilt.iitb.ac.in). The Hindi and Marathi WordNets (HWN and MWN) and the Hindi Verb Knowledge Base (HVKB) (Chakrabarty et al. 2007) have been given special attention. The WordNets more or less follow the design principles of the Princeton WordNet for English while paying particular attention to language-specific phenomena (such as *complex predicates*) whenever they arise.

While HWN has been created by manually looking up the various listed meanings of words in different dictionaries, MWN has been created by expansion from HWN. That is, the synsets of HWN are adapted to MWN via addition or deletion of synonyms in the synset.

Figure 1.1 shows the creation of the synset for the word *peR* 'tree' in MWN via addition and deletion of synonyms from HWN. The synset in HWN for this word is {*peR, vriksh, paadap, drum, taru, viTap, ruuksh, ruukh, adhrip, taruvar*} *'tree'*. MWN deletes {*peR,viTap, ruuksh, ruukh, adhrip*} and adds {*jhaaR*} to it. Thus, the synset for tree in MWN is {*jhaaR, vriksh, taruvar, drum, taruu, paadap*} *'tree'*. Hindi and Marathi being close members of the same language family, many Hindi words have the same meaning in Marathi. This is especially so for tatsama words, which are directly borrowed from Sanskrit. The semantic relations can be transferred directly, thus saving time and effort.[5]

1.3.1 Synset Making

The principles of *minimality, coverage,* and *replaceability* govern the creation of the synsets:

[5]Henceforth, we will use only Roman script for expressing Hindi text. This is to avoid any problem of font encoding and also for the readability of non-Hindi readers.

HWN entry:
{peR, vriksh, paadap, drum, taru, viTap, ruuksh, ruukh, adhrip, taruvar[5]} "tree"

← **synset**

jaR,tanaa, shaakhaa, tathaa pattiyo se yukt bahuvarshiya vanaspati
'perennial woody plant having root, stem, branches and leaves'

← **Gloss**

peR manushya ke lie bahut hi upayogii hai
'trees are veryuseful to men'

← **Example sentence**

MWN entry:
{jhaaR, vriksh, taruvar, drum, taruu, paadap} 'tree'

mule, khoR, phaanghaa, pane ityaadiinii yokt asaa vanaspativishesh
'perennial woody plant having root, stem, branches and leaves'

tii damuun jhaadacyaa saavlit baslii
'Being exhausted she sat under the shadow of the tree'

Fig. 1.1 MWN synset creation from HWN

(i) **Minimality**: Only the minimal set that uniquely identifies the meaning is first used to create the sysnet, e.g{*ghar, kamaraa*} (*room*)
ghar—which is ambiguous—is not by itself sufficient to denote the concept of a room. The addition of kamaraa to the synset brings out this meaning uniquely.

(ii) **Coverage**: Next, the synset should contain all the words denoting a particular meaning. The words are listed in the order of decreasing frequency of their occurrence in the corpus.
{*ghar, kamaraa, kaksh*} (*room*)

(iii) **Replaceability**: The words forming the synset should be mutually replaceable in a specific context. Consider,
Here, *svadesh* and *ghar* can replace each other (Fig. 1.2).

The replaceability criterion is observed with respect to synonymy (semantic properties) and not with respect to the syntactic properties (such as subcategorization) of a lexeme.

{ swadesh, ghar} (*motherland*)– apanaa desh (*the country where one is born*)
svadesh, ghar

amerikaa meN do saal bitaane ke baad shyaam svadesh/ghar lauTaa

America in two years stay after Shyam motherland returned

'Shyam returned to his motherland after spending two years in America'

Fig. 1.2 Illustration of replaceability

1.3.2 Lexical Relations

HWN incorporates several commonly used semantic and lexical relationships along with a few new ones.

(a) Antonymy is a lexical relation indicating 'opposites'. For instance, {**moTaa,** sthuulkaay}'fat' → {**patlaa**, dublaa} 'thin'. *Patlaa* (thin) is the antonym of *moTaa* (fat) and vice versa.
HWN indicates the criterion under which the antonymy holds. In the above example, the antonymy criterion is size. Other criteria are given in Table 1.2.
(b) Gradation is a lexical relation that represents possible intermediate states between two antonyms. For example, Fig. 1.3 shows the gradation relation among time words.
(c) Hypernymy and Hyponymy encode lexical relations between a more general term and specific instances of it.
{belpatra, belpattii, bilvapatra} *'leaf of a tree named bela'*
→ {pattaa, paat, parN, patra, dal} *'leaf'*
Here, *belpatra* (*a leaf of the bel tree*) is a kind of *pattaa* (leaf). *pattaa* is the hypernymy of *belpatra* and *belpatra* is a hyponymy of *pattaa.*
(d) Meronymy and Holonymy express the part-of relationship and its inverse.
{jaR, muul, sor} 'root' → *{peR, vriksh, paadap, drum} 'tree'*
Here, *jaR* (root) is a part of *peR* (tree), and therefore, *jaR* is the meronymy of *peR* and *peR* (tree) is the holonymy of *jaR* (root).
(e) Entailment is a semantic relationship between two verbs. A verb A entails a verb B, if the meaning of B follows logically and is strictly included in the meaning of A. This relation is unidirectional. For instance, snoring entails sleeping, but sleeping does not entail snoring.

Table 1.2 Criteria for antonymy

Criterion	Examples	Gloss
Size	(chhoTaa-badzaa, moTaa -patlaa)	Big-small, thick-thin
Quality	(achchhaa-buraa, pyaar-ghriNaa)	Good-bad, love-hatred
Gender	(betaa-beTii, maataa-pitaa)	Son-daughter, father-mother
State	(shuruu-ant)	Beginning-end
Personality	(raam-raavaN)	Rama-Ravana
Direction	(puurv-pashchim, aage-piichhe)	Eat-west, front-behind
Action	(lenaa-denaa, khariid-bikrii)	Take-give, buy-sell
Amount	(kam-jyaadaa, halkaa-bhaarii)	Little-much, light-heavy
Place	(duur-paas)	Far-near
Time	(din-raat, subaha-shaam)	Day-night, morning-evening

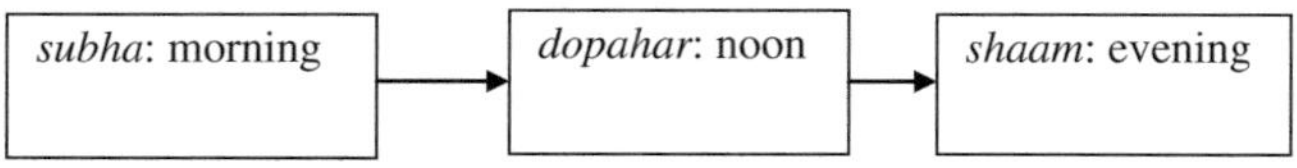

Fig. 1.3 Gradation

{*kharraaTaa lenaa, naak bajaanaa*} *'snore'* → {*sonaa*} *'sleep'*

(f) Troponymy is a semantic relation between two verbs when one is a specific 'manner' elaboration of another. For instance,
{dahaaRanaa} *'to roar'* is the troponymy of {bolanaa} *'to speak'*

(g) HWN also cross-links synsets across different parts of speech. Cross-links between 'nouns' and 'verbs' include the following:

(i) Ability link specifies the features *intrinsic to* a nominal. For example,
{machlii, macchii, matsya, miin, maahii} 'fish' → *{tairnaa, pairnaa, paunr-naa} 'swim'*

(ii) Capability link specifies the features that may be acquired by a nominal. For example,
{*vyakti, maanas*} *'person'* → {*tairnaa, pairnaa, paunrnaa*} *'swim'*

(iii) Function link specifies function(s) associated with a nominal. For example,
{*adhyaapak, shikshak*} *'teacher'* → {*paRhanaa, shikshaa denaa*} *'teach'*

Cross-links between 'nouns' and 'adjectives' are used to indicate typical properties of a noun. For example, {*sher*} *'tiger'* → {*maansaahaarii*} *'carnivorous'*. Links between morphologically derived forms mark the root form from which a particular word is derived by affixation. For example, {*bhaaratiiyataa*} *'indianness'* is derived from {*bhaaratiiya*} *'Indian'* and is linked to it.

1.4 The Process of IndoWordNet Creation

Seeing the enormous potential of WordNet, 16 out of 22 official languages of India have started making their WordNets under the leadership of IIT Bombay. These languages are as follows: (1) Hindi[6] (already discussed), (2) Marathi,[7] (3) Konkani,[8] (4) Sanskrit,[9] (5) Nepali,[10] (6) Kashimiri,[11] (7) Assamese,[12] (8) Tamil,[13] (9) Malyalam,[14] (10) Telugu,[15] (11) Kannad,[16] (12) Manipuri,[17] (13)

[6]Hindi/Khadi boli belongs to the Indo-Aryan language sub-group of Indo-European language family. It is a dialect continuum of the Indic language family in the northern plains of India. 2001 census of India noted 422,048,642 speakers of this language. It is spoken in the Indian states and union territories of Bihar, Chhattisgarh, Delhi, Haryana, Himachal Pradesh, Jharkhand, Madhya Pradesh, Rajasthan, Uttar Pradesh and Uttarakhand.

[7]Marathi is an Indo-Aryan language spoken by the Marathi people of south western India and is the official language of the state of Maharashtra. 2001 census of India noted 71,936,894 speakers of this language.

[8]Konkani is an Indo-Aryan language belonging to the Indo-European family of languages spoken in the Konkan coast of India. It has approximately 7.6 million speakers of its two individual languages, Konkani and Goan Konkani.

[9]Sanskrit is a historical Indo-Aryan language and as per the 2001 census of India, there are 6,106 speakers of this language.

[10]Nepali is a language of the Indo-Aryan branch of the Indo-European language family. 2001 census of India records 13,168,484 speakers of this language.

[11]The origin of Kashmiri language is uncertain. According to one view it belongs to the Dardic languages which form a sub-group of the Indo-Aryan languages whereas others believe that it belongs to the Iranian languages. It is spoken in eastern Afghanistan, northern Pakistan, and in the Indian region of Jammu and Kashmir. 2001 census of India recorded 5,527,698 speakers of this language.

[12]Assamese is the easternmost Indo-Aryan language. According to the 2001 census of India, there are 13,168,484 speakers of this particular language.

[13]Tamil is the only surviving classical language in the world and is a Dravidian language. According to the 2001 census of India, there are 60,793,814 speakers of this particular language.

[14]Malayalam is one of the four major Dravidian languages of South India. According to the 2001 census of India, there are 33,066,392 speakers of this particular language.

[15]Telugu is a Dravidian language mostly spoken in the Indian state of Andhra Pradesh. According to the 2001 census of India, there are 74,002,856 speakers of this particular language.

[16]Kannada is one of the major Dravidian languages of India, spoken predominantly in the state of Karnataka. 2001 census of India recorded 37,924,011 speakers of this language.

[17]Manipuri belongs to the Sino-Tibetan family of languages. It is the official language of south-eastern Himalayan state of Manipur, in north-eastern India. According to 2001 census, 1,466,705 speakers of this language are found in India.

Table 1.3 WordNets of different languages and institutes developing them

WordNet—language	Institute(s)
Assamese	Guahati University, Assam
Bengali	Indian Statistical Institute Kolkata, IIT Kharagpur and Jadavpur University
Bodo	Guahati University, Assam
Gugarati	DDU, Nadiad, Gujarat
Hindi	IIT Bombay
Kannad	Amrita University, Coimbatore
Kashmiri	Kashmir University, Srinagar
Malayalam	Amrita University, Coimbatore
Manipuri	Manipur University, Imphal, Manipur
Marathi	IIT Bombay
Nepali	Assam University, Silchar, Assam
Oriya	University of Hyderabad
Punjabi	Thapar Institute and Punjabi University, Patiala
Sanskrit	IIT Bombay
Tamil	Tamil University, Thanjavur and Amrita University
Telugu	University of Hyderabad and Dravidian University, Kuppam
Urdu	University or Hyderabad and International Institute of Information Technology, Allahabad

Bodo,[18] (14) Bangla,[19] (15) Punjabi[20], and (16) Gujarati.[21] These languages cover the length and breadth of India and are used by about 900 million people. Table 1.3 shows the WordNets and the corresponding institutes developing them.

The experiences of various language groups of building these WordNets have been presented in the 5th International Conference of Global WordNet (GWC2010) (Bhattacharyya et al. 2010).

WordNet creation for languages other than Hindi is going on using the expansion approach. Figure 1.4 below shows the big picture of the IndoWordNet.

[18]Bodo is a Tibeto-Burman language. 2001 census of India records 1,350,478 speakers of this language.

[19]Bangla is one of the major members of the Indo-Aryan family of languages, spoken by 215 million people. It is the national language of the country of Bangladesh and also the state language of the province of West Bengal in India.

[20]Punjabi is a member of the Indo-Aryan family spoken by about 88 million people. It is the state language of the province of Punjab in western India.

[21]Gujarati is a member of the Indo-Aryan family spoken by about 46 million people. It is the state language of the province of Gujarat in western India.

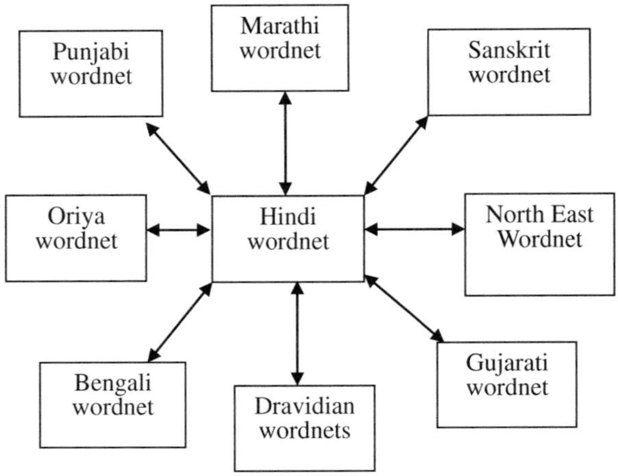

Fig. 1.4 Linked IndoWordNet structure

1.4.1 Selection of Core and Common Synsets

In the process of IndoWordNet creation, the first phase is the construction of synsets for most common concepts which are universal across languages. It was decided that all IndoWordNet members will first link to the core synsets.

To select the most common concepts from approximately 32000 synsets of HWN, the following steps were taken:

(1) Initially, 32K synsets were distributed among 6 people. Each one classified them into 4 categories, viz. (i) *Common*, (ii) *Uncommon,* (iii) *Common in Indian languages,* and (iv) *Region and language specific*. This was done with the help of a specially designed tool for synset classification. By this process, 16K synsets were filtered.
(2) These 16K synsets were again ranked by voting. 11K synsets were selected as common synsets.
(3) An online interface was provided to rank these 11K synsets by the NLP group at IIT Bombay.
(4) Bharatiya Vyavahar Kosha compiled by D.N. Narwane was used to create a set of core concepts necessary for everyday living and communication. 2000 synsets were selected as core synsets and distributed to other language groups.

Rest of the common synsets was also distributed, but these were linked only after finishing the 2000 core concepts. Table 1.4 shows the status of core and common synset linkage and the number of unique words covered thereby as on 1 March 2010.

Table 1.4 Statistics of total synsets and the unique words for WordNets of various languages

WordNet—language	#synsets/unique-words
Assamese	3530/19609
Bengali	8679/18563
Bodo	3837/13357
Gugarati	970/2125
Hindi	33900/82000
Kannad	5920/7344
Kashmiri	6569/8674
Malayalam	6154/8622
Manipuri	2744/5231
Marathi	9739/21223
Nepali	5802/10278
Oriya	To start
Punjabi	To start
Sanskrit	3340/17820
Tamil	4750/9821
Telugu	10639/18250
Urdu	6123/9641

The task of **linking the synsets of Hindi with those of English** has also been going on. As of now, 13693 synsets of Hindi have been linked with English. Efforts are also on to automatize this process of linkage.

1.4.2 Lexicographers' Interface for WordNet Building

To create a lexical resource like WordNet, one needs a user -friendly tool. Its use is made of the MultiDict tool developed at the Center for Indian Language Technology, Computer Science Department, IIT Bombay (Fig. 1.5). The tool provides an interface for linking the synsets that express the same meaning in different language. In this figure, a synset of Sanskrit meaning lotus is linked with the corresponding synset for Hindi. The left panel shows the Hindi synset and the right panel is for the synset of the target languages.

The linker tool (Fig. 1.6) is integrated in the interface for cross-linkage between the literals of source and target synsets. It allows a lexicographer to link a literal of the source language to one or more literals in the corresponding target language synset. The particular example shown in Fig. 1.6 depicts the word level linkage for words of Sanskrit and Hindi meaning *nail*.

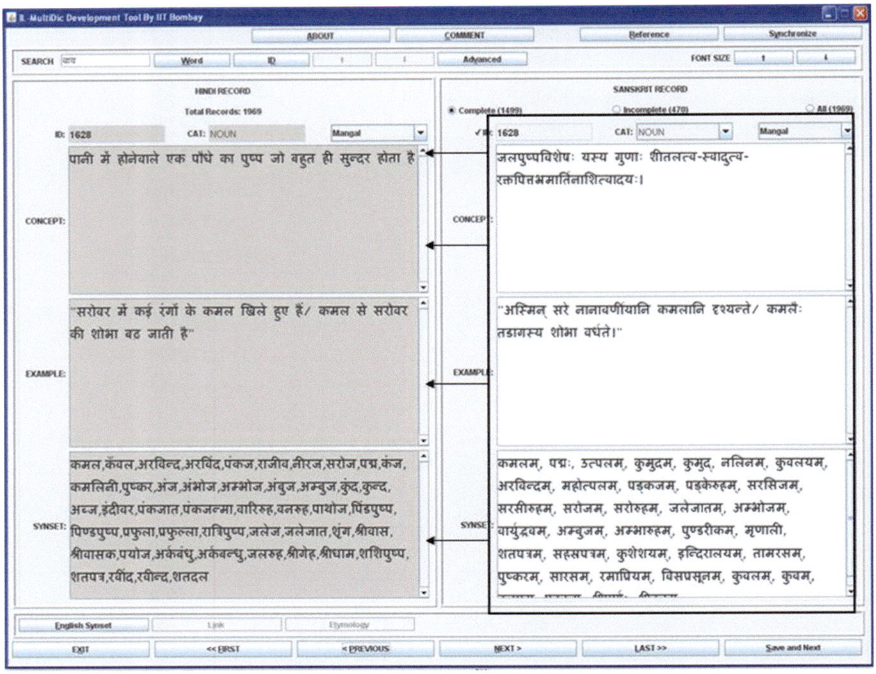

Fig. 1.5 Lexicographer's interface

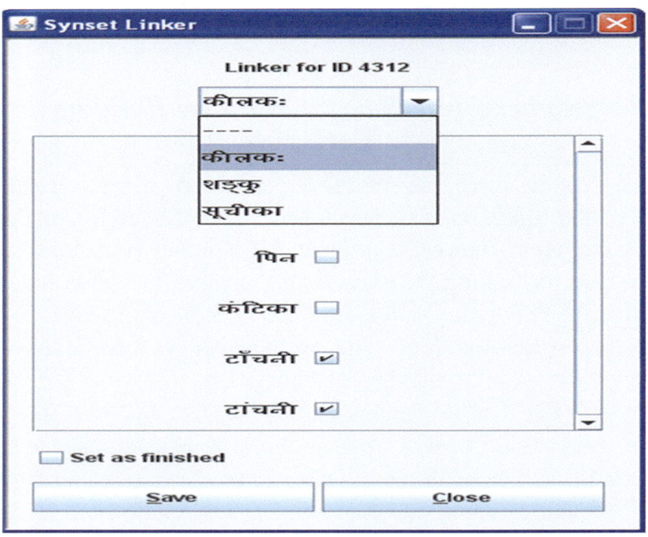

Fig. 1.6 The linker tool

1.5 Some Experiences of Lexicographers of Representative Indian Languages

Here, we record the IndoWordNet experience of three languages, by describing the challenges faced by lexicographers of these languages. We have chosen Sanskrit as a heritage language, Bodo as a member of the Tibeto-Burman family, and Telugu as a member of the Dravidian family of languages.

1.5.1 Sanskrit

Sanskrit is the oldest member of the Indo-Aryan language family, a subbranch of Indo-Iranian, which in turn is a branch of Indo-European language family. The WordNet for Sanskrit (Kulkarni et al. 2010) is being created from Hindi WordNet.

There is a traditional fourfold division of lexical units of Indian languages into:

(1) Tatsama[22]—words having their origin in Sanskrit and accepted in the modern Indo-Aryan languages without any change in their phonology.
(2) Tadbhava[23]—words which have their origin in Sanskrit, but their phonological forms are changed as per the rules of the modern Indo-Aryan languages.
(3) Deshī—words which are the native words of the particular language, and
(4) Videshī—words borrowed from foreign languages.

The links to *Tatsama* and *Tadbhava* words, in particular, will be a great pan-Indian linguistic resource for computational purposes.

The challenge faced in creating the synsets of Sanskrit WordNet in consonance with those of Hindi is mainly in finding equivalent words. For example, the word {chaaya} (tea) is a frequently used word. The concept of tea is explained as follows in the Hindi WordNet:

(1) *cAya ke paudhe kI pattiyon ko pAnI mein DAlkar cinI dUdha Adi milAkar banAyA huA peya padArtha* (A drink prepared by mixing the leaves of the tea plant with sugar, milk, and water)

But Sanskrit does not have a word of its own for this concept. Monier Williams in his Sanskrit–English dictionary (MW hereafter) suggests that *'cahA'* (which is actually is a Marathi word) should be used as a borrowed word. In the dictionary of spoken Sanskrit, we find two different regional words 'cAya' and 'cAyA' belonging to the languages of North and South

[22]Tatsama Shabda Kosha (Tatsama words dictionary) is published by Kendriya Hindi Nideshalaya, Shiksha Vibhaga, Manava Samsadhana Vikasa Mantralaya, Bharata Sarakara in 1988.

[23]See *Hindi ki Tadbhava Shabdavali* (Sarma 1968).

India, respectively. The gloss field in the synset of {kaSAyapeyaM, cAyaH, cAyA, cahA} in the Sanskrit WordNet is created as follows:

(2) *cAyaH cahA evaMvidhaiH shabdaiH bhAratIya-bhASAsu prasiddhasya kSupasya shuSka-parNAnAM cUrNam uSNajale abhipacya tasmin drave sharkarA-dugdhAdIn saMmishrya nirmitam uSNapeyam* (A hot drink which is prepared by first mixing the leaves of the plant, which is famous by the names such as *cahA and cAya.* in the Indian languages, into hot water and then mixing it with sugar and milk)

1.5.2 Bodo

The Bodo language belongs to the Tibeto-Burman branch of the Sino-Tibetan language family. It is a major language of the north-eastern part of India and has very close resemblance with the Rabha, Garo, Dimasa, Kokborok, Tiwa, Hajong, and other allied languages of north-eastern India. Bodo is a developing language. The language does not have rich linguistic and literary resources. New words and phrases are being discovered, coined, and added to the language. Few examples of synsets from Bodo WordNet (Sarma et al. 2010) are as follows:

[World, English]:	[prithvii, Hindi]: buhun, mulug, bhum, samsaAr, hAlur, baiso-mAthA, bilaThlAthA [Bodo]
[Jungle, English]:	[jangal, Hindi]:hAgrAmA, araN, hAgrA, hAgrAbAri, jAhAr, ArangA [Bodo]
[Body, English]:	SarIr, Hindi]: dehA, modom, solor, sAbtsri [Bodo]
[God, English]:	[bhagbAn, Hindi]: Isor, isAi, AnAn_gasAi, abanglAbari, abang[Bodo]

Some of the frequently encountered challenges faced by Bodo WordNet construction are as follows:

(1) Lack of proper vocabulary to mean the concept, or the example as given by the Hindi synset.
(2) Small size the Bodo synset. Two/three members synsets are very common.
(3) Multi-words in synsets which are often coined.

As is apparent, these challenges result from Bodo's relative newness as a language.

1.5.3 Telugu

WordNet for Telugu (Selvaraj 2010) is being constructed expanding from Hindi WordNet. Telugu belongs to the South Central Dravidian subgroup of the Dravidian family of languages.

The vocabulary of Telugu is highly Sanskritized in addition to the Persian-Arabic borrowings /kaburu/'It does have cognates in other Dravidan .balance'` / taraaju/Urdu ;answer'` /javaabu/ ,story'; village'` /uuru/ , tiger'` /puli/languages such as /.head'` /tala

Words in Dravidian languages, especially in Telugu, are long and complex. This is because of highly rich morphology and poly-agglutination.

In Telugu (as well as in other languages of the Dravidian family: *Tamil, Malayalam,* and *Kannad*), the lexicographers typically consult the English WordNet, even though they are expanding from the Hindi WordNet. The reason is the relatively lower level of proficiency with Hindi and much wider usage of English in the southern part of India. This is an interesting situation where both English and Hindi WordNets are consulted. IIT Bombay has provided both Hindi and English synsets for facilitating the expansion.

This gives rise to one of the main challenges in the construction of the Telugu WordNet. Sometimes, the Hindi and English synsets do not completely agree in the finer nuances of the meaning, and the lexicographers are left with the tough task of which language's meaning to choose.

The other challenge is that kinship terms differ between Hindi and Telugu. For example, for the Hindi synset with id #7379 containing the word {bhatiijaa} (meaning brother's son), Telugu has finer distinction between elder brother's son and younger brother's son. Currently, Telugu WordNet expands this particular Hindi synset into one with both these terms included, instead of the one with just {soudaaruni kumaarudu} (brother's son which is ambiguous in Telugu).

1.6 Some Guideline for IndoWordNet Construction

In developing the IndoWordNet, the following considerations have been kept in mind:

(1) WordNet's central concern is to express a concept unambiguously. To express concepts with a set of word (s), we can follow these options: (a) dictionary words, (b) transliteration (c) short phrase, and (d) coined word.

(2) Dictionary words are included in the WordNet according to the frequency of their use. Options (b), (c), and (d) are typically needed in expanding from a culture- or region-specific concept. However, these options should be used with discretion, respecting the native speakers' sensitivities.

(3) **Same synset ID has to be maintained across languages.**

(4) As for including newly coined words, it is felt that Standardization may be a problem. Coining of new words should be avoided till the method of coining and the procedure of standardization are decided. Some ways of standardization are proposed, but there is no consensus among the language groups. One possibility is to validate the words by keeping them on the Web and asking for opinions.

(5) Regarding region-specific and culture-specific words, the general policy adopted is to assign a specific **ID range** for such concepts. However, this needs synchronization among lexicographers. It was decided that IDs ranging from 0 to 50000 will be reserved for common concepts across languages. After that ID ranges will be allotted for specific languages, e.g. 50000–60000 for Marathi and 60000–70000 for Konkani.

(6) It was emphasized again and again to the lexicographers never to translate the words in the Hindi synset, but to understand the meaning expressed by the synset and its attached gloss and example sentence and then to put down the words in frequency order the words of the language.

1.7 Differences of IndoWordNet (IWN) from EuroWordNet (EWN)

The expansion approach of WordNet creation adopted and elaborated in EuroWordNet (Vossen 1998) is also the principal methodology for IndoWordNet construction. In EWN, English provided the Interlingual Index (ILI). In IWN, the same is provided by Hindi.

There are, however, some crucial differences between IWN and EWN:

(i) Right from the beginning, IWN insisted on storing lexical links expressing relationship of derivational morphology. Indian languages are rich in morphology. In Sanskrit WordNet, for example, the theory that all words are derived from verbal roots—*dhaatus*—is being seriously examined for its use as a fundamental guiding principle for storing and linking word.

(ii) *Causative verb forms* are a typically occurring phenomenon in Indian languages. For example, khaanaa (to eat), khilaana (to feed), and khilwaanaa (to cause to feed) are forms derived from the same root khaanaa. It has been decided to take special care to store causative forms in IWN and link them to their basic roots.

(iii) *Complex predicates* (CPs) (also known as complex verbs) abound in South Asian languages. They occur in the form of nominal + verb combinations (called *conjunct verbs*) and verb + verb combinations (called *compound verbs*). Key questions on complex predicates are as follows:

   (a) *Given a N(oun) + V(erb) combination, is the noun incorporated into the verb complex or is it an overt argument of the verb?*

   (b) *Given a V(erb) + V(erb) combination, is the second verb an aspectual/modal or is it the polar (intensifier) in a polar-vector combination?*

   IWN is drawing heavily on the research on complex predicates (Chakrabarty et al. 2007) and is devising means for storing them and linking them with their constituent N/V and Vs.

(iv) IWN has from the start taken cross part-of-speech linkages very seriously, especially between nouns and verbs. Ability and capability links discussed in Sect. 1.2—between nouns and verbs—are being incorporated exhaustively.
(v) IWN has finer categories for antonymy and gradation relations compared to EWN.

1.8 Conclusion

In this paper, we have described the India wide effort of creating the linked structure of Indian language WordNets—collectively called the IndoWordNet. Members of three language families spanning the length and breadth of the country are creating and linking lexical knowledge. Hindi is serving as the pivot language in this endeavour.

A key observation in this effort—which is by no means new, but important nonetheless—is that culture- and region-specific words do form a large component of the lexicography work, and provisions have to be made for their storage and linking. Language-specific ID ranges are an important step towards addressing this problem.

Our future work consists in putting in place a common background ontology for IndoWordNet. This will form the backdrop against which the synsets can be analysed for their quality.

Acknowledgments The support of the Department of Information Technology (DIT), Ministry of Communication and Information Technology, Government of India, and also Ministry of Human Resource Development is gratefully acknowledged.

References

Bhattacharyya, P., Fellbaum, C. & Vossen, P. (Eds.). (2010). Principles, construction and application of multlingual wordnets. In *Proceedings of the 5th Global Wordnet Conference, Mumbai*. India: Narosa Publishing House.

Chakrabarty, D., Sarma, V., & Bhattacharyya, P. (2007). Complex predicates in indian language wordnets. *Lexical Resources and Evaluation Journal, 40* (3–4).

Cruse, D. A. (1986). *Lexical Semantics*. Cambridge University Press.

Fellbaum, C. (Ed.). 1998. *WordNet: An electronic lexical database*. MIT Press.

Kulkarni, M., Dangarikar, C., Kulkarni, I., Nanda, A., & Bhattacharyya, P. (2010). *Introducing Sanskrit Wordnet, Global Wordnet Conference (GWC10), Mumbai, India.*

Mohanty, R., Bhattacharyya, P., Pande, P., Kalele, S., Khapra, M., & Sharma, A. (2008). *Synset Based Multilingual Dictionary: Insights, Applications and Challenges, Global Wordnet Conference (GWC08), Szeged, Hungary.*

Narayan, D., Chakrabarty, D., Pande, P., & Bhattacharyya, P. (2001). An Experience in Building the Indo WordNet—a WordNet for Hindi. In *1st International Conference on Global WordNet (GWC 02), Mysore, India.*

Sarma, S. (1968). Hindi ki TadbhavaShabdavali. College Book Depot.

Sarma, S. K., Brahma, B., Gogoi, M., & Ramchiary, M. B. (2010). A wordnet for Bodo language: Structure and development. In *Global Wordnet Conference (GWC10), Mumbai, India.*
Selvaraj, A. (2010). Telugu wordnet. In *Global Wordnet Conference (GWC10), Mumbai, India.*
Vossen, P. (Ed.). (1998). *EuroWordNet: A multilingual database with lexical semantic networks.* Dordrecht: Kluwer Academic Publishers.

Chapter 2
Insights on Hindi WordNet Coming from the IndoWordNet

Laxmi Kashyap, Salil Rajeev Joshi and Pushpak Bhattacharyya

Abstract In a multilingual country such as India, machine translation and crosslingual search are highly relevant problems. The WordNets, as crucial linguistic resources, play the most dominant role in the field of text processing and applications, such as machine learning, machine translation, information extraction, information retrieval, and natural language understanding systems. Therefore, no meaningful research in these areas can be complete without their help. This paper reports the categorization work of synsets of the Hindi WordNet (version 1.2), the challenges that were faced while doing the work, and solutions obtained for them thereafter. There are a number of concepts common to most of the languages, and linking these concepts with each other can provide an indispensable resource for Natural Language Processing and Language technology. The WordNet for Hindi language is created using the ab initio method while all the other Indian language WordNets are being created using the Hindi WordNet through expansion approach. The Hindi WordNet forms the foundation for the other Indian language WordNets as they are based on it and are being linked to it.

Keywords Language-specific synset · Hindi WordNet · IndoWordNet · In-family synset

---

L. Kashyap (✉) · S.R. Joshi · P. Bhattacharyya
Department of Computer Science and Engineering,
Indian Institute of Technology-Bombay, Powai, Mumbai, India
e-mail: yupu@cse.iitb.ac.in

S.R. Joshi
e-mail: salilj@cse.iitb.ac.in

P. Bhattacharyya
e-mail: pb@cse.iitb.ac.in

N.S. Dash et al. (eds.), *The WordNet in Indian Languages*,
DOI 10.1007/978-981-10-1909-8_2

2.1 Introduction

Among the Indian language WordNets, the Hindi WordNet (HWN) was the first one to come into existence from 2000 onward. It was inspired by the English WordNet which contains nouns, verbs, adjectives, and adverbs organized into synonym sets, each representing one underlying lexical concept. Different relations such as hypernymy and hyponymy link the synonym sets to each other. Soon, other Indian language WordNets started getting created. The WordNets for Marathi and Sanskrit followed the Hindi WordNet. All these three efforts are going on at Indian Institute of Technology, Bombay. Other Indian language WordNets are being linked to Hindi WordNet, paying particular attention to language-specific phenomena. Thus, linking Hindi WordNet to the English WordNet and then linking other Indian language WordNets to Hindi, in turn, will help to increase the linkage of concepts and will create a wide WordNet grid of shared concepts.

The Indradhanush project is formed to develop WordNets of Indian languages, which currently comprises seven major languages across India, viz., *Bengali, Gujarati, Kashmiri, Konkani, Panjabi, Oriya*, and *Urdu*. The construction of individual WordNet is carried out mostly by different Indian organizations. The **Bangla WordNet** is being created at the *Indian Statistical Institute*, Kolkata; the **Gujarati WordNet** is being created at the *DD University*, Nadiad; the **Kashmiri WordNet** is being formed at the *University of Kashmir*, Srinagar; the **Konkani WordNet** is being developed at the *Goa University*, Goa; the **Panjabi WordNet** is being generated at the *Thapar University*, Patiala; the **Odia WordNet** is being developed at the *Central University*, Hyderabad; and the **Urdu WordNet** is being developed at the *Jawaharlal Nehru University*, New Delhi.

The road map of the paper is as follows: Sect. 2.2 presents the creation of Hindi WordNet and its principles. Section 2.3 deals with the concept of categorization and relevant information. Section 2.4 describes the challenges involved in the task as well as the specific fields where they occur. Section 2.5 presents the solutions. Section 2.6 describes related tools and contains their snapshots. Section 2.7 presents the linkage statistics, and finally, Sect. 2.8 winds up discussion with conclusion and future work.

2.2 Creation and Principles of Hindi WordNet

Hindi WordNet creation started in the year 2000 with the help of a specially designed data entry tool. A common word from a Hindi dictionary is chosen. Then, the particular concept is made explicit with the help of elaborate gloss and example(s). Other synonyms according to that concept are taken and then definition, example, and ontology are added to the word. The part-of-speech is selected and, based on this, relations of the words are established.

To create a Hindi synset, three principles are adopted. They are as follows: minimality, coverage, and replaceability. However, the principle **minimality** implies that minimal sets of words are chosen to make the concept unique. For instance, both 'ghara' and 'griha' constitute a minimal set of words which denotes the concept of a 'house.'

The principle **coverage** implies that the maximal set of all possible words that stands for the sense and ordered by frequency in the corpus are included in the list of synonymous words. For instance, 'makaana,' 'sadana,' 'shaalaa,' 'aalaya,' 'dhaama,' 'niketana,' 'vaastu,' and 'paNa' are the synonymous words for the concept of 'house.'

Finally, the principle **replaceability** refers that the example sentences are such that the most frequent words in the synset can replace one another in the sentence without altering the sense, for instance, *isa ghara men paancha kamare hain* 'There are five rooms in this house.'

2.3 Categorization

2.3.1 Need for Categorization

When the IndoWordNet project started, there were about 32000 synsets in Hindi WordNet. The question arose about the set of synsets which were to be sent to language groups in which WordNets for respective languages were to be created as a part of this project. The reason for this activity was that the Hindi synsets were created alphabetically and not according to their most common uses. Since there are many uncommon synsets in the first five thousand synsets which do not have any lexeme in many of the languages falling under the project, it was difficult to send IDs serially. Hence, it was decided to categorize them according to their uses in different categories.

Synset categorization is an act of distributing synsets into categories of different kinds. This was done so that other WordNets can make the most commonly used synsets first and then go on to other categories such as (**a**) **Core**, (**b**) **Common**, (**c**) **Common in Indian language**, (**d**) **Common in Hindi**, and (e) **Uncommon**; the original categories are chosen for the purpose. This categorization was done at the IIT Bombay in March before the first IndoWordNet workshop was organized in Coimbatore from June 11 to June 14, 2009.

2.3.2 Original Categorization

In the original categorization, only **core** and **common synsets** were given more importance, since those synsets had to be linked in the first place. The **core synsets**, which are necessary for the day-to-day communication, were selected from

Bhaaratiiya Vyavahaara Kosha compiled by D. N. Naravane (1961). It is a multilingual dictionary which has lexical terms in sixteen (16) Indian languages for a particular concept. Nearly 2,000 concepts were selected as the core synsets from this book. These synsets were separated from the HWN senses.

After the core synsets, attention was devoted to **common synsets**. The common concepts were selected from remaining 32,000 synsets. The synsets were distributed among six (6) people to rank them into following categories with the help of a specially designed ranking tool (description and snapshot in Sect. 2.5): Common, Common in Indian languages, Common in Hindi, and Uncommon. In this way, 16,000 synsets were categorized as common synsets. These were again confirmed by manual voting and 12,000 synsets were finally selected in this process as common synsets.

2.3.3 Categorized Synsets to Be Linked to Other Indian Languages

The core and common synsets were the first lot of the synsets sent to the IndoWordNet group along with the off-line tool (description and snapshot in Sect. 2.6) to be linked with other Indian languages. IndoWordNet consists of *Assamese, Bengali, Bodo, Gujarati, Kannada, Kashmiri, Konkani, Manipuri, Malayalam, Marathi, Nepali, Oriya, Punjabi, Sanskrit, Tamil, Telugu*, and *Urdu* language groups (Bhattacharyya 2010).

2.3.4 Discrepancies in Categorization

The IndoWordNet language groups met at the Shillong Symposium held on April 12 to April 14, 2010, and discussed the synset categorization and raised the concerns regarding discrepancies in synsets and their categories. According to the opinion of different language groups, some synsets which were categorized as core synsets were actually belonged to common synsets category, and vice versa. Followings examples were categorized as core synsets while they should have been in the common category.

- ***anuvaada***—translation (Noun)
- ***aparaadhii***—criminal (Adjective)
- ***aastika***—theist (Noun)
- ***daana***—dotation (Noun)

In the reverse manner, the followings were categorized as common synset, while they should have been in the core category.

- ***sheranii***—lioness (Noun)
- ***saarangii***—a string musical instrument (Noun)
- ***godhulii Belaa***—dusk (Noun)
- ***karelaa***—bitter gourd (Noun)

2.3.5 New Categorization

The exercise of categorization was repeated to resolve the problems stated above. As a result, new categorization was done in May 2010 and this time synsets were categorized into six (6) categories instead of the initial four (4) categories by different WordNet groups.

The first group consisted of Gujarati and Konkani groups to whom synsets from 1 to 11,400 were given; Nepali and Punjabi groups were in second group to whom synsets from 11,401 to 22,800 were given, and third group included Telugu and IIT-B groups to whom the rest of the synsets in Hindi WordNet were given. Following are the new six (6) categories in which the synsets are divided:

(a) **Universal Synset:** Synsets which have an indigenous lexeme in all the languages of the world (e.g., *sun, earth*).
(b) **Pan-Indian Synset:** Synsets which have indigenous lexeme in all the Indian languages but no English equivalent (e.g., *paapaDa*).
(c) **In-family Synset:** Synsets which have indigenous lexeme in the particular language family (e.g., *bhatiijaa* in Dravidian languages).
(d) **Language-specific Synset:** Synsets which are unique to a language (e.g., *bihu* in Assamese)
(e) **Rare Synset:** Synsets which express technical terms (e.g., *ngram,* etc.).
(f) **Synthesized Synset:** Synsets created in the language due to influence of another language (e.g., *pizza,* etc.).

2.3.6 Challenges in New Categorization

Hindi synsets of some very core concepts did not have their counterparts in English. They, therefore, could not be categorized as Universal since the definition of it says that the concept should have an indigenous lexeme in all the Indian languages as well as in English, e.g., 'luhaarii' there is no English word for the Hindi concept of 'work of blacksmith.'

Hindi synsets having very core concept did not have the required equivalent synset in English WordNet. Therefore, these concepts could not be selected as Universal. For instance, 'soyaa huaa' 'dormant, sleeping,' but the English WordNet gives only one sense, that of lying with head on paws as if sleeping. This sense cannot be applied to humans; hence, the term cannot be categorized as a core concept. Similarly, 'anuvaada' refers to 'translation, interlingual rendition, rendering, version (a written communication in a second language having the same meaning as the written communication in a first language.' Since this sense cannot be applied to oral translation, the term cannot be categorized as a core concept.

Hindi adjectival concepts, for which mostly *-ed* and *-ing* forms of English adjectives are used, are not found in English dictionaries. Therefore, these concepts were also excluded from Universal categories, although, rightfully, they belong to here. For example, 'pisaa huaa' should be equivalent to 'milled.'

Many other Hindi words also do not find their matching terms in English lexicon. Therefore, these synsets were also not selected as the Universal synsets, for instance, 'daaniiya' 'donatable,' and the causative verb, such as 'sulaanaa' 'to make someone sleep'.

For many Hindi words that are used as adjectives as well as nouns, only noun forms are given but adjectives are not present in the English WordNet. This was another reason for excluding some synsets from Universal category although it was felt they were the core concepts, for instance, 'dalabadaloo' 'defector' (noun).

Lack of knowledge whether a synset has an indigenous lexeme in all other Indian languages or in a particular language family was also a hurdle for categorization.

Categorization of synsets between rare and synthesized categories was also not easy because of disagreement among the lexicographers, e.g., 'pneumonia' and 'diphtheria.'

2.3.7 Yet Another Categorization

Sighting the above obstructions, in the workshop held at the Indian Institute of Technology, Kharagpur, on December 8, 2010, it was decided to categorize all the 34,378 Hindi synsets again. These synsets were sent to all the IndoWordNet groups, along with a categorizer tool (description and snapshot in Sect. 2.7), in which they had following options to categorize the synsets:

(a) Yes : If an indigenous lexeme for the synset exists in the language
(b) No : If there is no indigenous lexeme for the synset in the language
(c) Not set : If the concept in Hindi is not clear to the group.

Depending on the responses from all the language groups, the following two categories were populated:

(a) **Universal synsets**: The synsets which were categorized as 'Yes' by all the groups, and also had equivalent English words or synsets, were classified here.
(b) **Pan-Indian synsets**: The synsets which were categorized as 'Yes' by all the groups, but did not have equivalent English words or synsets, were classified under this category.

2.4 Challenges in Linking

The linkage task has to do a fine balance between maintaining accuracy and providing maximum linkages. While linking with Hindi WordNet synsets, other language WordNets creator encountered several challenges. The problems have occurred because the languages belong to different language families. The specific areas where such problems were faced are listed below.

2.4.1 Challenges in Linking Synsets Across Languages

Other language groups had difficulties in linking with the Hindi WordNet synsets due to the following reasons:

2.4.1.1 Kinship Relation

Kinship relations in Hindi such as 'bhatiijaa' 'a brother's son' could not be linked directly in Dravidian languages since they have many terms to denote this concept, depending on gender of the speaker and whether the referent or speaker is elder or younger to him. In Manipuri, they have three different terms for the Hindi concept 'betaa' as a 'male child,' viz., 'nupaamachaa' for 'a boy,' 'ichaanupaa' for 'my son,' and 'machaanupaa' for 'his son' which is also a generalized term. The same kind of feature is in Bodo in the case of 'Maana.' For instance, 'bhatiijaa 'a brother's son' in Hindi has no equivalent lexeme in Telugu, but Telugu has different terms for this concept, a couple of which are mentioned below:

Telugu: Tam'muDu kumaaruDu
Hindi: (*chhote bhaaii kaa betaa*)
Meaning: 'younger brother's son'

Telugu: (Annayya kumaaruDu)
Hindi: (*bade bhaaii kaa betaa*)
Meaning: 'elder brother's son'

2.4.1.2 Change in Part-of-Speech

The predicative adjectives always become verbs in Manipuri language. Therefore, they cannot be linked as such. For instance, look at the following examples,

Manipuri: Nupi machhaa phajei
Hindi: (laDakii sundara hai)
Meaning: 'The girl is beautiful'

Some Hindi concepts cannot be linked with Sanskrit due to change in their part-of-speech in the language. However, these words are available in instrumental cases of nouns/adjectives in the same sense. For example:

Hindi: (shaantipoorvaka)
Definition: (shaanti ke saatha yaa shaanti se) (adverb)
Meaning: ‘quietly or with quietness’
Example: (aapa saba shaantipoorvaka merii baaton ko sunen)
English: ‘all of you listen to my speech quietly’

2.4.1.3 Different Terms in a Language for a Hindi Concept

There are two terms for water in Kashmiri language, whereas Hindi has only one term for water. The general term for water is ‘aaba’ and the term for drinking water is ‘tresh.’ Therefore, the question arises as to which one should be linked with the Hindi concept.

2.4.1.4 Language-specific Concept

The concepts which are very core to a language, such as its culture and food , are not there in the Hindi WordNet. So the question remains about how these terms can be linked with the Hindi WordNet. For instance, in *Marathi naoovaarii, navavaarii—naoo vaara laamba asalelaa* ‘tii naoovaari lugaDe nesate’ naoovaarii, navavaarii—which is nine yard long ‘She wears naoovaari saari.’

2.4.1.5 Challenges in Linking with English Synsets

Many challenges were encountered while linking Hindi synsets with English synsets. The problems have occurred because the two languages belong to cultures and social mores which are widely different. Musical instruments, kitchen utensils, tools, spices, grain, cast, occupation, wages, women, denoting cast and occupation, food, culture, etc. of Hindi synsets could not be linked to the English WordNet, since English does not have different terms for them (Saraswati et al. 2010), for instance, ‘tabalaa,’ ‘dhola,’ ‘mridanga,’ and ‘nagaadaa.’ There is only one term for all above-mentioned musical instruments in English which is ‘drum.’

2.5 Solutions

These were the steps taken to find solutions for the above-mentioned problems:

Fig. 2.1 Hypernymy linkages for kinship relations

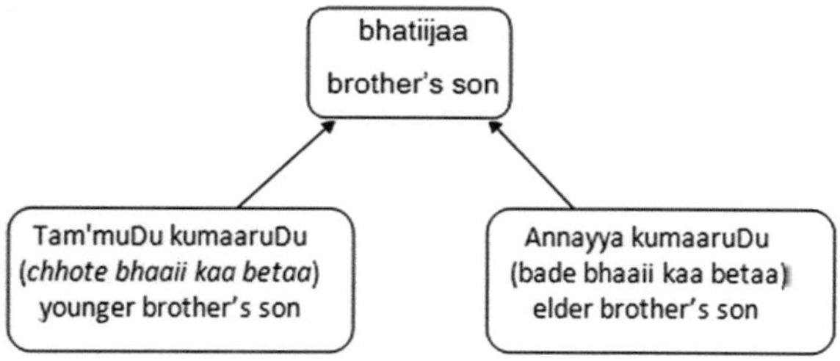

2.5.1 Kinship Relations

As mentioned above in challenges section that Hindi concept of *Bhatiijaa* could not be directly linked to some Indian languages where the gender of the speaker and youngerness or elderness of the speaker or referent plays a major role. In this case, it was decided to link the synsets of the particular language to Hindi synset of *Bhatiijaa* with a hypernymy relation, as the following diagram shows (Fig. 2.1).

2.5.2 Changes in Part-of-Speech

In Manipuri language, predicative adjectives cannot be linked as such, since in predicative position, adjectives become verb. Therefore, it has been decided that they will be changed to attributive adjectives and then the example sentences will be formed, e.g., *aada phajei nupii machaa eppii. vahaan sundar laDakii KhaDii hai*. 'A beautiful girl is standing there.'

There are Hindi concepts which cannot be linked with Sanskrit due to change in their part-of-speech in the language. However, since these words are available in instrumental cases of adjectives/nouns in the same sense, it has been decided to use the instrumental cases of sense instead of using them as adverb, e.g., 'shaantachetasaa,' 'shaantachitten,' 'shaantamanasaa,' and 'shaantahri' (instrumental cases of adjectives in Sanskrit which have been used as the adverb in language for 'shaantipoorvaka' of Hindi).

2.5.3 Different Terms in a Language for a Hindi Concept

In Kashmiri language, there are two different terms for water, one is for water in general and the other one is for drinking water, whereas Hindi has only one concept. The general term for water 'aaba' will be directly linked to the synsets for water 'paanii' of Hindi WordNet and 'tresh' which is a term for drinking water in Kashmiri will be linked to water 'paanii' of Hindi synset with a hypernymy relation, e.g., general concept of water 'aaba,' drinking water 'tresh.' The first concept can be directly linked to water 'paanii' and the second one can be linked through hypernymy to water 'paanii.'

2.5.4 Language-specific Synsets

To resolve the language-specific synsets, specific synset ids are allotted to each group. All groups will create synsets which are specific to their languages and culture in simple text file in the given id range. The groups will also generate parallel Hindi synsets for that concept in the same ids. This will be uploaded to the Hindi WordNet using the Hindi WordNet Data Entry Interface (description and snapshot in Sect. 2.6).

2.5.5 Challenges in Linking with English Synsets

To overcome the problem of Hindi–English synset linkage, this is the step taken. Hindi synsets can be linked with English synsets by two kinds of linkages, first is direct linkage and the other one is hypernymy linkage.

2.5.5.1 Direct Linkage

The Hindi synset having exact equivalents in English will be linked to them with direct linkage; e.g., 'paanii' is linked to water with direct linkage.

2.5.5.2 Hypernymy Linkage

Hindi synsets which cannot be linked directly to English concepts will be linked with hypernymy linkage; e.g., musical instruments which are part of Hindi WordNet, such as 'tabalaa,' 'dhola,' 'mridanga,' and 'nagaadaa' will be linked to 'drum' with a hypernymy relation (Fig. 2.2).

2.6 Tools for Hindi WordNet

Figure 2.3 shows the tools created at IIT Bombay for WordNet creation and maintenance along with their dependencies. Out of the tools shown in the diagram, the tools which help in WordNet creation in Hindi and other languages are discussed below.

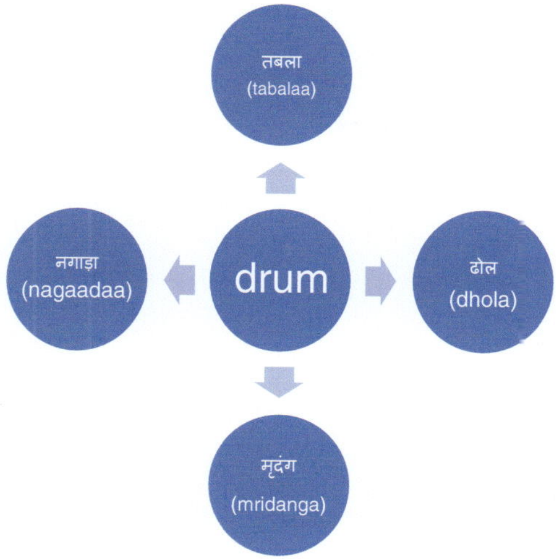

Fig. 2.2 Hypernymy linkage in action

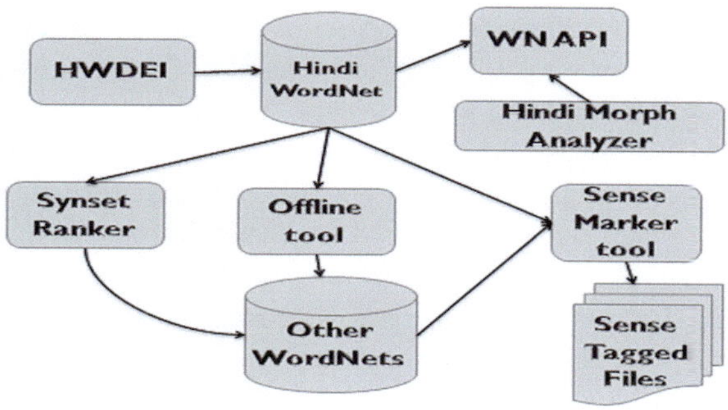

Fig. 2.3 All the tools and their dependencies

2.6.1 Hindi WordNet Data Entry Interface Tool

To facilitate a simple GUI-based synset insertion point for linguists working at IIT Bombay, this data entry interface was created. The interface allows the linguists to insert or modify the Hindi synsets easily.

This tool is designed for creating language-specific synsets and was originally created for Hindi language only. It is database-based tool, and the data entered using this tool are directly updated in Hindi WordNet database maintained at IIT Bombay. For this reason, this is used only within IIT Bombay by the linguistic team working on generation of Hindi WordNet (Fig. 2.4).

A similar interface was later on designed for Marathi WordNet as well, as the linguistic team for Marathi language is also part of IIT Bombay NLP group. This tool has facilities for faster lookup of category (nouns, adjectives, verbs, etc.)-specific search and includes options for specifying relations between synsets. The

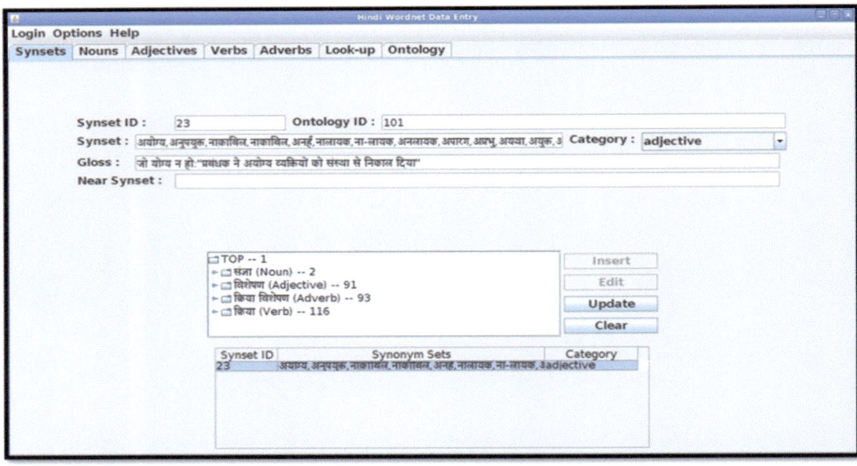

Fig. 2.4 Hindi WordNet data entry interface

tool allows the users to search for existing synsets using either the synset IDs or the synset words. It also keeps track of the ontology ID, category, and other fields which are related to the synset. It provides a facility of finding all synsets which contain a specific word or pattern. This is useful in cases where there are many synsets corresponding to a word or pattern, and the exact synset id is to be found out. The tool also includes user-friendly options for changing the font size, feel and look, etc. This tool is developed in java in order to make it as platform independent and works for Indic languages on platforms which support Unicode.

2.6.2 Off-line Tool

The off-line tool is a java-based open-source tool created for faster creation of Indic WordNets using Hindi WordNet as a pivot language. This tool provides a very similar feel to that of the online interface available for the Hindi WordNet and is publicly downloadable. The tool was created at IIT Bombay. Juxtaposed to HWDEI tool explained earlier, the off-line tool was created as a file-based tool for creation of WordNets. The tool uses Hindi WordNet as a pivot and provides a rapid way of constructing synsets for any language for the linguists (Fig. 2.5).

As shown in the screenshot, the left-side pane of the tool is where the Hindi synsets get loaded. The right-side pane is to be filled by the user in order to create synset in the target language (the screenshot is showing Sanskrit as the target language).

The tool provides some easy configuration options for setting the source and the target languages. By default the source language is Hindi (as it is the pivot language), but this can be changed to reflect any language of user's choice. The tool

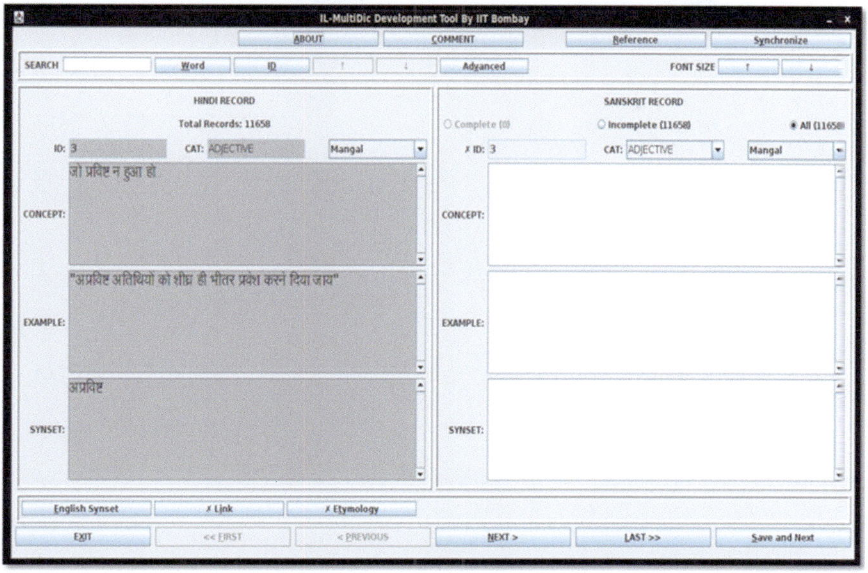

Fig. 2.5 Off-line tool

by default also allows the user to provide the English synset file (for reference) if it exists. Once the Concept, Example, Synset (words), Link, and Etymology fields are filled up for the target language, the synset is considered to be complete. This count helps the end user to gather data statistics and also to easily navigate through the incomplete synsets.

The latest version (v2.1) of the tool provides option for Secure Shell (SSH) Synchronization. This allows multiple users from same linguistic team to work on parallel for the same target language and then enables them to merge their work on a server through which the communication is done using SSH.

This tool provides standard options of changing the font size, navigation options, options for synset level comments, etc.

2.6.3 Synset Categorization Tool

As per the new distribution of synsets as decided in the 2nd IndoWordNet Workshop, there are six categories (ranks) of synsets for the Indian languages: Universal, Pan-Indian, Family-specific, Language-specific, Rare, and Synthesized. The Synset Categorizer or Ranker tool helps linguists categorize the synsets into one of the above six categories.

The Synset Categorizer tool is a very significant tool for IndoWordNet because synset making happens in a prioritized way in the following order: Universal → Pan-Indian → Family-specific → Language-specific → Rare → Synthesized (Fig. 2.6).

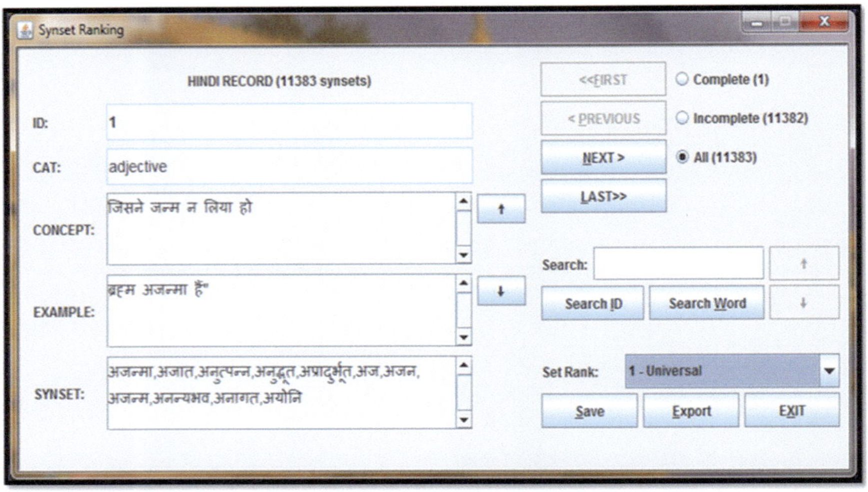

Fig. 2.6 Synset categorization tool

Besides, it automatically imposes a preliminary ontological structure on the synsets and if synsets are completed in this way, natural lexemes of the language get covered early, and the ambiguity that might have cropped up later is reduced at the initial stage.

The design for the tool is rather simple, compared to the previous tools. The tool shows the language synset in the left-side pane. The linguist's job is limited to deciding the category for this synset from the aforementioned categories.

Like off-line tool, this is a file-based tool and portable as it is written in Java. Since the tool follows the same syntax for the input file as that of the off-line tool, the file generated by off-line tool can be directly used for categorizing the synsets of that particular language.

As of now, for the task of identifying Universal and Pan-Indian synsets, the tool was modified to decide whether a particular Hindi synset is available in particular language, and the tool was distributed to all linguistic groups under IndoWordNet family to make a decision.

2.6.4 Morph Analyzer Tool

Morphology plays a crucial role in the working of various NLP applications. Whenever we run a spell checker, provide a query term to a Web search engine, explore translation or transliteration tools, use online dictionaries or thesauri, or try using text-to-speech or speech recognition applications, morphology works at the back of these applications.

Natural Language Processing (NLP) systems aim to analyze and generate natural language sentences and are concerned with computational systems and their interaction with human language. Morphology accounts for the morphological properties of languages in a systematic manner, enabling us to understand how words are formed, what their constituents are, how they may be arranged to make larger units, what are the semantic and grammatical constraints involved, and how morphological processes interact with syntactic and phonological ones. An analysis of the inflectional morphology of Hindi has been presented here in the theoretical framework of Distributed Morphology, as discussed by Halle and Marantz (1993, 1994); Harley and Noyer (1999). The theory has been used to develop the rules required to analyze and describe the various inflectional forms of Hindi words. Our tool takes an inflected word as input and outputs its set of roots along with its various morphological features using the output of the stemmer. The suffixes extracted by the stemmer are used to get the various morphological features of the word: gender, number, person, case, tense, aspect, and modality. The tool consists of two parts—Stemmer, which takes inflected word as input and stems it, to separate root and suffix and Morphological Analyzer, which takes pair as input and outputs a set of features along with the set of roots (Bahuguna et al. 2014).

2.6.5 Sense Marker Tool

Annotation plays a key role in today's NLP scenario. And, one of the toughest annotation tasks is sense marking. In a given text, the occurrence of a particular word will correspond to only one sense and assigning the word with the correct sense from Hindi WordNet (or any other WN) is sense marking.

For machine translation of English to any Indian language, word sense ambiguity is a prominent issue. A huge amount of data needs to be sense-marked accurately by humans using an authentic and standard lexicon is essential (Fig. 2.7).

The sense marker tool is a Graphical User Interface-based tool which uses Java for manual sense marking. It can be used for any language, provided that the language has its own data base and morph analyzer. The tool displays the different senses of a word with gloss and entries of each synset to which the word belongs. It allows the user to select the correct sense of the word from among all the senses. Word can be tagged by just a single click on the correct synset (Fig. 2.8).

2.7 Web Interface

The current Hindi WordNet interface conforms to the Web standards and the latest UI/UX designs. The interface boasts of a 'card-ed' interface where each synset along with all its properties is shown in the form of a color-coded card. The cards are color coded according to their part-of-speech categories.

The interface also supports all the handheld devices and can be viewed at varied resolutions. In this era when a lot of Internet browsing is done through mobile devices, it is a preliminary need of Web-based design to be mobile supportive. Hence, we have modified the interface to support all such devices and, thus, all kinds of resolutions. The current interface not only does search for words based

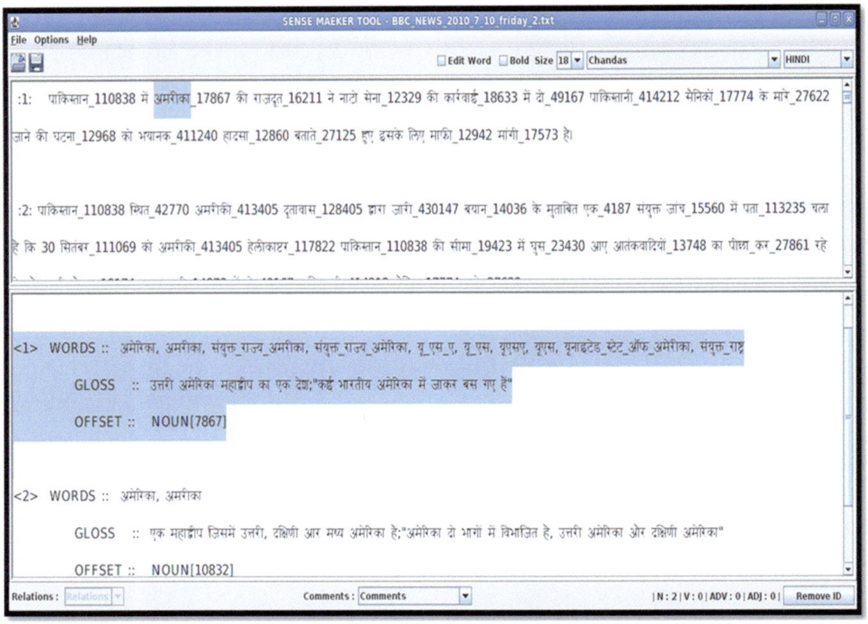

Fig. 2.7 Sense marker tool

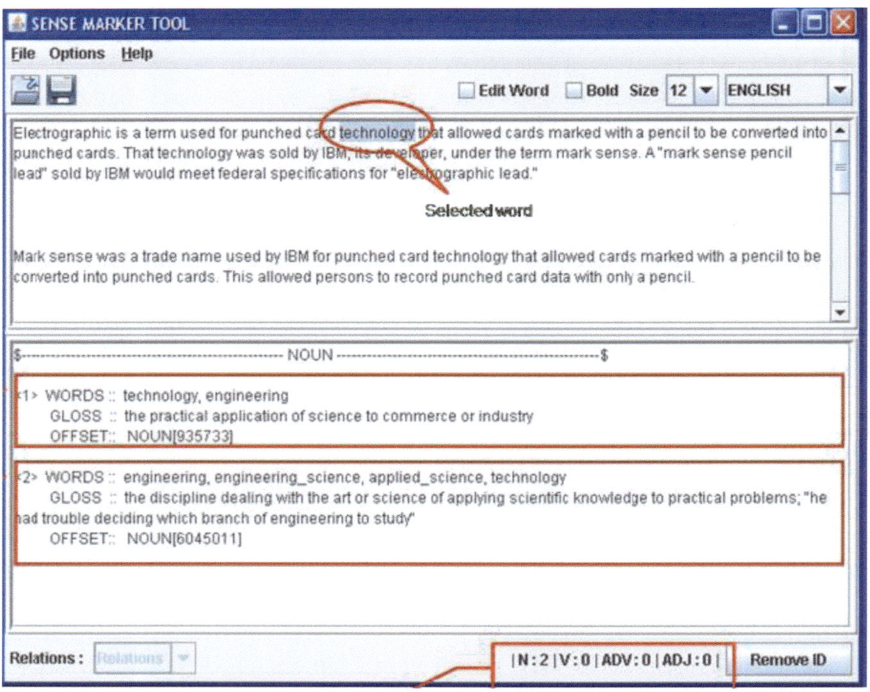

Fig. 2.8 Sense marker tool

on their senses, but also inculcates a lot of facilities such as Morph Analyzer, Root form suggestions, Nukta Normalization, and Transliteration for easy typing, Traditional Devanagari keyboard, and a hierarchical synset display for related synsets. The Hindi WordNet is also available for off-line browsing and content search via a downloadable off-line HWN browser. Its database is updated daily, and it can be downloaded from the HWN Web site itself (Figs. 2.9, 2.10 and 2.11).

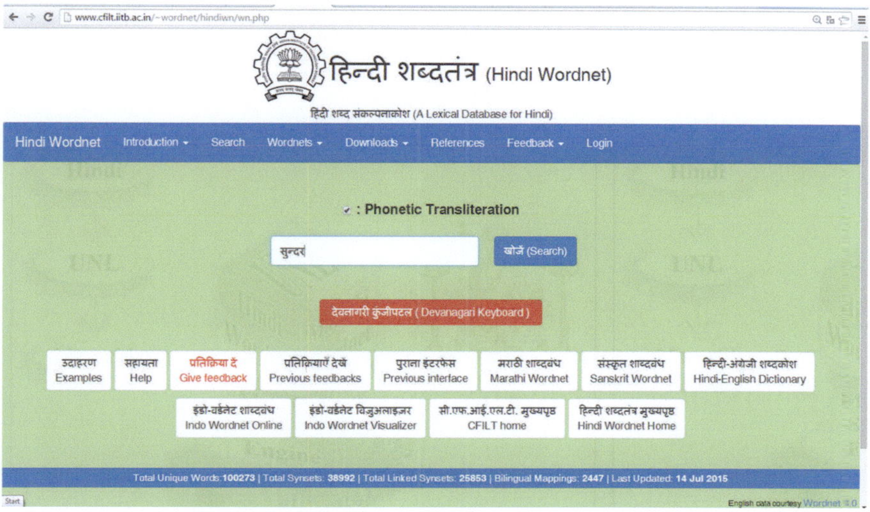

Fig. 2.9 HWN web interface

Fig. 2.10 HWN web interface

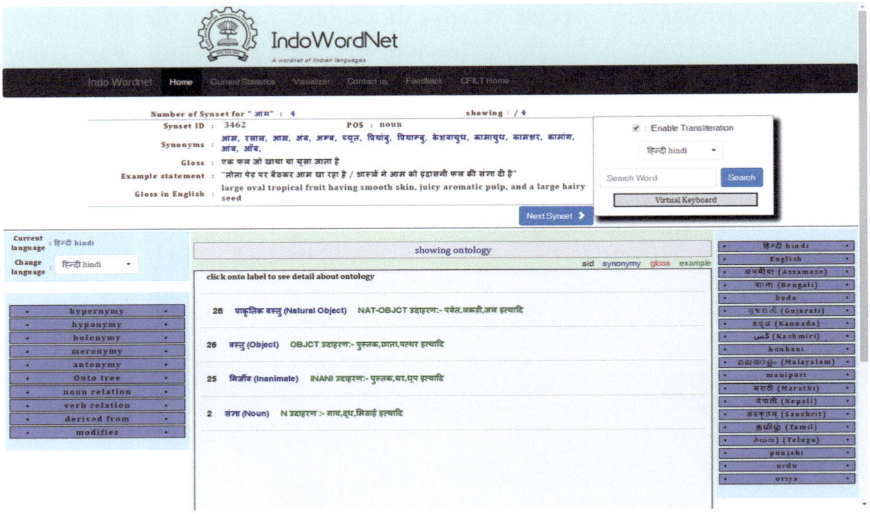

Fig. 2.11 IndowordNet web interface

2.8 IndoWordNet Visualizer

IndoWordNet visualizer (Chaplot et al. 2014) is a graphical user interface for exploring the IndoWordNet lexical database. The interface is made publically available on IndoWordNet Web site. It takes the input word from a user and displays the IndoWordNet subgraph for the concepts of a given word. The interface is enhanced with various features to provide flexibility to the user. User can hover a mouse pointer over a particular node and an edge for highlighting the information about the synset and semantic relations associated with the synsets. User can click, drag, zoom

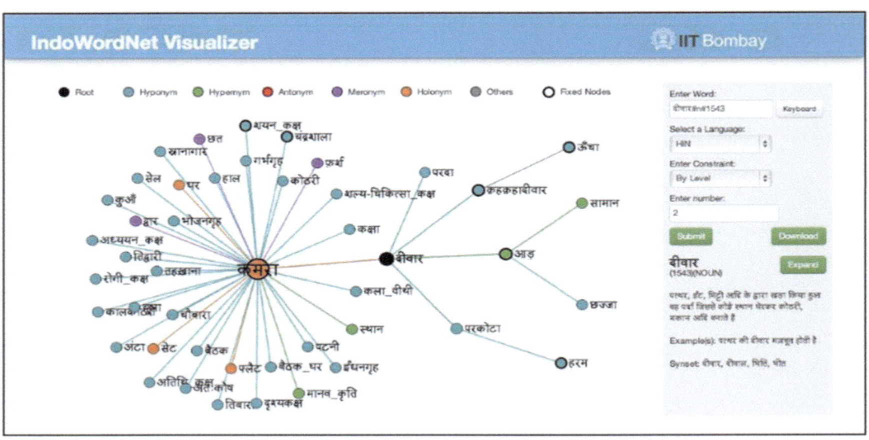

Fig. 2.12 IndoWordNet visualizer—graph for the Hindi word 'diiwaara'

in/out, expand, and fix nodes for better visibility. The screenshot for the Hindi word 'diiwaara' is shown in the figure given below. This interface is very useful in various NLP applications, viz., WordNet Validation, Semantic Relatedness, Word Sense Disambiguation, Information Retrieval, and Textual Entailment (Fig. 2.12).

2.9 Hindi WordNet Mobile Application

In this era of handheld mobile devices, there is a great need to make available the traditional Web services as mobile applications (Kanojia et al. 2016) which are extremely popular. Web browser-based interfaces are available but are not suited for mobile devices, which deters people from effectively using WordNets. We developed mobile applications for the Android and iOS platforms for Hindi WordNet which allows users to search for words and obtain more information about them along with their translations in English and other Indian languages.

India is a country in the world with massive language diversity. According to a recent census in 2001, there are 1365 rationalized mother tongues, 234 identifiable mother tongues and 122 major languages. Of these, 29 languages have more than a million native speakers, 60 have more than 100,000 and 122 have more than 10,000 native speakers. With this in mind, the construction of the Indian WordNets, the IndoWordNet (Bhattacharyya 2010) project was initiated which was an effort undertaken by over 12 educational and research institutes headed by IIT Bombay.

It is common knowledge that Web sites such as Facebook, Twitter, LinkedIn, and Gmail can be accessed using their Web browser-based interfaces but the mobile applications developed for them are much more popular. This is a clear indicator that browser-based interfaces are inconvenient which was the main motivation behind our work. We studied the existing interfaces and the WordNet databases and developed applications for Android, iOS, and Windows Phone platforms. We believe that such an application can be quite helpful in a classroom educational scenario, where students, often belonging to different cultural and linguistic background, would be able to access this application as a dictionary for multiple Indian languages.

The current application for Hindi WordNet has been launched on Android and Windows Phone stores, which are available for free download. It can be used to search for words using Hindi as the pivot language and then results are multilingual connected to each other based on the same sense. Another possible use of this application can be where tourists traveling to India use this application for basic survival communication needs.

Hindi is fairly new to the Web, and despite of standard UTF encoding of characters, there remain a few steps to be taken to sanitize the input for WordNet search. We inculcated steps such as nukta normalization and morphological analysis of the input word to ease the search in our mobile application. The results returned by the server are interpreted by the application pages and displayed in a very simplistic manner. We display all synsets for each part-of-speech and all senses of that word and initially showing the synset words, gloss, and example.

These senses are categorized by their part-of-speech categories. We have conformed to the principles of good user interface design and provided for an incremental information display.

We plan to make efforts toward improving this application to enable searching for words belonging to all languages which have a common interface via language detection. We also plan to inculcate Word Suggestions as they are being typed so that the user is presented with better lexical choices (Fig. 2.13).

Fig. 2.13 Hindi WordNet mobile application

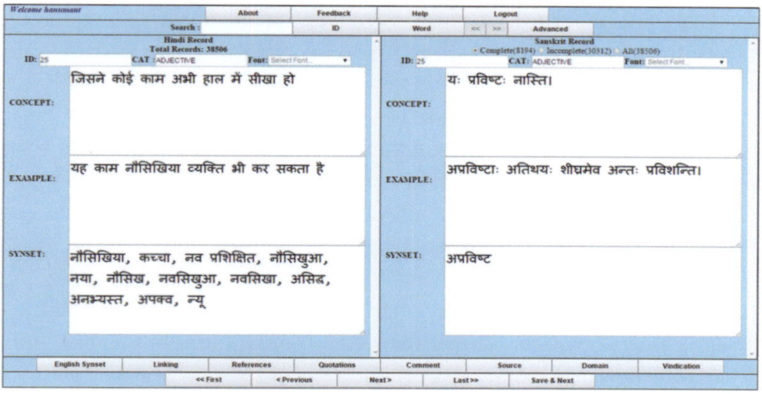

Fig. 2.14 Online synset creation interface

2.10 Online Synset Creation Interface—Synskarta

Synskarta (Redkar et al. 2014) is an online interface designed for creating synsets from source language to target language by following the expansion approach. It is a centralized Web-based system which uses relational database to store and maintain synset and related data. The difficulty of maintaining data in flat files is taken care of by Synskarta. It is developed using PHP and MySQL. The IndoWordNet database structure is used for storing and maintaining the synset data while IndoWordNet APIs are used for accessing and manipulating these data (Fig. 2.14).

2.10.1 Some of the Salient Features of Synskarta are as Follows

- User Registration Module—This module allows the system administrator to create user profiles and provide necessary access privileges to his/her role. The user can login using the access privileges provided to him and accordingly the user interface is displayed to that particular user.
- Configuration Module—This module sets all the necessary parameters such as source language and target language and enables or disables certain features such as Source, Domain, Linking, Comment, and References.
- Main Module—This module allows the user to enter data in the target language panel by referring to data in the source language panel. The source panel and the target panel vertically divide the main module into two equal sized panels. Following are the major components of this module:
- Source language panel—This panel is placed on the left of the screen which has fields for synset id, POS category, gloss, example(s), and synonyms of the source language synset.

- Target language panel—This panel is placed on the right of the screen. This panel has non-editable fields such as synset id, POS category and editable fields such as gloss, example(s), and synonym(s) of the target language synset. The user is expected to enter the data in these editable fields.
- Search—User can search a synset either by entering 'synset id' or a 'word' in a synset.
- Advanced Search—Here user is allowed to search synset data by entering various parameters, such as POS category and words appearing in gloss or in example.
- Comment—User can comment on a particular synset being translated.
- English Synset—User can check the corresponding English synset for better clarity in translation process.
- Navigation Panel—This panel allows the user to navigate between synsets. Button 'Save & Next' allows inserting or updating a current target synset and the data are directly stored in the IndoWordNet database.
- Vindication—This feature allows the user to record the special feature of a particular word in a current synset.
- Source—This feature allows the user to record the information about source of the synset.
- Domain—This feature allows the user to record the information about domain of the synset.
- Linking—Many-to-many linking of words is supported in this feature.
- Quotations—The feature is to add quotations as additional examples are supported.
- Root Verb—This feature allows the user to enter the root verb of a given word.
- Feedback—Feedback related to the tool and its features are captured here.
- Word Options—Provides specific features which can be specific to a particular word in the synset. There are features which are specific to the Sanskrit language. Some of these features can also be applicable to other languages. As far as Sanskrit is concerned, some of the features are Indication of Word Type, Indication of Accent, Identification of Gender, Indication of Proverbs, Indication of Class, Etymology, Indication of Transitivity, Indication of Iṭtva, Indication of Pada, and Indication of Verbal Root Types.

2.10.2 *Advantages and Limitations of Synskarta*

2.10.2.1 Major Advantages of Synskarta are as Follows

- Centralized system—Online access from anywhere in the world
- No data redundancy and inconsistency.
- No text files to maintain data
- Faster processing and updating
- Multiple users can work at the same time
- Can be used by all the language WordNets

Table 2.1 Synset linkage status

No.	Languages	Linked status
01	Assamese	14,958
02	Bodo	15,785
03	Manipuri	16,351
04	Nepali	11,713
05	Tamil	25,431
06	Telugu	21,091
07	Malayalam	27,180
08	Kannada	20,033
09	Kashmiri	29,469
10	Konkani	32,370
11	Marathi	30,817
12	Sanskrit	23,176
13	Gujarati	35,599
14	Panjabi	32,364
15	Bengali	36,346
16	Urdu	34,280
17	Oriya	35,284

2.10.2.2 Disadvantage

The major limitation of Synskarta is it is heavily dependent on Internet access or networking.

2.11 Linkage Statistics

The table shows linkage status of synsets of other language WordNets with Hindi WordNet as mentioned earlier, and these seventeen (17) languages follow Hindi WordNet as pivot for creation of WordNets in the respective language (Table 2.1).

The status mentioned in the table shows the counts of synsets from these languages which are linked to Hindi language as of July 2015.

2.12 Conclusion

In this paper, we have discussed problems faced in categorization of Hindi synsets and the different categories chosen. The paper presents challenges faced while categorizing and in linking Hindi synsets with different languages. The solution suggested accommodates culture-specific concepts such as different types of cuisines of different places, folk dances, and folk songs in a particular language WordNet.

A suggestion of using Hypernymy linkage has been proposed to solve the problem of linkage of culture specific or uncommon synsets in different languages. Current linkage statistics for all languages in IndoWordNet has be mentioned. Near-future plan is to link language-specific synsets with Hindi WordNet.

The paper also presented different tools which were developed for WordNet synset data entry, linkage, categorization, etc.

Acknowledgments The support of the Dept. of Information Technology, Govt. of India, toward the WordNet development effort through *Indradhanush* project is thankfully acknowledged.

Appendix: Some of the Universal Synsets Selected by IndoWordNet Members

Id	Synset	Id	Synset	Id	Synset	Id	Synset
27	*moorkha* (fool)	273	*masooDaa* (gum)	561	*tarjanii* (index finger)	779	*jyeshTha* (name of a lunar month)
30	*yogya* (capable)	278	*hiiraa* (diamond)	562	*anaanikaa* (ring finger)	780	*saavana* (name of a lunar month)
31	*sabhya* (decent)	293	*Boonda* (drop)	568	*arahara* (toor pulse)	781	*bhaadrapada* (name of a lunar month)
44	*apamaan* (insult)	298	*khoona* (blood)	591	*maaranaa* (to hit)	782	*pousha* (name of a lunar month)
46	*sammaana* (respect)	332	*pinjaraa* (cage)	592	*latiyaanaa* (kick)	787	*chaadara* (bed sheet)
47	*iishwar* (God)	335	*choohaa* (mouse)	600	*jaala* (net)	788	*asatya* (lie)
51	*achaanaka* (suddenly)	344	*sariiyaa* (rod)	604	*mastaka* (fore head)	792	*dhanusha* (bow)
75	*sadguNa* (virtue)	345	*kalama* (pen)	605	*cheharaa* *(face)*	798	*dvaara* (door)
120	*prema* (love)	346	*kaagaja* (paper)	610	*tanaa* (stem)	801	*paradaa* (curtain)
121	*sneha* (love)	370	*baansurii* (flute)	617	*kala* (yesterday)	802	*bichhounaa*
129	*anuvaad* (translation)	373	*paasa men* (nearby)	623	*laala ranga* (red)	806	*kambala* (blanket)
142	*ghriNaa* (hatred)	406	*sitaara* (name of a string instrument)	624	*haraa* (green)	808	*maagha* (name of a lunar month)

155	*oura* (other)	409	*taanapooraa* (name of a string instrument)	625	*niilaa* (blue)	822	*puraskaara* (prize)
171	*aparadha* (crime)	417	*motaa* (plump)	630	*poornimaa* (full moon)	849	*sinha* (lion)
172	*aparaadhii* (criminal)	422	*paira* (leg)	631	*madhya raatri* (midnight)	858	*aadamii* (man)
203	*baraamadaa* (veranda)	444	*biskuta* (biscuit)	632	*kala* (tomorrow)	890	*taaraa* (star)
208	*graha* (home)	452	*mandira* (temple)	635	*makkhii* (fly)	893	*khulaa* (uncovered)
217	*lohaa* (iron)	464	*moorti* (statue)	642	*tahanii* (twig)	965	*qaanoona* (law)
225	*budha* (Mercury)	470	*rangamancha* (theater_ stage)	643	*konpala* (foliage)	976	*taalaa* (lock)
226	*shukra* (Venus)	473	*dhaagaa* (thread)	644	*shaakhaa* (tree branch)	984	*darshaka* (spectator)
227	*brihaspati* (Jupiter)	474	*dhaatu* (metal)	647	*haddii* (bone)	985	*naaka* (nose)
228	*shani* (Saturn)	476	*duma* (tail)	648	*chaitra* (name of a lunar month)	987	*kaana* (ear)
229	*varuNa* (Neptune)	491	*bhujaa* (arm)	652	*avastha* (state)	990	*nathunaa* (ale)
231	*pradesha* (province)	492	*poshaaka* (clothing)	661	*pasalii* (rib)	991	*niraashaa* (hopelessness)
233	*zillaa* (district)	504	*kalaaii* (wrist)	667	*polaa* (hollow)	1011	*naraka* (hell)
235	*ronaa* (cry)	505	*kuhanii* (elbow)	679	*haara* (defeat)	1012	*damaa* (asthma)
236	*gaanna* (sing)	511	*ulkaa* (meteoroid)	720	*mitrataa* (friendship)	1013	*prasannataa* (cheerfulness)
247	*satyavaadii* (honest)	521	*jhandaa* (flag)	749	*koyala* (cuckoo)	1017	*Indradhanusha* (rainbow)
268	*riiDa* (spine)	526	*vaakaii* (actually)	752	*pankha* (wing)	1029	fena (foam)
269	*shakti* (strength)	528	*spashta* (clear)	753	*choncha* (beak)	1036	*mahaavata* (mahout)
270	*munha* (mouth)	531	*praaNa* (spirit)	758	*phana* (hood)	1038	*Imalii* (tamarind)

271	*daanta* (tooth)	532	*naayikaa* (heroine)	762	*magar* (crocodile)	1045	*shaanti* (peace)
272	*taaloo* (palate)	558	*choolhaa* (stove)	778	*vaishaakha* (name of a lunar month)	1046	………

Note Hindi words are written in *italic* and English meanings are given in the brackets in the above table

References

Bahuguna, A., Talukdar, T., Bhattacharyya, P., & Singh, S. (2014). HinMA: Distributed morphology based hindi morphological analyzer. In *International Conference on Natural Language Processing 2014 (ICON 2014), Goa University,* Goa, India, 19–20 December 2014.

Bhattacharyya, P. (2010). IndoWordNet. In *Lexical Resources Engineering Conference 2010 (LREC 2010),* Malta, May, 2010.

Chaplot, D. S., Bhingardive, S., & Bhattacharyya, P. (2014). IndoWordnet visualizer: A graphical user interface for browsing and exploring wordnets of Indian languages. In *Global WordNet Conference 2014 (GWC 2014),* Tartu, Estonia, 25–29 January 2014.

Halle, M., Marantz, A. (1993). Distributed Morphology and the Pieces of Inflection. In Kenneth Hale & S. Jay Keyser (Eds.), *The view From Building 20* (pp. 111–176). Cambridge: MIT Press.

Halle, M., Marantz, A. (1994). Some key features of Distributed Morphology. In Andrew Carnie and Heidi Harley (Eds.), *MITWPL 21: Papers on phonology and morphology* (pp. 275–288). Cambridge: MITWPL.

Harley, H., Noyer, R. (1999) Distributed morphology. *Glot international, 4*(4), 3–9.

Kanojia, D., Dabre, R., & Bhattacharyya, P. (2016). Sophisticated Lexical Databases-Simplified Usage: Mobile Applications and Browser Plugins For Wordnets. In Global WordNet Conference (GWC 2016), Bucharest, Romanian, 27–30 January 2016.

Naravane, V. D. (1961). *Bharatiya Vyavahara Kosha: Solah Bhasao ka kosha.* Triveni Samgama. (in Hindi).

Redkar, H., Paranjape, J., Joshi, N., Kulkarni, I., Kulkarni, M., & Bhattacharyya, P. (2014). Introduction to Synskarta: An online interface for synset creation with special reference to Sanskrit. *In International Conference on Natural Language Processing 2014 (ICON 2014),* Goa, India, 19–20 December 2014.

Saraswati, J., Shukla, R., Goyal, R. P., & Bhattacharyya, P. (2010). Hindi to English WordNet linkage: Challenges and solutions. In *Proceedings of 3rd IndoWordNet Workshop, International Conference on Natural Language Processing 2010 (ICON 2010),* Indian Institute of Kharagpur, India, 8–11 December 2010.

Chapter 3
Defining Language-Specific Synsets in IndoWordNet: Some Theoretical and Practical Issues

Niladri Sekhar Dash

Abstract A WordNet is a digital network of semantically linked words, which are organized around the notion of synsets of a language. A synset is a set of synonyms with same part-of-speech (mostly), which are potential to be interchanged in usage at certain contexts of expression and information interchange within or across languages. The presence of synsets in a WordNet attests the basic argument that a single word can refer to multiple concepts (i.e., polysemy), and reversely, several words can point to a single concept (i.e., synonymy). Based on the general notion of WordNet, it is possible to assume that synsets can be universal or language specific. In this chapter, I have made an attempt to critically evaluate the concept of 'synset' in WordNet as well as the problems of defining language-specific synsets (LSSs) for the Indian languages with special reference to Bangla. Defining LSSs, unlike those of universal synsets, is a real challenge, since the very idea of language specificity is still a fuzzy notion in the domain of lexicology, lexical knowledge representation and language understanding. Therefore, I shall first try to address the question of language specificity; explore the existence and use of LSS in a language; define the methods for LSS selection; and finally refer to the process of LSS generation in a language, with reference to Bangla, within a network of cross-cultural lexical percolation.

Keywords WordNet · Synset · Concept · Community · Bangla · Language · Culture · Geography

N.S. Dash (✉)
Linguistic Research Unit, Indian Statistical Institute, Kolkata, India
e-mail: ns_dash@yahoo.com

N.S. Dash et al. (eds.), *The WordNet in Indian Languages*,
DOI 10.1007/978-981-10-1909-8_3

3.1 Introduction

The concept of WordNet is a complex proposition, since it asks for adequate and explicit elaboration for conceptualization of the concept. In its simplest sense, a WordNet is a web-based digital network of words expressing different concepts and ideas—either linked or delinked (Fellbaum 1998). These concepts and ideas are explicated through several denotative and connotative functions of words when these are utilized in natural language texts. That means the basic architecture of a WordNet is actually built up on the concepts expressed by the lexical stock of the vocabulary of a language. Since there is no concept for which there is not a word in a language, and reversely, since there is not a single word which does not refer to a concept, it is understood that each and every concept represented within a WordNet is definitely fabricated within a lexical item, and reversely, each lexical item included in the WordNet invariably refers to a concept or an idea—either unique or regular (Whorf 1956, pp. 207–219).

The most typical and unique feature of a WordNet is that words are functionally defined in terms of their semantic relations to others. Following this scheme of lexical relations, an ontological structure is designed to express beliefs, notions, items, customs, concepts, and physical properties of the world as encapsulated in the vocabulary of the language (Vossen 2004). What I understand here is that in a WordNet each concept is aptly represented within an interface of a multilayered digital network in such a manner that it is possible to extract relevant linguistic terms relating to particular concept, idea or physical item by a set of synonymous forms and vice versa (Miller 1985). This is possible only when there are well-formed and well-framed word–sense pairs that are interlinked through unambiguous definitional elaborations of the concepts and supported with a large number of synsets retrieved from a language with intimate reference to their multidimensional usage varieties recorded in the actual empirical texts (Apresjan 1973).

The concept of 'synset' is not beyond question. It is assumed in a WordNet that there exists some words in a language which may be treated as conceptual equivalents to each other on the ground that these are semantically same or functionally similar, although our practical realization is that a word in a language is normally endowed with a single lexical identity with single form, single function (i.e., part-of-speech) and single meaning, which eventually leads us to argue that in true sense, there is no synonyms in a language.

I also understand that, on principle as well as on reality, each natural language can have a WordNet of its own to showcase the concepts expressed by its vocabulary in a uniform pattern of lexicalization to represent the internal structure of sense relations as well as for representing the global knowledge shared by the members of the language community (Magnini and Cavagliá 2000). However, linking up the synsets of language-specific concepts to a general network of universal WordNet generates far more applicational and referential implications as a digital resource of this kind can open up many cross-lingual avenues for exchanging linguistic information, concepts, and ideas across the languages of typological, genealogical and geographical diversities.

3.2 The IndoWordNet

The arguments presented above provide the basic rationale for designing the IndoWordNet where the implicit ontological structures of synsets of each Indian language are preserved and represented in a unique interface within a multilingual synset database covering all major Indian languages (Chakrabarti and Bhattacharyya 2004). Within this interface, the IndoWordNet is visualized as a cross-lingual ontology rather than an isolated language-specific ontology for making inferences only. It is a WordNet in the true sense of the term, which aims at capturing valuable information about the concepts that are lexicalized in the Indian languages—not only the concepts available from words and expressions of the languages, but also for substitutable sense similarities of words and expressions across the Indian languages (Cruse 1986, p. 135).

With a common consensus, in IndoWordNet, the entire lexical stock is conveniently divided into six major subcategories, namely *Universal Synset, Pan-Indian Synset, In-family Synset, Synthesized Synset, Rare Synset* and *Language-specific Synset*, which in a combined mirror reflects on the hierarchical structure of vocabulary of the Indian languages (Bhatt and Bhattacharyya 2011).

Based on this ground structure, in this chapter, I have made an attempt to understand the nature and character of LSS—one of the most crucial components of the IndoWordNet. I have also tried to show how the process of selection, collection, and validation of LSS is a real challenge as the very basic notion of language specificity is, at present, under rapid change due to vibrating cross-cultural fusions triggered from the dynamics of localization and globalization where all language communities—large and small, well known and less known, dialect and standard, imperialistic and endangered, relic and focal—are put within a transient cauldron of cultural exchange and sharing and thus are made open and accessible for the recurrent processes of cross-cultural fusion and lexical percolation.

3.3 Goal of IndoWordNet

The IndoWordNet is a plurilingual Internet-based network interface where the general goal is to develop a WordNet for each Indian language and link up an individual WordNet with the other in a frame where structure and content of each WordNet is similar to other in the frame as well as similar to that of EuroWordNet and Princeton WordNet. The IndoWordNet thus represents a larger showcase that includes several WordNets of *Assamese, Bangla, Bodo, Gujarati, Hindi, Kannada, Kashmiri, Konkani, Malayalam, Manipuri, Marathi, Nepali, Odia, Punjabi, Sanskrit, Tamil, Telugu* and *Urdu* (Narayan et al. 2002; Kulkarni et al. 2010; Selvraj 2010; Bhattacharya 2010). It is expected that once such a digital lexical database across Indian languages is generated, it will serve, besides other things, the following basic purposes:

(a) Search out language-specific words and terms for obtaining the language-specific ideas and information about the lexico-semantic relations among the words (e.g., synonymy, antonymy, hypernymy, meronymy, usages, sense variation and collocation).
(b) Initiate search into cross-lingual lexical matching, lexical mapping, sense parallelism, translation equivalent extraction, information exchange, and knowledge sharing between the closely as well as distantly related Indian languages.
(c) Develop useful digital monolingual linguistic database and lexical resource (e.g., thesauruses, dictionaries, terminology databases and parallel translation corpora) for Indian languages.
(d) Devise systems and tools of language technology for machine translation, multilingual search, multilingual information retrieval, bilingual and multilingual language teaching, and e-governance.
(e) Globalize lexical stock as well as linguistic identities of the less known Indian languages.

An important attribute of the IndoWordNet is noticed in its sincere attempt for establishing the conceptual equivalence relation among the synsets of the member languages. This is different from the traditional bilingual and/or bilingual–bidirectional dictionaries in the sense that while in a bilingual (as well as in bidirectional) dictionary, an attempt is made to explicate sense relations between the individual words or word pairs across the languages considered for the dictionary (e.g., English–Bangla); in the IndoWordNet, an effort is initiated to match and map up sense relations among the words across all the Indian languages taken in the IndoWordNet. Therefore, compared to any bilingual and/or any bidirectional bilingual dictionary, the lexical stock furnished in the IndoWordNet supplies more varied and comprehensive overview of concept lexicalization both in the source and in the target languages, from which one can easily select the best candidate required in a particular search. In this sense, IndoWordNet makes use of the 'shake and bake' methodology in lexical sense representation, where an abstraction is first made from the structural properties in the source language to produce a neutral conceptual level (i.e., shake), from where a new structure is possible to generate in the target language (i.e., bake) (Whitelock 1992).

What I understand and argue is that it is absolutely necessary for the IndoWordNet to represent the autonomous language-specific ontology for each language, because identification and attestation of language specificity is an essential component of this interface. On the contrary, ignoring linguistic uniqueness of a particular language or a variety within the interface will not only delimit the referential value of the resource, but also will lose much of its functional relevance in the activities of data sharing, information exchange, e-governance, e-learning, knowledge sharing, and translation.

However, for generating the sense equivalence relations across all the Indian languages, the central database of the IndoWordNet needs to employ an interlingual indexing system by which it is possible to provide an efficient mapping interface across the autonomous language-specific WordNets. This indexing system should also include concepts for all the lexicalized words of the member languages with direct reference to the semantically equivalent words in the other languages. In future, when WordNets of all the Indian languages will be integrated together within this interface, it will be a highly useful resource for one and all in all kinds of applied and descriptive linguistic works including cross-lingual translation, knowledge sharing, information extraction, lexical mapping, data exchange, and language education.

3.4 What Is Language-Specific Synset?

Although it has been rigorously argued that each and every natural language has its own sets of ideas and concepts which are based on the process of lexicalization that is very much active and operational in a language over centuries (Vossen 2004), the very concept of the Language-Specific Synset (LSS) does not reside beyond any question. Let us first understand clearly the concept before we agree to find out LSS from a language or the other. In principle, it is argued that the idea of LLS refers to a unique concept, which is available only in a particular language or a variety, and which has no conceptual match or equivalence in other languages (Buitelaar and Sacaleanu 2001). In reality, it is very much possible that a particular language community (say, L_1) has some ideas, concepts or practices which are not observed in other language communities. In this case at least, we can argue that L_1 has some unique concepts and the words that express these concepts are language-specific synsets. This is quite possible, as we know that every speech community has certain items or practices which are its own assets and which may not be known to or shared by others.

Since finding out the LSS in a language is a challenging task and lengthy process, it is difficult to compile a list of words, which, to my assumption, may be termed as 'unique synsets' with a claim that they have no conceptual equivalence in other languages. However, it must be admitted that it is not beyond question that there is 'no match' in other languages, since, on principle, a living language is open for continuous change or upgradation of linguistic knowledge and information retrieved from neighbouring or other languages. Therefore, it is very much possible that the concepts which we like to consider to be 'specific' to a language today may be shared by other languages tomorrow, as with the progress of time, linguistic communities are free to assimilate ideas and concepts of each other to enrich their knowledge and existence. So, what is claimed to be 'specific' for a language, or for any language for that matter, may not remain the same after a few years, and if this happens, the very concept of LSS may need to be reconstructed with new insights and arguments. The ongoing process of concept generation within a language community and its percolation to other language groups is an age-old phenomenon, and it is more active and operational in the present global situation where sharing of knowledge and information is an easy practice among the engaging social networking groups where members come and join across all linguistic, geoclimatic and sociocultural boundaries. It is, therefore, to be kept in mind that multiple stages of dynamic verification are absolutely necessary before a LSS is confidently identified as 'language specific' or 'culture specific'.

This definition of LSS triggers some theoretical as well as conceptual complexities in understanding the idea, since the very concept of LLS is a deceptive one. The first question that may arise in this context is a theoretical one that warrants our attention to know whether the phrase 'language specific' is equal to 'culture specific' and 'community specific'. If these phrases are identical in denotation, then the following questions will be raised:

(1) Are monolingual concepts really monolingual?
(2) Can monolingual concepts remain 'monolingual' in a pluricultural society?
(3) How monolingual concepts percolate across the languages to become multilingual?
(4) What linguistic–cognitive interface is invoked to assimilate monolingual concepts by others?

Such questions are actually based on the dichotomy of two opposite theories formulated below.

3.4.1 Monolingual Concept Theory

Each language has some ideas, concepts and practices which are mostly alien to the members of other language communities. These concepts evolve from the sociocultural, ecolinguistic and geoclimatic factors unique to a particular language and are understood only by the members of the language only. These concepts may become accessible and intelligible to the members of the other languages only when these are shared with the members of other languages as a result of various linguistic and extralinguistic interactions. I call this theoretical postulation as **Monolingual Concept Theory** (MCT).

In support of this argument, I can cite reference to many words and terms that denote some concepts which are available to a particular language community but not found in other communities. For example, *bhairavjap* is a unique practice of the specific religious community of Gujarat which is hardly known to other speech and cultural communities in India. This term refers to the act of embracing death by jumping from the top of a high mountain—as a part of self-sacrificing yajna or prayer to the Almighty.

3.4.2 Plurilingual Concept Theory

The very idea of 'language specificity', on the other hand, is on the platform of strong challenge as the theoretical existence of monolingualism is at stake due to the emergence of plurilingual societies where mixing of members across languages is the practice of the new age. Since, on principle, no language community is monolingual any more, except some remote communities located at some relic areas far away from the mainstream human civilization and detached from all communicational strategies used by civilized human societies, the idea of monolingual concept becomes a myth because a concept, however unique it may appear, remains no longer monolingual and thus becomes a shared property of the members of the language community as well as of the members of other neighbouring language communities. Moreover, within a large language community, we come across several linguistic subgroups (i.e., dialects groups), and the members of these subgroups often share their unique ideas and concepts with the members of other linguistic subgroups, due to which no idea remains individual or monolithic. Therefore, on principle, there is no idea or concept which is unique or extremely specific to any language or a variety. Whatever concepts are there in a language are shared by the members of other linguistic subgroups—partially or completely. This theoretical postulation leads to generation of a theory I like to call the **Plurilingual Concept Theory** (PCT). For instance, the idea of *raja* festival which is considered to be unique to the Odia language community only is actually not a language-specific concept, as it is practised by several linguistic subgroups of Odia, even though it remains unknown to Gujarati, Marathi or Tamil language communities.

Keeping these arguments in view, we have to consider the languages or the varieties, where LLS is available. We have to also keep in mind that certain amount of sociocultural uniqueness must be there which are designed and developed due to various geographical, topographic, demographic, and ecological factors. And because of these factors, any two related (typologically, genealogically or geographically) languages are assumed to possess certain concepts and ideas, which are not attested and shared by their sister or neighbouring languages. Therefore, it is rational to consider that the concept of LLS is not altogether utopian, rather very much a reality, which needs to be captured as well as represented in an organized manner in the LLS of a WordNet developed for a language. This leads to the formation of the following two questions that are directly related to this issue, and these questions are addressed in two different sections.

(a) Need for LSS selection, and
(b) Methods of LSS selection.

3.5 Need for LSS Selection

The first issue refers to the question of why LSS is needed to be selected for a language or a variety. Is it necessary to show that a language community has certain concepts that are not found in others, by which it is able to establish its unique linguistic identity among the peer communities living within a wider geographical area? This is a crucial question as this may lead to explore the events of linguistic convergence and divergence among the neighbouring communities as well as the practice of cross-lingual data paring and cross-cultural information sharing. In reply argument, it may be said that while one is trying to develop a multilingual WordNet including several languages within a single platform, it is necessary to identify the concepts and concept-denoting terms that are considered unique to the language communities on the ground that this practice, beside supporting the other things stated below, may help in finding out how a language, in spite of being similar to others, is still unique in its in-built concepts, lexical coverage, and linguistic identity.

3.5.1 Lexical Uniqueness

It refers to special lexical load denoting unique concepts in a language. It is known that each natural language has a large set of lexical items that are capable of denoting certain concepts and ideas, which are clearly intelligible to the speakers of other language communities, at least to a large group of members of the neighbouring languages. This happens to all the natural languages, and this common lexical stock is represented as ‘A’ in the diagram (Fig. 3.1).

On the other land, each natural language does posses a limited stock of unique lexical items, which refer to certain unique concepts and ideas for which no conceptual equivalents are available in the related or neighbouring languages (represented as ‘B’ in Fig. 3.1). These are not intelligible to the members of other language communities for many reasons—distance between two the communities, less exchange of mutual information, less exposure to the concepts, less cross-cultural assimilation or motivation for hiding specific concepts from others—may be some of them. These unique lexical items should be treated as the most suitable candidates to be included in the list of LSS because they are unique, language specific and indigenous. In the IndoWordNet, it is necessary to showcase these concepts and the terms as far as it is possible and feasible.

Fig. 3.1 Conceptual uniqueness leading to LSS generation

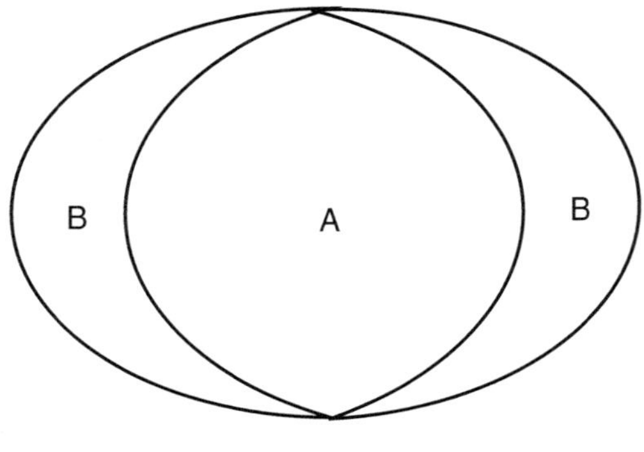

3.5.2 Lexical Gap

This refers to the phenomenon of lack of lexical equivalence between any two languages, closely or distantly related on the parameter of genealogy, geography or typology. We argue that when there is a lexical gap in one language or when the meanings of words of a particular language do not exactly fit into the meanings of words of the other language, those lexical items, which exhibit differences in the meanings, may be treated as unique and therefore stored in the LSS. Let us consider, for instance, the Bangla word *khāoyā* which is capable of denoting all three different meanings expressed by three different English words *eating, drinking* and *smoking*. This clearly shows distinct lexical gap between the two languages where three different concepts are expressed in three different words in English, but all these senses are represented by just one expression in Bangla. This kind of lexical gap needs to be accounted for in the act of developing LSS for any language pair.

3.5.3 Cultural Gap

Cultural gap normally originates from the sociocultural differences that exist between the languages. The concepts or words which are identified as LSS in a language may belong to culture and literature domains. This simply establishes our long-preserved assumption that a language community normally differs from its neighbouring communities due to its own cultural elements and practices which may not be available in neighbouring language communities. It is observed that a particular language community observes certain sociocultural rites, rituals, customs, festivals, practices, norms, etc., which are not known to the members of the other language community. Therefore, it is quite natural that the specific synsets denoting these concepts may not be available in other languages. For instance, the Odia people observe *raja* festival—a unique sociocultural ritual, which is not practised by other language groups of the Indian subcontinent. Lexical items relating to such events should, therefore, be recorded in the LSS of Odia as well as adequately elaborated with audio-visual illustration for proper comprehension by the members of the other language communities.

3.5.4 Pragmatic Gap

Pragmatic gap is caused due to differences observed in lexicalization process between the two languages. It says that although the basic concept is known to both the languages, it is not expressed in the same manner in the concerned languages. While it is expressed in a single lexical form in one language, it may be expressed in the form of a multi-word expression (i.e. *compounds, phrases and idioms*) in another language.

For example, the English term *nephew* may be represented in Bangla in different forms where each form reflects on conceptual differences expressed in the multi-word forms, such as, *khuṛtuto bhāi, jyeṭhtuto bhāi, māmāto bhāi, pistuto bhāi and māstuto bhāi.* Similar examples may be found in many Indian languages, and if found, such forms should be stored in the LSS of the respective language.

3.5.5 Lexical Mismatch

This refers to a unique linguistic phenomenon where a particular idea or a concept is referred to by a particular term of a language, while the same term refers to a different concept in another language. That means, although the terms in both the languages are identical in form or similar in orthographic representation, they actually refer to two different concepts. This is a common linguistic feature in many of the Indian languages, and these forms are often identified as the **false cognates** (Parkes and Cornell 1992) or the **false friends** (Zuckermann 2003, p. 102). Such terms may be considered for inclusion in the list of LSS for proper understanding of the terms as well as the concepts denoted by the terms. For instance, let me present below some Hindi and Bangla terms which clearly exhibit this phenomenon (Table 3.1), where words have almost same spellings in both the languages but refer to two different meanings vis-à-vis concepts.

Table 3.1 Similar orthography but different meaning

Hindi	Gloss	Bangla	Gloss
abhimān	'rage or anger'	abhimān	'state of being hurt'
bacan	'oath'	bacan	'word/number'
bādal	'cloud'	bādal	'rain'
bāli	'tender age'	bāli	'sand'
cāul	'boiled rice'	cāul	'non-boiled rice'
dard	'pain'	darad	'sympathy'
ghaṛi	'hour'	ghaṛi	'watch/clock'
hāṅgāmā	'bumper sale'	hāṅgāmā	'chaos'
khāli	'vacant'	khāli	'empty'
khiṛki	'window'	khiṛki	'backyard'
khun	'blood'	khun	'murder'
magarmāch	'crocodile'	māgurmāch	'a kind of cat fish'
mārg	'road'	mārg	'means or way'
nāriyel	'green coconut'	nārikel	'ripe coconut'
pataṅg	'kite'	pataṅga	'insect'
phā̆kā	'empty'	phā̆kā	'lonely'
sāmānya	'all'	sāmānya	'minimum'
sandeś	'news'	sandeś	'sweets'
sucnā	'information'	sūcanā	'introduction'

These examples can adequately illustrate how the terms of similar orthographic form can exhibit different concepts in two different languages. Although Hindi and Bangla are related in terms of etymological ancestry, a large number of words used in Hindi express different concepts when used in Bangla. We need to investigate why and how these two closely related languages have developed so many concepts vis-à-vis words, which are not intelligible to each other. It can be one of the highly captivating areas for cross-cultural sociolinguistic investigation, the understanding of which may ventilate into the unexplored meanders where two closely related languages may evolve with separate linguistic identity and texture due to geoclimatic and sociocultural differences. If we take all these issues into consideration, then we can perhaps justify the necessity for representing the LSS within the frame of the IndoWordNet with the following diagram (Fig. 3.2).

The diagram presented above (Fig. 3.2) shows, in a gross manner although, that all the Indian languages considered for the IndoWordNet can have (in reality it has) large number of concepts which are shared by each other. These concepts, therefore, are eligible to be portrayed within the common core vocabulary (CCV) of the pan-Indian multilingual lexical equivalence database to justify that each Indian language does possess appropriate or nearly appropriate lexical items to express the concepts found other languages. On the other hand, the six small triangles (i.e. L1, L2, L3, L4, L5 and L6) of the diagram (Fig. 3.2) refer to those LSS, which are found to be unique to a particular Indian language and are not available in other Indian languages. Therefore, along with the common core vocabulary, these LSSs are also entitled to have their legitimate places in the central database of the IndoWordNet with special tags assigned to each lexical item to mark their language-specific identity. Such an interactive interface will invariably benefit the target IndoWordNet users in the following two ways:

(a) IndoWordNet users may translate these terms across languages based on the notion of conceptual equivalence among the terms stored in the common core vocabulary;
(b) People may refer to the LSS of a particular language to grab the concept foreign to their native tongues and thus get ideas how unique concepts are available in other languages to be assimilated into his/her mother tongue.

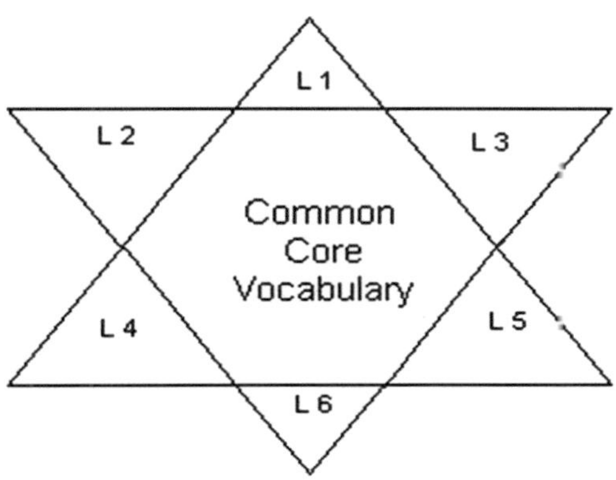

Fig. 3.2 Interface of common and LSS for the languages of IndoWordNet

Thus, the act of cross-lingual knowledge sharing will be an event of learning and cultural assimilation—two vital components for the nation to grow as a country of cross-lingual affinity.

3.6 Reasons for LSS Selection

Since the argument for having LSS in IndoWordNet is no more a deceptive proposition, it has to be agreed unanimously what is to be a considered as a concept or idea specific to a language or a variety. In general, it has been argued that we can adopt the following approaches to decide whether a specific concept vis-à-vis a word belongs to a particular language community or not (Krstev et al. 2007).

First, we have to find out whether any particular concept actually belongs to a particular language or not. For instance, consider the Assamese word *bihu* which refers to a 'special kind of harvest festival of Assam', or the Bangla term *rasagollā* which refers to a 'kind of special sweet item made with mixing posset and milk in Bengal', or the Odia term *chānāpoṛā* which refers to a 'special kind of sweet made by burning posset in fire in Orissa', etc. We can argue that these terms should be selected in the LSS list on the ground that although these terms have percolated into other Indian language communities due to various sociocultural assimilation and lifestyle sharing, in reality, these terms first belonged to those languages wherefrom these are originated. Therefore, these concepts are language specific and should be treated accordingly, even though these have turned into pan-Indian concepts in the later periods. I am, however, not sure whether this argument actually kills the underlying assumption based on which the idea of LSS is postulated. If these concepts have percolated into other languages, then these cannot be treated as language specific, and thus, these terms lose their place in the list of LSS of a language.

Second, we have to find out whether any concept is originated from a language, and if it is so, it may be considered as LSS for that language. Based on this argument terms such as *iḍli, dosā, sambar* 'unique south Indian food items', *bhāṅṛā* 'unique Punjabi dance type', *bāul* 'a unique Bangla folk song', should be in the list of LSS, since these terms originally were language-specific concepts. In reality, however, these are no more language specific, because these have already percolated into other languages due to various extralinguistic factors. Therefore, there may be arguments that such LSS terms should not be treated as language specific because the concepts are already known to other language communities. However, the general opinion is that in view of future applications and diachronic reference of the IndoWordNet, it is better to have all these lexical items in the list of LSS, since these are etymologically recognized items of that particular language. That means, since these are originally the lexical items (and concepts) of particular languages, they should be given the status of LSS.

Third, the most sensible means of finding LSS is to refer to those words and expressions which are tagged as *deśi* (i.e. local) words and terms in the dictionaries of a language. For instance, in Bangla, I can select the local terms such as *goṭ* 'a kind ornament used at the waist by women', *ghulghuli* 'a small round hole in wall', *gharāñci* 'a small table made of bamboo sticks' or *cāṛi* 'a big earthen bowl used to drink watered rise'. The quicksand, however, lies hidden in the act of blind selection of the local terms without verification, as the same concept or word may prevail in neighbouring languages but with a different name and with slight modification of shape size and function of the item. This strategy may be further extended to the dictionaries and wordbooks of different dialects of a language to select the LSS denoting unique concepts and ideas. That means we need to delve into diverse local varieties of a language through the lanes of dialects for selecting words and terms, which are less known, less general and less exposed. Similarly, meandering through the lanes of antiquity, we have to select old words and antique terms, which are known to be less intelligible as well as less conceivable even to the members of that speech community.

Fourth, it is necessary to find out the concepts or words which are not necessarily specific to a particular language or a variety, but which are recognized as common concepts or lexical items in the language, while at the same time, the concepts or lexical items have not been attested and not found to be used in other languages. This generally refers to the borrowed words and terms from foreign languages into a language but not borrowed in other or neighbouring languages. For instance, the Bangla word *bargī* (<Pers. *bārgīr*) refers to the 'Maharashtrian cavalry that invaded Bengal centuries ago', and *phiriṅgi* (<Protugue: *Franeez*) refers to 'a cross-breed of European and India parents'. These terms may be considered for inclusion in LSS, but before that, we have to cross-check and confirm that these terms are not available in other Indian languages.

Fifth, we need to find out the instances of lexical incorporation (alternatively, lexical naturalization) which is a powerful and productive system in generating new lexical stock in a language (Dash et al. 2009). Through some productive strategies of adoption, adaptation and naturalization, a language can produce large number of words expressing clearly different concepts and ideas. For instance, the Bangla words such as *ḍhapār, ḍhapist, gultānist and khepist* are produced by combining English agentive suffixes such as *-er,* and *-ist,* with the Bangla words to accommodate new concepts and ideas in the language. Such forms may be considered for inclusion in the LSS.

Sixth, although it is possible to show that the concepts considered unique to a particular language can have existence in the same sense in the genealogically related languages as these languages have evolved from the same source and have exhibited adequate amount of ecological, geographical, demographic and topographical affinity and have close intercultural communication relations, it has been argued that lexical items of the same origin do not necessarily pertain to the same concept in the both languages (Vossen 2004). For instance, we can refer to several terms relating to food items, recipes, dresses, festivals, rites, rituals, etc., which are different in Bangla and Odia speech communities although both the languages have evolved from the same source and both the language communities have been living side by side for centuries.

3.7 Method of LSS Selection

Taking into consideration various reasons involved in the process of selection of LSS for IndoWordNet (as discussed in the previous section), I like to propose the following stages to be adopted in the act of LSS selection from the Indian languages (Fig. 3.3).

Stage 1: Each language group of the IndoWordNet may be encouraged to prepare an exhaustive list of the terms and words, which they consider suitable to be included in the list of LSS. A note of caution may be raised here to highlight that over or greater exposure of a language (such as Hindi and English) may put the language in the risk of losing language specificity and thereby causing paucity in the list of LSS.

Stage 2: Each group may also be encouraged to provide explanatory definitional meaning and examples of usage in the form of an elaborate sentence so that the concept becomes clear for recognition and conceptualization by member groups. If required, each LSS should be supported with visual (and animated presentation) illustrations for better conceptualization and comprehensibility of the concepts.

Stage 3: The list of LSS may be put to cross-lingual comparison to identify whether any concept is essentially unique to a language or whether it already exists in other languages. Thus, the lists of all the member languages may be compared and verified to know whether the chosen terms are indeed representing unique concepts to a particular languages, and they do not exist in the other languages. That means, even if a particular concept appears to be a natural candidate for LSS of a particular language or a variety, it cannot be considered so if it is already included in the LSS of other languages.

Stage 4: After cross-verification across Indian languages, it may be confirmed whether any concept offered by a particular language group is indeed unique to that language. If the concept (or the lexical item) is not recognized by the members of other groups, then only one can certify the term as a language-specific lexical item and can suggest for its inclusion in the LSS.

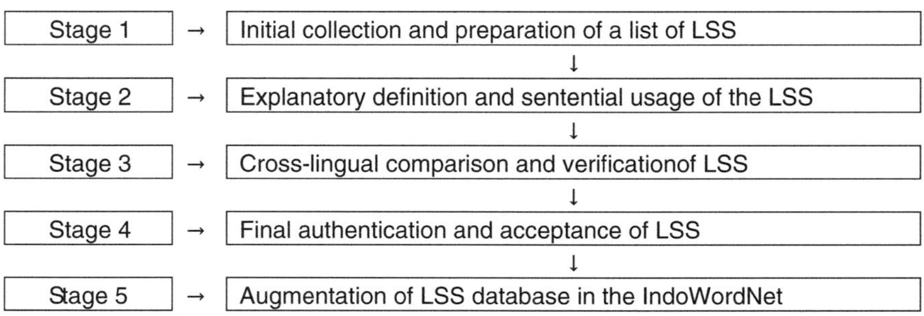

Fig. 3.3 Process of selection of LSS for the IndoWordNet

Stage 5: Once the initial list of LSS is selected and approved for the IndoWordNet consortium, each group is encouraged to augment more and more unique concepts that are found important for their languages, in the same process mentioned above.

However, final selection, validation and acceptance have to be done in the same manner proposed in the first four stages before the LSS is augmented for any Indian language. In essence, cross-lingual verification is mandatory before claiming a synset unique and including it in the LSS.

3.8 Creation of LSS in Bangla

Based on the observations and arguments stated above, I have attempted to select LSS for the Bangla language. After much deliberation, a list of 356 words is selected as LSS for Bangla that constitutes three hundred nouns, five verbs, forty-five adjectives and only one adverb, which are believed to be unique to the language. The words and terms that are considered to be included in the LSS for the Bangla language are categorized in the following domains:

(a) **Tools and Instruments**: This category contains various tools and instruments (including musical instruments) along with those items of constructions that are characteristic of regional architecture, e.g., *kaṛibargā, āṭhākāṭhi, ḍugi, kāchi, ḍhāk, ḍhẽki, dhāmsā, śābal, śālti, śike, ḍhyāṛā and bācāṛi.*

(b) **Evaluatives**: This category contains adjectives and other terms that evoke some kind of value judgment specific to Bangla culture. For instance, the word *nekā* in Bangla describes a bundle of feigning features observed in somebody's character. At the same time, it bears a negative or pejorative association. Some more instances include *apayā, aruci, āṭkuṭe, alppeye, bakhāṭe, bũd, bhije beṛāl, bhusimāl, bheto, ragcaṭā, rāybāghinī, sakṛi and ẽṛe.*

(c) **Descriptives**: There are the terms that become instrumental in portraying certain traits and trends characteristic of a group or an individual in the Bangla speech community, such as *ekśā, eyoti, śāradīyā, eoji, sahajiyā and siddhāi.*

(d) **Ethnic Groups**: This category includes terms that refer to an ethnic race, cultural group or a social clan, etc., such as *gõsāi, bāul, nācni, loṭo, śabar and sahajiyā*. Similarly, there could be evaluative and descriptive terms and others that overlap with this. The interesting thing is that there are social classes with which some kinds of value judgment and description are associated.

(e) **Occupation**: This can be treated as organically related to the groups of people who were holding certain kinds of profession for the generations in the society, which in return does assume to form a social class, such as *hũkobardār, nuliyā, hāluikar and tolābāj.*

(f) **Food items**: It includes local foods, drinks and beverages available in particular geographical location, where the Bangla speech community resides, such as, *khājā, khai, gajā, bāluśāi, mihidānā, mālpoyā, śākbhāt, lāughaṇṭa and kaṭkaṭi.*
(g) **Songs, Music and Dance**: These actually refer to folk songs and music, which are typical to the Bangla speech community, e.g., *sārigān, bāul, bhāṭiyāli, nācni, loṭo, jārigān, tarjā and jhumur.*
(h) **Flora and Fauna**: The varied flora and fauna that constitute the ecology of the region come under this category, such as, *sundarī, garān, śuśni, bādā, bādāban, rui, khayrā, benebau, boyāl, telapiyā, phalsā and khalśe.*
(i) **Festivals and Rituals**: Different folk or local festivals and rituals and words that are related to such events are brought under this category, such as, *āiburobhāt, kalābau, jāmāiṣaṣṭhi, dūrgāpūjā, gājan, kathakatā, caṛak and kāṅālibhojan.*
(j) **Mythology**: These relate to those mythological figures and events which have originated in the classical Sanskrit mythology but have localized, e.g., *bhādu, ṭusu, bhadrakālī,* or owe their origin in the folk culture of the speech community. For instance, many words find their origin in the local culture of tiger worship in the region of Sundarban and south Bengal, e.g., *olābibi, banbibi and dakṣiṇrāy.*
(k) **Games and Sports**: Many of the terms related to local sports (mostly of the children) are also included in the list of Bangla LSS. These sports are highly localized and hardly practised beyond the arena of the speech community, e.g., *dāṅguli, kitkit, kāṭhinãc, kānamāchi, ekkādokkā and bāghchāgal.*

However, it must be categorically mentioned here that this list is not final, since each of the terms included here needs further investigation across other Indian languages to confirm its existence as LSS for the Bangla language.

3.9 Problems Related to LSS Creation

Minute inspection of the LSS database of the Bangla language, however, reveals that most of the so-called unique concepts are rather general in nature as many of them might be available in many other Indian languages, if not in all the Indian languages considered in the IndoWordNet. Moreover, the meanings of most of the LSS are more or less predictable from the semantically similar or near-similar terms available in other Indian languages. Therefore, it does not hold sense to claim their uniqueness to be registered within a particular language. I, therefore, like to argue that it is better to exclude all the derivations with predictable meanings to make the concepts language neutral so that the other language groups can map equivalence regardless to the part-of-speech of the words.

The wide geopolitical and ethnocultural range of the Bangla speech community entails for Region-Specific Terms (RST) rather than LSS. For instance, we might find some words and expressions used in the southern most part of the state (say, Medinipur district) to be quite unfamiliar in the northern most part (say, Darjeeling district) of the state. On the contrary, certain items and ideas prevalent in the Medinipur district of West Bengal are also found in the Balasore district of Odisha, although people living in these two districts belong to two different language communities (i.e., Bangla and Odia) of the two respective states. They exhibit similarities in concepts and terms among themselves just because of their geographical proximity, even if they do not belong to the same language. What I argue here is that since due to different types of diaspora and extensive language contact, people have developed a whole gamut of naturalized vocabulary, which have at least partially blocked many of the Bangla words from being selected in the LSS, it is better to go for RST than for LSS.

Prevalent concepts in a post-globalized society are also getting globalized and replacing, in many cases, the original forms generated inside a language community. For instance, in Bangla, the term *lāṅgal* is being gradually replaced by a newly borrowed term from English *tractor*. Similar observation stands valid for the Bangla terms sucha as *kāli* and *doyāt* which are no longer in use and are being replaced by the English terms such as *pen* and *refill*. In fact, several such language-specific terms (and concepts) are on the brink of extinction and hence hard to find out, such as *kumkum, cuyā, miśi, nolak and narun.*

In many cases, LSS could be the terms of old origin (archaisms), archaic forms, obsolete terms and expressions derived from a part of the non-urban cultural life (especially from folk art and literature). However, it should be remembered that unlike many other countries, in India, many languages share large amount of common mythology recorded in the purāṇas, scriptures and epics. Therefore, all the mythological and cultural terms cannot be easily and indiscriminately designated as 'language specific'. It might be sensible to look into the literature and old texts of other religion and culture of this region in search of language-specific words as instances of loan translation and calquing from the texts of different religion and culture are quite evident in the language of this region.

If we adopt the notion of speech community as depicted in Gumperz (1962), we might extend the Bangla speech community to a cross-linguistic interactive arena, where we are permitted to include lexical items (and concepts) already known and used in her sister languages such as Odia, Assamese, Maithili and Bhojpuri. Historically, there are so many evidences of exodus along the eastern line that it would be hard to find out words and terms that are exclusive to the region of Bengal and are alien to other neighbouring states. This might be true of other Indian languages as well.

3.10 Concluding Remarks

After introducing as many LSS as possible in the IndoWordNet according to the procedure described above, we can continue to expand the list of LSS by way of adding new LSSs from each language group highlighting the local and regional issues and events, since many terms well known in the regional variety of a language may not exist in the standard variety. Addition of such terms into IndoWordNet may be of considerable interest for all language groups, since most of the terms are not likely to be found in many languages.

In essence, the establishment of attested pertinence of LSS within the IndoWordNet demonstrates that besides concepts specific for particular languages and domains, concepts specific to a language group can also exist (e.g., Hind–Urdu, Manipuri–Mizo, Bangla–Odia, Tamil–Malayalam and Telegu–Kannada, etc.). Therefore, introducing a procedure for identifying region or group-based synsets can be useful as it might help in enlarging the number of common or shared concepts and semantically similar words across the language groups.

There may be further similarities among the geographically proximal languages, which could be used for expansion of the regional common synsets. For example, consider the Odia language and the Telugu language, which, although do not belong to the same language family, do share some common concepts vis-à-vis words due to their close geographical proximities. Such synsets can also contribute in understanding the nature of conceptual interfaces shared by the members of the respective speech communities as well as may reflect on the degree of interlingual communication and the nature of information exchanges between the two speech communities.

Since LSS of a particular language is not always explicit to be easily discernible to the members of other languages, let me argue for providing necessary visual support in the form of images, pictures and animation with the synsets, wherever possible, so that any confusion relating to LSS selection may be settled with additional information obtained from the visual illustrations. Moreover, this method may help in better conceptualization of terms (and concepts) in future works of language teaching, knowledge accumulation, information sharing, and translation.

References

Apresjan, J. (1973). Regular polysemy. *Linguistics, 142*, 5–32.

Bhatt, B., & Bhattacharyya, P. (2011). IndoWordNet and its linking with ontology. In *Proceedings of the 9th International Conference on Natural Language Processing (ICON-2011),* Anna University, Chennai, India, 16th–19th Dec 2011.

Bhattacharyya, P. (2010). IndoWordNet. In *Proceedings of the 7th International Language Resource and Evaluation Conference (LREC-10), Valletta, Malta*, May 19–21, 2010.

Buitelaar, P., & Sacaleanu, B. (2001). Ranking and selecting synsets by domain relevance. In *Proceedings of the NAACL 2001 Workshop on WordNet and Other Lexical Resources, Pittsburgh*, June 2001.

Chakrabarti, D., & Bhattacharyya, P. (2004). Creation of English and Hindi verb hierarchies and their application to Hindi WordNet building and English-Hindi MT. In *Proceedings of the Second Global WordNet Conference, Bruno, Czech Republic,* 20–23 Jan (pp. 83–90).

Cruse, D. A. (1986). *Lexical semantics*. Cambridge: Cambridge University Press.

Dash, N. S., Dutta Chowdhury, P., & Sarkar, A. (2009). Naturalization of English words in modern Bangla: A corpus-based empirical study. *Language Forum, 35*(2), 127–142.

Fellbaum, C. (Ed.). (1998). *WordNet: An electronic lexical database*. Cambridge, Mass: MIT Press.

Gumperz, J. (1962). Types of linguistic communities. *Anthropological Linguistics, 4*(1), 28–40.

Krstev, C., Obradovic, I., & Vitas, D. (2007). An approach to the development of language specific concepts in the WordNets. *Southern Journal of Linguistics, 29*(1), 77–90.

Kulkarni, M., Dangarikar, C., Kulkarni, I., Nanda, A., & Bhattacharyya, P. (2010). Introducing Sanskrit Wordnet. In *Global Wordnet Conference (GWC10), Mumbai, India.*

Magnini, B., & Cavagliá, G. (2000). Integrating subject field codes into WordNet. In *Proceedings of the 2nd International Conference on Language Resources & Evaluation LREC'2000, Athens* (pp. 1413–1420).

Miller, G. A. (1985). WordNet: A dictionary browser. In *Proceedings of the 1st International Conference on Information in Data*. University of Waterloo, Waterloo, Canada.

Narayan, D., Chakrabarty, D., Pande, P., & Bhattacharyya, P. (2002). An experience in building the IndoWordNet: A WordNet for Hindi. In *Presented in the 1st International Conference on Global WordNet (GWC 02), Mysore, India.*

Parkes, G., & Cornell, A. (1992). NTC's dictionary of German false cognates. National Textbook Company, NTC Publishing Group.

Selvaraj, A. (2010). Telugu wordnet. In *Proceedings of the Global Wordnet Conference (GWC10), Mumbai, India.*

Vossen, P. (2004). EuroWordNet: A multilingual database of autonomous and language-specific WordNets connected via an Inter-Lingual-Index. *International Journal of Lexicography, 17*(2), 161–173.

Whitelock, P. (1992). Shake-and-bake translation. In *Proceedings of the 14th International Conference on Computational Linguistics (COLING'92)* (Vol. 2, pp. 784–790). Nantes, 23–28 August.

Whorf, B. L. (1956). Science and linguistics. In J. B. Carroll (Ed.), *Language, Thought and Reality: Selected Writings of Benjamin Lee Whorf* (pp. 207–219). Cambridge, Mass: MIT Press.

Zuckermann, G. (2003). *Language contact and lexical enrichment in Israeli hebrew*. Houndmills: Palgrave Macmillan.

Chapter 4
Problems in Translating Hindi Synsets into the Bangla WordNet

Niladri Sekhar Dash

Abstract In this chapter, I have made an attempt to look into the problems and challenges I have faced in developing the Bangla synsets that will stand as conceptual equivalents for the Hindi synsets used in the IndoWordNet. The Bangla synsets that I have developed so far are to be represented in the IndoWordNet, which is meant to be linked up with the unique concepts represented in the IndoWordNet—a digital semantic net that aims at representing parallel concepts available in the EuroWordNet and the *Princeton WordNet of English* of the *Pennsylvania University,* USA. In this chapter, I have also tried to highlight some of the crucial problems relating to Hindi to Bangla translation of sentences used to elaborate the concepts captured in the Hindi synsets. There are many problems and challenges in translation between the languages (e.g., lexical divergences, convergences, reordering of phrases, ambiguities, and lexical mismatches), which have been briefly addressed in this chapter due to paucity of space. Moreover, our primary focus is on the problems related to synset generation rather than on the problems of translation in general from Hindi to Bangla.

Keywords Synset · Hindi · Bangla · Concept · Lexical gap · Translation · Semantics · WordNet

4.1 Introduction

The task of designing an interlingual WordNet system has its own pros and cons. A WordNet, although keeps words as basic units, includes idiomatic expressions, collocations, and phrasal expressions, making the task of a dictionary maker

N.S. Dash (✉)
Linguistic Research Unit, Indian Statistical Institute, Kolkata, India
e-mail: ns_dash@yahoo.com

N.S. Dash et al. (eds.), *The WordNet in Indian Languages*,
DOI 10.1007/978-981-10-1909-8_4

substantially different from just finding equivalents of given words (Fellabaum 1988, p. 5). A WordNet, therefore, forces a lexicographer to delve into the domain of cultural fabric for providing panoramic information related to the words. In such cases, translating the source language, and in turn the source culture in the target language, poses serious challenges and problems before the lexicographers.

In this chapter, I seek to look into the problems and challenges I have faced while I have tried to develop the Bangla synsets parallel to *Hindi WordNet* synsets for the *IndoWordNet* (Bhattacharyya 2010). Most often the challenges I have faced have stemmed from the differences in lexicon, meaning, grammar, phraseology, discourse, and sociocultural differences of the respective languages. In the following sections of this chapter, I have tried to illustrate some of these issues in a sequential order with adequate explanation and examples obtained from the Hind synset databases (Chakrabarty et al. 2002) provided to us for analysis and generation.

I have tried to classify all the translational problems into three broad types, namely (a) lexical anomalies, (b) semantic anomalies, and (c) syntactic anomalies. Lexical anomalies (Sect. 4.2) include paradigmatic lexical gap, onomatopoeic word formation, the use of diminutives, and the differences in flora and fauna. Semantic anomalies (Sect. 4.3) include lexical mismatch and false cognates. Syntactic anomalies (Sect. 4.4) discusses about gender differences, the use of copula, the treatment of gerundial forms, and the construction of causative forms in Hindi and Bangla. The theoretical-cum-functional importance of this study has been attested in conclusion (Sect. 4.5) which may provide adequate insights and guidelines for developing strategies of translation from Hindi to Bangla and vice versa—both at manual and automatic enterprises.

4.2 Lexical Anomalies

Instances of lexical anomaly between Hindi and Bangla are simply galore. There are many cases where an entire paradigm of words in Hindi does not find any equivalence in Bangla. On the other hand, where the situation is not so overtly acute, I have to deal with those concepts of Hindi for which there is no single word equivalent in Bangla. In this section, I have provided a brief account on such problems and the strategies I have adopted to deal with such lexical anomalies.

4.2.1 Paradigmatic Lexical Gap in Wage Terms

Hindi often exhibits the presence of a unique paradigm of words relating to wage terms (WTs) that does not find translational equivalents in Bangla. It leads to the generation of a unique problem in translation called as **paradigmatic lexical gap (PLG)**—a theoretical-cum-practical problem in translation between

Table 4.1 Paradigmatic gap in translation of wage terms

No.	Concepts	Hindi words	Bangla equivalents
1	Wage for rubbing something	ragRaai, ghisaai	ragṛānor majuri
2	Wage for scattering something	chiDkaai	chaṛānor majuri
3	Wage for cutting something	kaTwaai	kāṭār majuri
4	Wage for catching something	pakDaai	dharār majuri
5	Wage for spreading something	bichaai	bichānor majuri
6	Wage for washing something	dhulaai	dhoyār majuri, kācār majuri
7	Wage for stitching something	silaai, silwaai	selāiyer majuri
8	Wage for ploughing land	jutaai, jotaai	lāṅgal karār majuri
9	Wage for cleaning Ieds	niraai, nindaai	āgāchā pariṣkār karar majuri
10	Wage for painting something	putaai, potaai	raṅg karār majuri, lepan karār majuri

two typologically related languages. From our study, I have found that the main domains where PLG makes itself evident quite consistently are the domains of WTs, which refers to the payment of wages against the service provided by people in various forms of physical and mental activities. For instance, consider some of the examples given below in the list (Table 4.1).

In the following examples, it is found that while Hindi has a single-word expression for each *wage term*, Bangla does not have such a single-word expression to stand as a synset equivalent. Therefore, as a possible solution, I have used two-word (sometimes multiword) expressions where the first word (W_1) is a gerundial form tagged with genitive case marker -er 'of' and the second word (W_2) is a fixed noun for 'wage'. Interestingly while W_2 acts a constant, W_1 acts as a variable, as the following schema shows:

Schema 1 $[[W_1 + er]_{N\_Gen}] + [W_2]_N : WT$

The last three examples (8, 9, and 10) of the table reveal far more complexities that demand direct use of multiword expressions to deal with the problems. Here, I have to introduce a new helping verb 'karā' with which the genitive case marker '-er' is to be tagged, while the W_1 remains as an unchanged noun, e.g. *lāṅgal karār majuri* "wage of ploughing lands", *āgāchā pariṣkār karar majuri* "wage for cleaning Ieds", *raṅg karār majuri* "wage for painting something", and *lepan karār majuri* "wage for pasting something".

What is interesting in these examples is that while I seek help of multiword expressions in generating nearly equivalent translation in Bangla, the specification of a particular type of wage as expressed in the source Hindi synset is lost as it misses out on a few connotations relating to language-specific culture. For instance, when the Hindi synset *'bichāi'* is used to refer to kind of wage paid for laying beds for the newly married couple as a part of a marriage ceremony, it adorns an extra shade of cultural connotation, which is missed if it is literally translated into Bangla as *bichānor majuri* "wages of laying something". Although in Bangla I do not have any cultural synset with payment made for the preparation of bed for the bride and the groom, I have another unique compound known as *śajyā tolā* that conversely refers to the act of rolling up bed used by newly married couple. Since a WordNet is meant to bring out the beliefs and properties of all the cultures encapsulated in the vocabulary of various languages (Fellbaum 1988, p. 32), such cultural differences should invariably lead to the cross-cultural sociolinguistic investigation as reflected in use of synsets in Hindi and Bangla—an unexplored avenue the study of which may lead to birth of diachronic lexicological investigation across language boundaries.

Even if there are large PLG with regard to the use of 'wage terms' between the languages, Bangla, indeed, cites one or two forms where the suffix *'-ī'* is tagged with a verb or noun to refer to the same concept, such as *'khorākī'* "wage given for food" and *'bājanī'* "wages given for playing drums". One or two stray instances, however, do not stand for a system or a general rule of a language.

What is most striking is that almost in all cases, there is a strong lexical gap between Hindi and Bangla in this area, although it is not clear to us why these two genealogically related languages with exhibited conceptual linkages reveal this kind of difference in their linguistic expression of the concepts. Surely, a discourse-based multidimensional crosslingual investigation is required to attest and address this phenomenon in minute details the information of which may be adopted to design better WordNets as well as better systems for machine translation between the two languages.

4.2.2 Gerundial Onomatopoeic Words

There are a host of onomatopoeic words in Hindi, which by way of adding suffix '-ā' assume the form of gerundial nouns and infinite verbs. Although this is a volatile morphological process in Hindi, it is hardly used in Bangla, as shown in the following sentences (1–10) where translation of Hind sentences in Bangla is also provided to show how gerundial nouns in Hindi are treated differently in Bangla translation.

1a. ajj subah se hi hawa sarsraa rahi hai
1b. āj sakāl theke śõśõ kare hāoyā baiche
1c. Wind is blowing strong today from morning

2a. ma bacche ko pyar se thapthapa rahi hai
2b. mā baccāke ādar kare piṭh cāpṛe dicche
2c. Mother patting the back of her child

3a. rat se hi mera sara badan chunchuna raha hai
3b. rāt theke āmār sārā śarīr ciṛciṛ karche
3c. I am having a burning sensation in body from night

4a. desh ki simao par kabhi kabhi goliyan dandnati hai
4b. deśer sīmāy kakhano kakhano guli damdam kare
4c. Sometimes bullets burst at the border of the country

5a. atyadhik thandi ke karan mere dant kiTkiTaa rahi hai
5b. atyadhik ṭhāṇḍāy āmār dā̃t kiṭkiṭ karche
5c. My teeth are shivering in cold

6a. aj merā ghora bahut hinhina raha hai
6b. āj āmār ghoṛāṭā khub cī̃hī̃ cī̃hī̃ śabda karche
6c. My horse is neighing very much today

7a. pulis ko dekhte hi chor ka dil dhakdhakane lagaa
7b. puliśke dekhei corer buk dhukpuk karte lāglo
7c. The thief started trembling seeing the police

8a. bacchon ke kudne ki karan chat dhamdhama rahi hai
8b. bāccāder lāphālāphir kārane chāt dhamdham śabda karche
8c. The roof creates 'dhum dhum' sound when children jump

9a. khet se chiriya ko bhagane ke liye Tin ko paTpaTate hai
9b. khet theke pākhi tāṛānor janya ṭin paṭpaṭ karā hay
9c. Tin is tapped to scary birds from field

10a. chiriya apne pankh phaRphaRa rahi hai
10b. pākhiṭā nijer ḍānā phaṛphaṛ karche
10c. The bird is flapping its wings

I have noted that only a few onomatopoeic words in Bangla have such gerundial entities by adding the special nominal suffix '-ni', such as the following:

- kirkirāni: "an sensation of continuous irritation"
- dapdāpani: "a sensation of something sullen in forehead"
- gungunāni: "act of ceaseless humming"
- śanśanāni: "sound of strong breeze"
- khiṭkhiṭāni: "state of continuous displeasure"
- dhukpukuni: "a feeling of strong fear"
- śirśirāni: "a feeling of eerie sensation"
- chaṭpaṭāni: "state of restlessness"
- pyānpyānāni: "state of repeated requests of something"
- ghyānghyānāni: "state of constant complain".

In most cases, however, these are used in some special stylistic situations to describe the mental or physical state of the persons concerned.

What is important is that although Bangla has many productive word formation strategies through which I can create large number of onomatopoeic words,

Table 4.2 Onomatopoeic words in Hindi and Bangla

No	Hindi word	Bangla word
1	sarsarānā	śõśõ karā
2	thapthapānā	piṭh cāpṛe deoyā
3	chunchunānā	ciṛciṛ karā
4	dandanānā	damdam karā
5	kitkitānā	kiṭkiṭ karā
6	katkatānā	kaṭkaṭ karā
7	Hinhinānā	cĩhĩ cĩhĩ śabda karā
8	dhakdhkānā	dhukpuk karā
9	dhakpakānā	dhukpuk karā
10	dhamdhamānā	dhamdham karā
11	paTpatānā	paṭpaṭ karā
12	phaRphaRānā	phaṛphaṛ śabda karā
13	pharpharānā	phaṛphaṛ śabda karā
14	phurphurānā	phaṛphaṛ śabda karā

I hardly take help of the suffix '-ni' to create onomatopoeic words as Hind does with the suffix '-ā'. Therefore, to overcome the problem, I have adopted again the process of lexical diversion by which I had to take help of multiword units in place of single-word units used in Hindi. For instance, consider the examples given above (Table 4.2) which sums up the use of specific lexical items in Bangla concerned with problems of translation of Hindi gerundial onomatopoeic forms.

In the examples given above, it is to be noted that some Hindi onomatopoeic words, when translated into Bangla, need a support of the helping verb 'kar' "to do" (not the 'do support' of the transformational-generative grammar) to generate same kind of sense. Moreover, when this helping verb fails to yield expected sense, it requires the support of another fixed lexical expression, namely 'śabda' "sound" (refer to examples 6, 8, and 10 in Table 4.2) to generate the sense of making sound.

Such a process, however, does not guarantee for natural translation in Bangla, as many of the Hindi onomatopoeic words do not find conceptually equivalent expressions in Bangla. In case of examples 4, 5, 8, and 9, for instance, I have faced this problem, which I have solved by way of adopting one of the two following strategies:

(a) Transliteration of Hindi expressions into Bangla or
(b) Coinage of new equivalent terms in Bangla.

In case of the first method, I need to apply further linguistic operations as conversion of Hindi gerundial forms into onomatopoeic words in Bangla also asks for addition of causative forms of the helping verb 'kar' with the newly generated onomatopoeic word. The event of morpholexical metamorphosis through which these expressions pass may be described in the following stages:

Stage 1: Input of Hindi onomatopoeic word: paṭpaṭānā
Stage 2: Deletion of infix '-ā' and gerundial suffix: '-ā'
Stage 3: Generation of a string in Bangla: 'paṭpaṭ'
Stage 4: Addition of causative form of helping verb: 'karā'
Stage 5: Generation of final Bangla word: 'paṭpaṭ karā'.

Since this method has been used as a makeshift means of translation, the issue of naturalness in sense equivalence of the concepts in Bangla is at stake. Also, combination of certain lexical items within a sentential form resists the use of an onomatopoeic expression in Bangla. For instance, in example (4), Hindi makes use of an onomatopoeic form 'dandanānā' to refer to the process of ceaseless firing of bullets. In Bangla translation, however, it is extremely unnatural to retain this form as it is, since I do not use this onomatopoeic form in Bangla. Therefore, I prefer to use multiword string such as *'lāgātār golāguli calche'* "Bullets are being fired ceaselessly" as the most appropriate translation of the Hindi expression.

In example 8, I come across almost similar problem. The Bangla speakers do not usually use a sentence such as *'chāt dhamdham śabda karche'* "roof is making dhamdham sound". Rather I form a more natural sentence such as *'chāte dhumdhum śabda hacche'* "dhum dhum sound is being made on the roof". Logically, if the first sentence is S_1 and the second one is S_2, then these may be schematized in the following ways where the note of preference of the native Bangla speakers will surely tilt towards the second one.

(a) S_1: $N_{\text{\_Nominative Onomatopoeia sound}}$ 'do'
(b) S_2: $N_{\text{\_Locative Onomatopoeia sound}}$ 'be'

There are also cases where an onomatopoeic expression in Hindi has a non-onomatopoeic equivalent in Bangla. In example 2, it has been noted that Hindi 'thapthapānā' has a Bangla equivalent expression 'cāpṛāno' that can denote almost the same sense, although the gerundial form of the expression, e.g. 'cāpṛāni', has not been used here because the gerundial Bangla form fails to produce equivalence of the sense of the Hindi expression.

4.2.3 Use of Diminutives in Hindi and Bangla

Hindi has a regular pattern of using '-ā', '-ni', and '-I' to refer to the items of smaller size. For expressing diminutive sense, Hindi uses these diminutive suffixes in a consistent manner irrespective to [± ANIMATE, ± HUMAN, ± GENDER] attributes of nouns. Hindi, therefore, does not need to take help of any additional lexical item to imply diminutive sense of nouns.

The use of diminutive terms is not foreign in Bangla as the language possesses some such terms that are frequently used to denote diminutive sense of items, such as

Table 4.3 Use of Bangla 'choṭa' in diminutive sense

Concept	Hindi word	Bangla word
Small cot	khaṭolā	choṭa khāṭ
Small cot	khaṭolnā	choṭa khāṭ
Small pitcher	luṭiyā	choṭa ghaṭi
Small lotus plant	kamalini	choṭa padma gāch
Small lotus plant	padmini	choṭa padma gāch
Small anklet	kinkni	choṭa ghuṅur
Small pulley	rahaṭi	choṭa kapikal
Small pulley	rahāṭi	choṭa kapikal
Small metal backing pan	tauni	choṭa tāoyā
Small metal backing pan	tai	choṭa tāoyā
Small metal backing pan	tavi	choṭa tāoyā
Small umbrella	chatri	choṭa chātā
Small muller made of stone	loṭi	choṭa noṛā
Small muller made of stone	loṭiyā	choṭa noṛā

'pũṭli' "a small packet" and 'bũcki' "a tiny bag". Also, we sometimes tag the diminutive suffix '-kā' with base forms to generate words with diminutive sense, e.g. 'peṭikā' "a small bundle", 'pustikā' "booklet", 'nāṭika' "playlet", and 'patrikā' "leaflet", etc.

However, the suffix '-kā' is not always used in the diminutive sense in Bangla. It is also used to denote feminine gender, e.g., 'nāyikā' "heroine", 'pāṭhikā' "female reader", 'jātikā' "girl child", and 'bālikā' "girl", as well as for formation of adjectives, e.g., 'ḍābkā' "big and juicy", 'ṭhunkā' 'petty", 'palkā' "fragile", 'damkā' "gusty", and 'jhaṭikā' 'stormy", etc.

This implies the use of diminutive marker '-kā' is morphologically limited and lexically restricted in Bangla. Therefore, while translating Hindi diminutive terms, it appears impossible to provide a single-word unit from Bangla that can stand as an appropriate translational equivalent for the Hindi term. As a strategic solution, I have used endocentric compounds in a schema of 'choṭa X' where 'choṭa' stands for diminutive sense, while X stands as a variable in place of Hindi nouns, as the list (Table 4.3) shows.

4.2.4 Systematic Lexical Gap

Bangla also exhibits a kind of systematic lexical gap for many female counterparts of [+ANIMATE, -HUMAN] objects of Hindi. The morph denoting femininity '-nī', which is widely used in Hindi to refer to the lexical gender, has a restricted use in Bangla as it is affixed only to those words that refer to human beings. Therefore, in these cases also, I have used similar schema of endocentric compound formation with the use of 'mādī X', where 'mādī' stands for feminine gender and X stands for a +ANIMATE noun (Table 4.4).

Table 4.4 Use of 'mādī' for feminine gender of +ANIMATE, - HUMAN in Bangla

Concept	Hindi word	Bangla word
Female camel	ũṭni	mādī uṭ
Female parrot	toti	mādī totā
Female parrot	suggi	mādī totā
Female rat	chuhiā	mādī ĩdur
Female rat	chuhi	mādī ĩdur
Female crow	kāuyi	mādī kāk
Female crow	kālikā	mādī kāk

Table 4.5 Hindi–Bangla differences in feminine forms

Sl. No.	Concept	Hind	Bangla
1	A lady of goldsmith community	sunarin	Not Available
2	Wife of a goldsmith	sunarin	syākrānī
3	A lady of carpentry community	barhain	Not Available
4	Wife of a carpenter	barhain	chutornī

I have observed that some sociolinguistic issues play significant role in distribution of '-ni' in both Bangla and Hindi. While Hindi WordNet is marked with concepts such as 'a female blacksmith' or 'a female member of the tribe/profession X', Bangla does not usually have such formations. Following the regular tradition, there are certain professions in Bengal that are practiced by male members only. In these cases, 'X + -ni' normally refers to the wife of X, not to a female professional engaged in the profession. For instance, consider some of the Hindi examples and their counter formations in Bangla (Table 4.5).

The list (Table 4.5) shows that Bangla does not have any term to stand as equivalent to the Hindi 'sunarin' (1) or 'barhain' (3), because these concepts are hardly realized in Bangla. On the contrary, Bangla has 'syākrānī' (2) and 'chutornī' (4) to stand as equivalents to Hindi 'sunarin' (2) and 'barhain' (4), respectively, when these terms refer to the concepts of "wife of a person belonging to profession X". So to deal with the concepts in (1) and (3) in the list (Table 4.5), I have generated multiword expressions such as 'syākrā jātir mahilā' and 'chutor jātir mahilā', since I understand that these will be accepted by the native speakers.

4.2.5 *Difference in Flora and Fauna*

It is observed that Bangla does not have equivalent lexical terms for some flora and fauna found in Hindi synset. This directly substantiates the argument for creation of Language Specific Synset (LSS) in which a particular concept of a particular language community, which is missing in another language community, should be represented. Since many concepts of Hindi flora and fauna are not found

Table 4.6 Transliterated names of flora and fauna in Bangla

Concept	Hindi word	Bangla word
lal rang ka ek jalpari jo akar me battakh se chota hota hai	silhii, silkahii	silahi
ek chota samudri jantu jiske sharir par gol, kantedar kabac hota hai	Jalsahi	jalsāhī
sunhale rang ki ek chiriaa	sonchRiyaa	sonciṛiyā
ek prakar ki machli	karwaa)	karbā māch
ek prakar ki supari jo chikni hoti hai	chiulii	cakcake supuri
titir ke akar ka ek jalpaksii	jalkapot	jalkapot
ek jalpaksii jo akar mein titiri se baRaa hotaa hai aur jiske sharir ka upri bhaag kala tathaa nichlaa bhaag saphed hota hai	gajpaaon	gajpāon
Sambhaar jheel ke nikat paayaa janewaalaa ek jalpaksii	chaniyaarii	caniyārī
ek ekvarsiiya ausodhiya banaspati se prapta beej	barraa	barrā
Ek briksa ka phal	kaayphal	kāyphal
Kaamrakh kii jaati kaa ek paiR	bilambi	bilambi
ek prakar ka bahut chotaa kiiRaa	kebakii	kebakī

in Bangla I have tried to directly transliterate the names of these flora and fauna into Bangla (Table 4.6) as a readymade solution. However, I apprehend that these transliterated concepts are entirely new to Bangla people and therefore will mostly remain unacceptable to them.

4.3 Semantic Anomalies

There are indeed large numbers of lexical items which are orthographically identical both in Hindi and Bangla, but are very much different in meaning and sense denotation in respective languages. For understanding the phenomenon I call them 'semantically mismatched expressions', which are sometimes identified as **'false cognates'** (Parkes and Cornell 1992) or **'false friends'** (Zuckermann 2003, p. 102) in the domains of lexicography and WordNet development. Some examples from Hindi and Bangla are given in the next page (Table 4.7).

There are sociocultural issues inherent with the lexical expressions presented in the list. For example, the term 'parv' in Hindi means a social festival or ceremony, e.g., *āj bāhā parb hai* "Today is Baha festival", which is almost similar in sense in Bangla when the term is used as 'parab' meaning some social or cultural events. However, the Bangla term 'parba' is more frequently used in a different sense meaning a part of an episode of a play, drama, or literary text, e.g., *eṭā nāṭaker pratham parba* "this is the first act of the play".

The example of Hindi synset 'dhanī', however, presents a curious case. The term is metaphorically used in Hindi to mean a talented and enlightened person. In Bangla, the word is normally used to mean a wealthy person. Therefore, at the

Table 4.7 Semantic mismatches in Hindi and Bangla

Hindi meaning	Words with similar orthography	Bangla meaning
rage	abhimān	state of being hurt
request	abhyarthana	hospitality
request	āgraha	eagerness
exception	apabād	bad name
relative	atmajaniya	son, daughter
disconnected	aŷathā	without reason
oath	bacan	word/number
cloud	bādal	rain
tender age	bāli	sand
irritation, indifference	birti	rest, break
boiled rice	cāul	non-boiled rice
pain	dard	sympathy
talented	dhanī	rich
hour	ghaṛi	watch/clock
bumper sale	hāṅgāmā	chaos
many	katipay	few
vacant	khāli	empty
window	khiṛki	backyard of house
blood	khun	murder
road	mārg	means or way
green coconut	nāriyel	ripe coconut
festival	parv	episode
kite	pataṅg	insect
empty	phankā	lonely
revenue tax	pot	boat
new leaf	prabāl	coral
any vegetable	śāk	leafy vegetable
all	sāmānya	minimum
information	sandeś	sIets
to pay back	śodh	revenge
information	sūcnā	introduction
to find out	talab	to summon
commodity put to use	Upabhogya	enjoyable

time of translation of Hindi synset, I have to depend on contextual information of the Hindi sentence to decide how the subtle sense of the term can be accommodated in the Bangla text. Both the examples reiterate our argument that contexts call for adequate attention and interpretation while preparing translational equivalent synsets in the two languages (Dash 2005).

These examples amply illustrate how words of similar orthographic representation can exhibit different manifestations of meaning in two different languages. This again confirms that although Hindi and Bangla are closely related languages in terms of etymological ancestry, there are large numbers of words which express different concepts and meanings in the two languages—potentially one of the highly captivating domains for cross-cultural sociolinguistic investigation.

4.4 Syntactic Anomalies

Anomalies are not only attested at the lexical and semantic levels, but also at the syntactic level. I have come across many syntactic anomalies at the time of translating Hindi synsets into Bangla for explaining the concepts captured within the synsets. In fact, the number of anomalies observed in this area is more than the anomalies observed in other two areas. Some of our observations are elaborated below with examples.

4.4.1 Treatment of Gender in Hindi and Bangla

The gender factor brings in a twofold problem in translation of Hindi synsets into Bangla: First one is grammatical and the second one is lexical-cum-semantic. The syntactic problem stems from the structural anomalies between the two languages. For instance, while Hindi shows clear gender agreement in sentence formation, Bangla is entirely free from it. So when a Hindi speaker writes 'laDkā ýātā hai' "The boy is going" and 'laDki ýāti hai' "The girl is going"—using two different forms of the verb based on the gender of the subject—a Bangla speaker simply uses just one form of the verb, i.e., 'ýācche' irrespective of the gender of the subject, e.g., 'cheleṭi ýācche' "The boy is going" and 'meyeṭi ýācche' "The girl is going".

4.4.2 The Presence and Absence of Copula

Sentences in simple present tense in Hindi necessitate the use of 'hai' as a copula that needs to be physically present immediately after the main verb. This mandate is not relevant for Bangla, since sentences in simple present tense in Bangla are usually formed without the physical presence of a copula. In fact, the presence of a copula in Bangla sentence of simple present tense might reflect on the feature of paucity of naturalness in the construction. A few instances of this phenomenon are evident in the following examples (11–24).

11a. janme pranio ki mrityu nischit hai
11b. jāta prāṇīder mṛtyu niścit
11c. Born animals are sure to die

12a. Shyam anaaj kaa byapaari hai
12b. śyām ānājer byāpāri
12c. Shyam is a seller of raw vegetables

13a. gaon ki apeksaa shahero meim khaadya bastueM bahat mahengi hai
13b. grāmer tulanāy śahare khāoyar jiniṣer dām anek beśi
13c. Foods are costlier in cities than in villages

14a. dayaaluta sajjan purusoM ka abhusaN hai
14b. dayā sajjan puruṣer alaṅkār
14c. Mercy is an ornament of honest person

15a. Woh is khel main anubhavhin hai
15b. Se ei khelāy anabhijña
15c. He is a non-expert in this game

16a. Bhaskar meraa choṭaa bhaai hai
16b. Bhāskar āmār choṭa bhāi
16c. Bhaskar is my younger brother

17a. Shyam mera chacheraa bhaai hai
17b. śyām āmār khuṛtuto bhāi
17c. Shyam is my paternal brother

18a. Raam ka baRaa bhaai adhyapak hai
18b. Rāmer baṛo bhāi adhyāpak
18c. Ram's elder brother is a professor

19a. Kashmir amshle par bharat pak samjhota abashyak hai
19b. Kāśmīr prasaṅge bhārat o pākistāner samjhotā ābaśyak
19c. India and Pakistan should negotiate on Kashmir

20a. manobhav par niyantran karnaa kathin hota hai
20b. manobhābke niyantraṇ karā kaṭhin
20c. It is difficult to control mentality

21a. Meri maa ek kaamkaaji mahila hai
21b. āmār mā ekjan karmaratā mahilā
21c. My mother is a working lady

22a. yeh rastrapati ke anreji pustak ki anudit kriti hai
22b. eṭi rāṣṭrapatir iṅreji pustaker anudita kṛti
22c. It is a translation of President's book

23a. Godan Premchand ki maulik kriti hai
23b. Godān Premchchder maulik sṛṣṭi
23c. Godan is an original writing of Premchand

24a. tulsidas ka ramcharitmanas prasiddha sahityik kriti hai
24b. Tulsīdāser Rāmcaritmānas ekṭi prasiddha kṛti
24c. Ramcharitmanas is famous literary work of Tulasidas

When I look at the examples given above (11–24), it is evident that while 'hai' is a mandatory in Hindi sentences of simple present tense, the use of 'hay' as a translational equivalent in Bangla sentences is strictly prohibited. A native Bangla user will never use 'hay' in such sentences, since the use of 'hay' will invariably destroy naturalness of the sentences. In simple present tense, Bangla permits verbless construction because such constructions are obvious grammatical forms where the role of a copula is made redundant in expressing the meanings of the sentences. Therefore, while translating simple present tense sentences from Hindi to Bangla I have been extra cautious in dealing with such constructions in the language. It is a unique feature of Bangla—almost similar to the feature of gender agreement in Hindi.

4.4.3 Treatment of Gerundial Forms

The Hindi gerund system puts forth a challenge before us as I find a consistent Paradigmatic Lexical Gap (PLG) between the two languages. Although Bangla has single-word gerundial forms made with affixation, e.g., 'thābṛā': 'thābṛāno', 'ṭana': 'ṭānāno', and 'karā': karāno', these are mostly used as single-word verbs and rarely as compound verb forms. Moreover, since this process does not work for many of the Bangla verb forms, I have to depend on the use of compound verbs (i.e., complex predicates) to express gerundial sense generated by the single-word gerunds of Hindi as the following examples shows (Table 4.8).

4.4.4 Causative Constructions

Hindi has two different causative constructions. Both the types are schematized in the following algorithms where A stands for a subject, B stands for an object, C stands for second object and D stands for an action:

Table 4.8 Gerundial forms in Hindi and Bangla

Concept	Hindi word	Bangla word
Samkalpa karne kii kriya ya bhaab	samkalpan, samkalpanaa	saṃkalpa karā
Chaukne kii kriya ya bhaab	chaunknaa, chaunk, chaundh	camke ẏāoyā
Eisa kaam jisme mastisk kiii bahut adhik shakti byay ho	mathapacchi	māthā khāṭāno
akRane ya enThne ki kriya ya bhaab	akaD, eNTh, tanaw	ṭān dharā
God ya dattak lene ki kriya	raas	dattak neoyā
Pair ke kisi nas ya nason ki sikuRan	Taans	ṭān dharā

Schema 2 A causes B to do D and

Schema 3 A causes B to do C do D.

The Hindi verbal suffixes '-nā' and '-vānā' correspond to both the 1st and 2nd causatives, respectively, although there are cases where this rule does not always hold. This pattern generates several difficulties in translation of Hindi causative constructions into Bangla as the following examples show (25–36).

25a. rikshabalo ko paise dene ke liye usne panc sau ka note bhunaya
25b. rikśāoyālāke ṭākā deoyār janya se pancśo ṭākār noṭ bhāṅgālo
25c. He exchanged five hundred rupee note to pay fare to the rickshaw puller

26a. samira ne apne gehno lokar main rakhwaye
26b. Samīrā nijer gaynā lakāre rākhiyeche
26c. Samira has employed someone to keep her jellries in locker

27a. Usne baccho ke liye bhi khub sara bhojan parsaya
27b. tini bāccāder janyeo bohu bhojan paribeśan karālen
27c. He made others to distribute foods to children

28a. darji apni biwi se karDe turpata hai
28b. darji nijer strīke diye kāpaṛ selāi karāy
28c. The tailor makes his wife to stick cloth

29a. sarpanch ne gaon walon se ek talaw khudwaya
29b. pañcāyet pradhāṇ grāmbāsīder diye ekṭi pukur khanan kariyechen
29c. The panchayat head made the villages dig a pond

30a. kal hi maine us khet ko ramelu se gauDwaya
30b. kāli āmi Rameluke diye oi khetṭi karṣaṇ kariyechi
30c. Yesterday I made Ramelu to cultivate the field

31a. Mangala ne apne paise bablu se ginwayi
31b. Maṅgalā nijer ṭākā Bāblu ke diye goṇālo
31c. Mangala made Bablu count her own money

32a. Nani ne naukarani se bistar bichwaya
32b. Didā paricārikāke diye bichānā pātālo
32c. Grandmother made the maid prepare the bed

33a. Adhyapika ne Rajib dwara mujhe bulwaya
33b. Adhyāpikā Rājībke diye āmāke ḍeke pāṭhālen
33c. Professor made Rajib to call me

34a. dadaji mazduron se khaT bunwa rahe hai
34b. dādu majurke diye khāṭ bonācchen
34c. Grandfather makes the servant prepare the cot

35a. Ojha rogi ko mantra ke pratap se jhumwate hai
35b. ojhā rogīke mantrer prabhābe (diye) nācācche
35c. The exorcist makes the patient dance with mantras

36a. seiThanee ne nauktanee se daree jhatakwaai
36b. gṛhakartrī paricārikake diye gālicā jhāṛāla
36c. The landlady made the maid clean the carpet

The examples furnished above show that the use of '-nā' and '-vānā' as verbal suffixes have a kind of consistency with regard to number of people involved in execution of the work. While '-nā' is used to get the works done by a person directly, the form '-vānā' is used when the third person is needed to carry out the work. The translation of this pattern generates multiword causative expressions in Bangla to act as proper equivalents.

In the examples above, one can also note consistency in distribution of '-nā' and '-vānā' in Hindi, which correspond to the first and the second causative forms. While the use of the second causative construction is not present in Bangla, the formation of the first causative form is quite normal in the language. Hence while writing the equivalent of the second causative form or translating the example sentences of this type in Bangla, I have to insert an indirect object to evoke the sense of 'A causes B to make C do D', in which no morphosyntactic change occurs within the VP. It assumes the following schema in Bangla.

Schema 4 $NP_{Subject}$ $NP_{Indirect\ Object\ 1}$ $NP_{Indirect\ Object\ 2}$ $NP_{Direct\ Object}$ $VP_{First\ Causative}$

The list of examples given below (Table 4.9), on the other hand, shows some special cases where the causative inflection '-vānā' denotes the first type of causative formation, i.e., it assumes the form of the following type.

Schema 5 $NP_{Subject}$ $NP_{Indirect\ Object}$ $NP_{Direct\ Object}$ $VP_{First\ Causative}$

Table 4.9 Second causative marker denotes first causative sense

No	Hindi 2nd causative	Bangla causative verb
1	bichwaanaa	aparke diye bichānā pātāno
2	bulwaanaa	aparke diye ḍeke pāṭhāno
3	bolnaa	aparke diye ḍākāno
4	bunwanaa	aparke diye khāṭ bonāno
5	jhumwanaa	ekjanke diye anya ekjanke nācāno
6	jhatakwaanaa	aparke diye gālicā jhāṛāno

Here again, it is observed that the suffix '-vānā' cannot be taken for granted only for the second causative forms and translators have to be judicious in the choice of meanings at the time of generating appropriate translation in Bangla.

4.5 Conclusion

In this chapter, I have tried to delve into the linguistic as well as extralinguistic issues that have cropped up during the preparation of Bangla synsets that are meant to be used as translational equivalents for the Hindi synsets in the IndoWordNet. While working with the Hindi synset databases tagged with examples and explanation, I have observed that there are indeed several problems that crop up from constraints such as lexical gap, morphological structure, grammatical formation, and extralinguistic issues. Some of the problems are briefly highlighted with possible solutions that I have adopted to solve these problems.

It should, however, be clearly informed that the data and information presented in this paper are actually the tip of an iceberg, which propels serious problems in translation of Hindi texts into Bangla. Also, there are several other issues such as divergence, convergence, reordering of phrases, lexical mismatches, sense modifications, and lexical selection, which also need to be addressed adequately for solving the syntactic and lexical ambiguities faced in translation.

What I understand from this pilot enterprise that there are several cultural, ecological, geographical, religious, and ethnic issues that call for serious attention at the time of synset generation between any two languages (addressed in snapshots in the chapter on generation of language-specific synset in Bangla (in this volume). I have presented here only some sample cases to explicate the problems and challenges I had to encounter in our work for generating synsets in Bangla.

Acknowledgments I would like to express my thanks to Abhisek Sarkar, Dipshikha Bose, and Soumi Banerji who worked with me in the Bangla WordNet project at the Linguistic Research Unit, Indian Statistical Institute, Kolkata, India.

References

Bhattacharyya, P. (2010). IndoWordNet. *Proceedings of the 7th International Language Resource and Evaluation Conference (LREC-10)*, Valletta, Malta, May 19–21, 2010.

Chakrabarty, D., Pande, P., Narayan, D., & Bhattacharyya, P. (2002). An experience in building the Indo WordNet—a WordNet for Hindi. *International Conference on Global WordNet (GWC02)*, Mysore, India.

Dash, N. S. (2005). Role of context in word sense disambiguation. *Indian Linguistics., 66*(1–4), 159–176.

Fellbaum, C. (Ed.). (1988). *WordNet: An electronic lexical database, Cambridge*. MA.: MIT Press.

Parkes, G., & Cornell, A. (1992). *NTC's dictionary of German false cognates*. National Textbook Company, NTC Publishing Group.

Zuckermann, G. (2003). *Language Contact and Lexical Enrichment in Israeli Hebrew*. Houndmills: Palgrave Macmillan.

Chapter 5
Development of Punjabi WordNet, Bilingual Dictionaries, Lexical Relations Creation, and Its Challenges

R.K. Sharma and Parteek Kumar

Abstract WordNet is an electronic lexical database and is a powerful resource for computational linguistics and natural language processing. WordNet for Hindi language has already been developed by IIT Bombay. The Indian languages WordNets are being created using expansion approach from Hindi WordNet under IndoWordNet project. This paper describes the process of creation of Punjabi WordNet, where semantic relations are borrowed from the Hindi language, while the lexical relations are created for Punjabi language, as these relations are language dependent. To create lexical relations, a lexical relation tool has been proposed in this paper. The development of bilingual Hindi–Punjabi and Punjabi–Hindi dictionaries through this process has also been presented in this paper. This paper also discusses the challenges in the development of Punjabi WordNet and creation of language-specific synsets with reference to Punjabi WordNet.

Keywords Wordnet · Semantic relations · Lexical relations

5.1 Introduction

WordNet is a large lexical database of a language, where words are grouped together according to their similarity of meanings. WordNet maintains concepts in a language, relations between concepts and their ontological details. Each concept in a language represents a synset. Synsets are basic building blocks of WordNet. Synset is composed of gloss, example sentences, and set of synonym

R.K. Sharma · P. Kumar (✉)
Department of Computer Science and Engineering, Thapar University, Patiala, India
e-mail: parteek.bhatia@thapar.edu

R.K. Sharma
e-mail: rksharma@thapar.edu

N.S. Dash et al. (eds.), *The WordNet in Indian Languages*,
DOI 10.1007/978-981-10-1909-8_5

words that can be used for concept. Synsets are created for content words like nouns, verbs, adjectives, and adverbs (Khapra et al. 2010). Besides synset data, WordNet also maintains lexical and semantic relations within these synsets. Lexical relations like antonomy and gradation are between the words in a language whereas semantic relations like hypernymy, hyponymy, meronymy, holonymy, entailment, troponymy, and casuation are between concepts in a language. The major applications of WordNet are text categorization (Gabrilovich and Markovitch 2004), text summarization (Bellare et al. 2004), and word sense disambiguation (Banerjee and Pedersen 2002; Rana and Kumar 2015) and machine translation etc.

India is a multilingual country and creation of lexical resources for all Indian languages is a complex and huge task. To create WordNets for all Indian languages, Department of Electronics and Information Technology (DeitY) initiated an IndoWordNet project. WordNets for Indian languages are being created using the expansion approach from the Hindi WordNet which was developed in 2006. Using expansion approach, there is an advantage of being able to borrow the semantic relations of a given source WordNet (Bhattacharyya 2010). However, there are some challenges in this approach, for example, the lexicographer can be distracted by synsets which denotes region-specific concepts. Also, there is a probability of ignoring target language's 'own concepts.' Lexical relations cannot be borrowed from source WordNet using expansion approach as they are language dependent. In order to create lexical relations for IndoWordNet languages, a lexical creation tool has also been discussed in this paper with a provision to create lexical relations from source WordNet as well as to create lexical relations for those words which are not covered in source WordNet.

This paper is divided into 10 sections. Section 5.2 gives a brief account on features of Punjabi language. Section 5.3 provides an overview of related work that has been done in this field. Section 5.4 provides the details of semantic and lexical relations of WordNet with respect to Punjabi Language. The process of creation of bilingual Hindi–Punjabi dictionary is discussed in Sect. 5.5 while the development of Punjabi WordNet is discussed in Sect. 5.6. Section 5.7 provides details about the development of lexical creation tool. The challenges faced in the development of Punjabi WordNet have been provided in Sect. 5.8, while Sect. 5.9 describes creation of language-specific synsets. Section 5.10 concludes this paper.

5.2 Punjabi Language

Punjabi language is world's 10th most widely spoken language. Punjabi language is used in both parts of Punjab, in India and Pakistan. Punjabi is syllabic in nature. There are relatively less efforts in the field of computerization and the development of lexical resources of this language.

5.3 Related Work

English WordNet is the first WordNet created in this field. Its development began in 1985 and is being maintained at Princeton University. The success of English WordNet has inspired several projects that aim at constructing the WordNet for other languages or to develop multilingual WordNet. EuroWordNet is a system of semantic network for European languages. The EuroWordNet project dealts with Dutch, Italian, Spanish, German, French, Czech, and Estonian languages (Vossen 1998). In 2004, BalkaNet WordNet project has been initiated for the development of WordNets for Bulgarian, Greek, Romanian, Serbian, and Turkish languages (Tufis et al. 2004).

In India, Hindi WordNet has been developed by IIT Bombay. Later on, Hindi WordNet was extended to Marathi WordNet. Currently, IndoWordNet project, a linked structure of Indian languages is in progress in India. Moreover, Indradhunush project aims at developing WordNets for seven major Indian languages: Bengali, Gujarati, Kashmiri, Konkani, Oriya, Punjabi, and Urdu.

5.4 WordNet Relations

The synsets in the WordNet are linked through two types of relations, i.e., lexical and semantic relations. Lexical relation exists between the word forms while semantic relation exists between the concepts (Miller et al. 1990).

5.4.1 Semantic Relations

Semantic relation is a relation between meanings, and since meanings can be represented by synsets, semantic relations can be considered as pointers between synsets (Narang et al. 2013). For example, hypernym/hyponym is a semantic relation. Consider two synsets given in (5.1) and (5.2).

$$\{paud\bar{a}\,'plant', b\bar{u}\d{t}\bar{a}\,'plant'\} \tag{5.1}$$

$$\{c\bar{a}h\,'tea'\} \tag{5.2}$$

Here, {*paudā ‘plant’*, *būṭā ‘plant’*} is hypernym of {*cāh ‘tea’*} and {*cāh ‘tea’*} is hyponym of {*paudā ‘plant’*, *būṭā ‘plant’*}. There are total thirteen semantic relations, namely hypernymy, hyponymy, meronymy, holonymy, entailment, causation, troponymy, ability link, capability link, functional link, attributes, modifies noun, and modifies verb exist in a WordNet.

Using expansion approach there is an advantage of being able to borrow the semantic relations of a given WordNet. For example, consider two synsets in the source WordNet given in (5.3) and (5.4).

$$\{chaie\,'tea'\} \tag{5.3}$$

$$\{paudha\,'plant',\, pauda\,'plant'\} \tag{5.4}$$

In Hindi WordNet (source), synset given by (5.4) is hypernymy of synset given by (5.3) and synset given by (5.3) is hyponym of synset given by (5.4). These two synsets also share hypernymy/hyponymy relation in Punjabi (target) language. Since, the synset ID are kept same for all the languages, therefore, semantic relations from the source WordNet (Hindi) can be extended to all target languages with expansion approach.

5.4.2 *Lexical Relations*

Lexical relations are the relations between members of two different synsets. For example, consider two synsets given in (5.5) and (5.6).

$$\{m\bar{o}t\bar{a}\,'fat',\, bh\bar{a}r\bar{i}\,'fat',\, sath\bar{u}l\,'fat',\, th\bar{u}l\,'fat',\, vajn\bar{i}\,'fat'\} \tag{5.5}$$

$$\{patl\bar{a}\,'thin',\, dubl\bar{a}\,'thin',\, kamz\bar{o}r\,'thin',\, m\bar{a}t\bar{a}\,'thin'\} \tag{5.6}$$

Here, synsets (5.5) and (5.6) are opposites but they do not share antonym relation. Antonym relation exists between two words, not between two synsets. Here, words *mōṭā 'fat'* and *patlā 'thin'* are in antonym relation.

5.5 Creation of Bilingual Hindi–Punjabi Dictionary Using Punjabi WordNet

Hindi and Punjabi both belong to same language family and therefore they have a lot of semantic and syntactic similarities. But these languages use different scripts. This inspired us to develop Hindi–Punjabi bilingual dictionary from Punjabi and Hindi WordNets. The structure of this bilingual dictionary is given in Table 5.1.

Algorithm 1 describes the process of creating Punjabi WordNet, while the algorithm used in developing Hindi–Punjabi bilingual dictionary is described in Algorithm 2.

Algorithm 1: Creation of Punjabi WordNet

(1) Read the text file of Punjabi words and generate a linked list *L* for the file.
(2) Input the word to be searched in a string *W*.

Table 5.1 Structure of Hindi–Punjabi bilingual dictionary

Concept	*vh sthaan jo pvitr maanaa jaataa ho*
L1 (Hindi)	*pvitr sthaan, kaity sthaan, puny bhumi, puny-sthl, puny sthl*
L2 (Punjabi)	*pratīkūltāpvittar-sathān, dhārmiksathān, pavittar-asathān, pavittar-thāṃ, punn-bhūmī, pāvan bhūmī*

(3) For each word *W* to be searched

   (a) Search the linked list L for the occurrence of word *W* in synset.
   (b) If *W* is found in the list, then retrieve all the related ID numbers and store them in an array.
   (c) Search the linked list *L* for each of the ID number stored in array.

      (i) If ID match occurs, then retrieve the associated information with each ID number and store in a list *F*.
      (ii) Display the linked list *F*.

Algorithm 2: Creation of Hindi–Punjabi dictionary

(1) Read the text file of Hindi words and generate a linked list *L1* for the file. Similarly, read the text file of Punjabi words and generate a linked list *L2* for the file.
(2) Input the word to be searched in a string *W*.
(3) For each word w to be searched

   (a) Search the linked list *L1* for the occurrence of word *W* in synset.
   (b) If *W* is found in the list, then retrieve all the related ID numbers and store them in an array.
   (c) Search the linked list *L2* for each of the ID number stored in array.

      (i) If ID match occurs, then retrieve the associated information with each ID number and store in a linked list *F*.
      (ii) Display the linked list *F*.

      This is worth noting here that if we interchange the roles of L1 and L2 in this algorithm, we will be able to create Punjabi–Hindi dictionary.

5.6 Development of Punjabi WordNet

Figure 5.1 depicts the GUI of the Punjabi WordNet. Punjabi keypad is used to enter the word which is to be searched. The user can use the View keyboard button to use the Punjabi keyboard. Then on the click on the Submit button the various senses of the word in which it can be used will be shown on the page. The number of senses in which it can be used is shown at the top. It will show the category, concept, one example usage, and synonymous words for each of the sense.

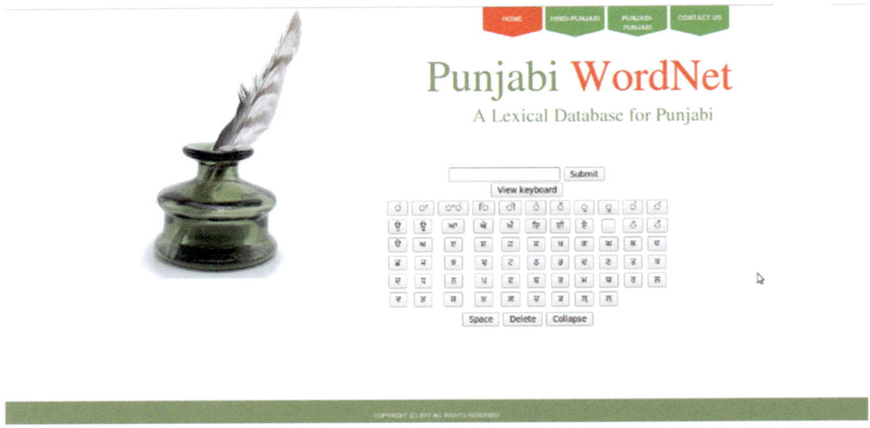

Fig. 5.1 Interface for Punjabi WordNet

Fig. 5.2 Interface showing first sense of the word *pratīkūltā*

The Next and Previous links can be used to move to the next sense and to the previous sense of the word.

For example, the one of the senses of word *pratīkūltā* is shown in Fig. 5.2.

5.7 Development of Lexical Creation Tool

In order to create the lexical relations for all the participating languages of IndoWordNet project, a lexical creation tool has been developed with provision to create lexical relations in target language on the basis of relations created in Hindi

WordNet and with another provision to create lexical relations in target language without referring to Hindi WordNet. Lexical creation tool can create the following lexical relations.

- Antonym
- Compounding
- Conjunction
- Gradation

In the subsequent subsection, the lexical creation tool has been presented by considering Punjabi as target language (Kumar et al. 2014). However, the system is able to handle all languages participating in IndoWordNet project.

5.7.1 Antonymy Creation Tool with Reference to Hindi WordNet

Antonymy is a lexical relation that exists between a pair of words that represent opposite meaning. The antonyms for Hindi WordNet have already been created. Antonyms for the Punjabi WordNet can be created from the antonyms of Hindi WordNet, but database design of Punjabi WordNet is different from Hindi WordNet. There is a need to design an interface which can bridge the gap between two different database designs and create the antonyms for the Punjabi WordNet from Hindi WordNet.

Algorithm 3 has been used for creation of antonyms from Hindi WordNet. The algorithm is developed using IndoWordNet database design (IndoWordNet Database design 2011) and Hindi WordNet database design followed by IIT Bombay.

Algorithm 3: Creation of antonyms with reference to Hindi WordNet

1. Extract ***synset_id*** of source Hindi ***synset_word*** from ***HWN_DB*** table
2. Extract ***word_ids*** from ***wn_synset_word*** table for the ***synset_id*** found in step 1.
3. For each ***word_id*** found in step 2, extract the corresponding words in target language from ***wn_word*** table
4. Extract ***synset_id*** of antonym Hindi ***synset_word*** from ***tbl_noun_anto_direction*** table
5. Extract ***word_ids*** from ***wn_synset_word*** table for the ***synset_id*** found in step 4.
6. For each ***word_id*** found in step 5, extract corresponding words in target language from ***wn_word*** table.

Description of algorithm 3

For example, for the word *purav 'east'* in Hindi, system searches for source word in ***tbl_noun_anto_direction*** table and extracts corresponding ***synset_id***, i.e. 6898as shown in Fig. 5.1. For the given ***synset_id*** 6898, system refers to ***wn_synset_word*** table to extract the ***word_ids*** as shown in step 1 of Fig. 5.3. For each of

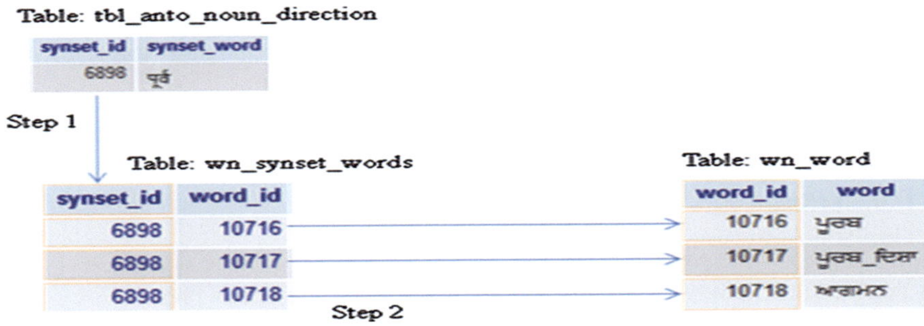

Fig. 5.3 Extracting words corresponding to synset_id 6898

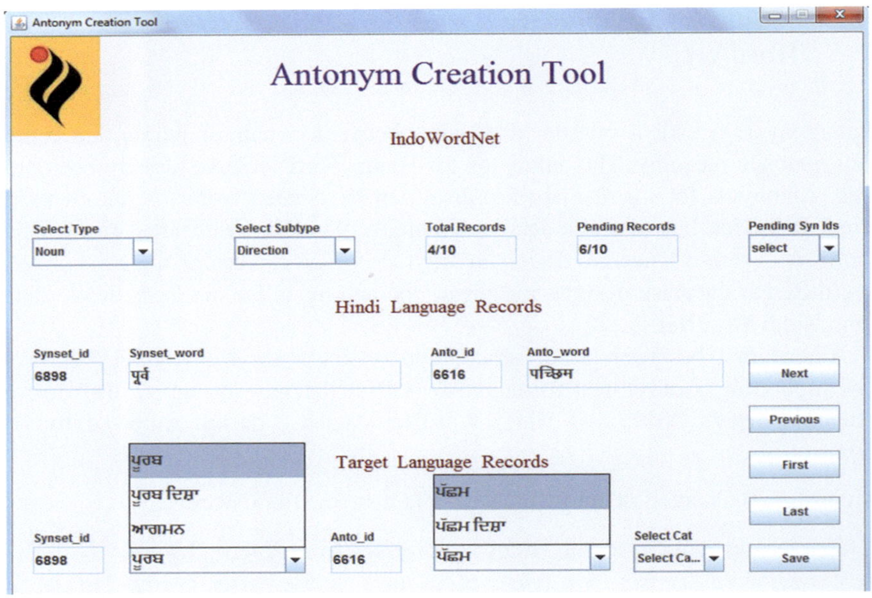

Fig. 5.4 Interface for antonym creation tool with reference to Hindi WordNet

the ***word_id*** found, system retrieves the corresponding words in target language, i.e., Punjabi from ***wn_word*** table as shown step 2 of Fig. 5.1. The similar approach has been followed to find the antonym words for antonym ***synset_id.*** A user interface has been designed in Java to provide the relevant information to the end user as shown in Fig. 5.4.

5.7.2 *Antonymy Creation Tool Without Reference to Hindi WordNet*

The antonym relation may also exist between the words which are not covered in Hindi WordNet, but may exist in the target language. This is a very common case for those Indian languages that do not belong to same language family as Hindi. There is need to design a tool which can create the antonyms for such words.

The algorithm 4 has been designed for the creation of antonym for these words. The algorithm is developed using IndoWordNet database design (IndoWordNet Database design 2011).

Algorithm 4: Creation of antonyms without reference to Hindi WordNet

1. Extract ***word_id*** of the input word in target language from ***wn_word*** table
2. Extract ***synset_ids*** from ***wn_synset_word*** table for ***word_id*** found in step 1.
3. For each ***synset_id*** found in step 2, extract the corresponding concepts from ***wn_synset*** table
4. Extract ***word_id*** of the input antonym word in target language from the ***wn_word*** table
5. Extract ***synset_ids*** from ***wn_synset_word*** table for ***word_id*** found in step 4.
6. For each ***synset_id*** found in step 5, extract the corresponding concepts from ***wn_synset*** table.

Description of algorithm 4

Let us consider an example for creation of antonym for input Punjabi word, *caṅgā 'good character'*, and the system refers to ***wn_word*** table to extract corresponding ***word_id*** as shown in Step 1 of Fig. 5.5.

For a given ***word_id***, system extracts ***synset_ids*** from ***wn_synset_word*** table. Concepts for extracted ***synset_id*** have been retrieved from ***wn_sysnset*** table as shown in step 3 given in Fig. 5.5. The similar approach has been followed for corresponding input antonym word. The process of extraction of antonym word information is depicted in Fig. 5.6.

A user interface has been designed in Java to provide relevant information to end user as shown in Fig. 5.7.

5.7.3 *Compounding Creation Tool*

Compounding relation relates a compound word with its part word. A compound word is formed when two words are joined to form a new word. An interface has been designed to create such relations from compounding relations that already exist in Hindi WordNet. The tool reduces manual typing effort for the creation of compounding relation. The snapshot of compounding creation tool taking Hindi WordNet as basis is given in Fig. 5.8.

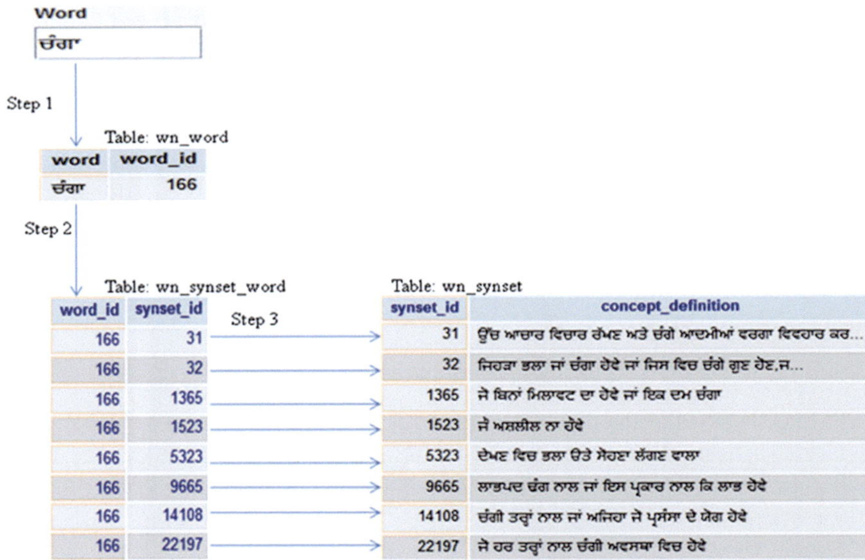

Fig. 5.5 Extraction of concepts for the word *caṅgā 'good character'*

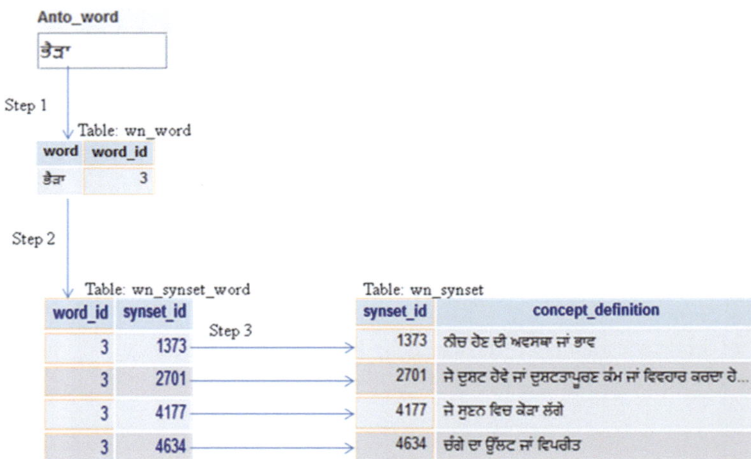

Fig. 5.6 Extraction of concepts for the word *bhaiṛā 'charactterless'*

A compounding relation may exist in target language between those words that are not covered by Hindi WordNet. For this, a tool has been developed. The snapshot of compounding creation tool without taking Hindi WordNet as basis is given in Fig. 5.9.

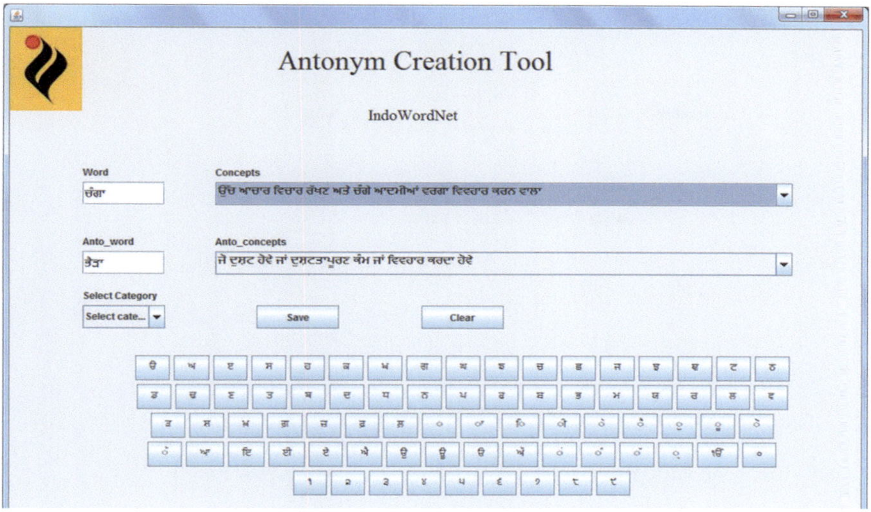

Fig. 5.7 Interface for creation of antonyms without Hindi WordNet

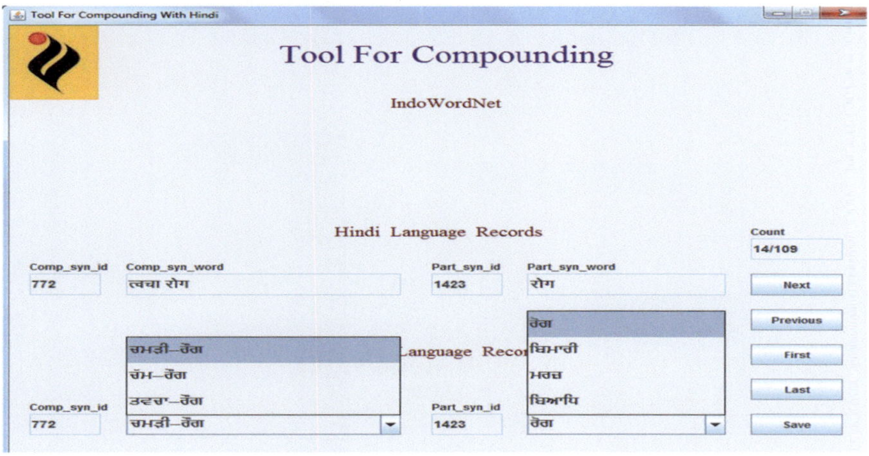

Fig. 5.8 Compounding creation tool taking Hindi WordNet as basis

5.7.4 Conjunction Creation Tool

Conjunction relation relates a conjunction word with its part word. The snapshot of conjunction creation tool taking Hindi WordNet as basis is given in Fig. 5.10.

The snapshot of conjunction creation tool without taking Hindi WordNet as basis is given in Fig. 5.11.

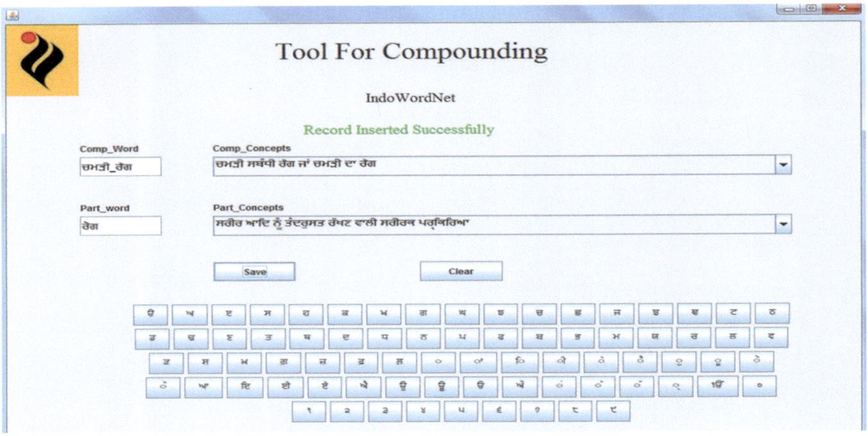

Fig. 5.9 Compounding creation tool without taking Hindi WordNet as basis

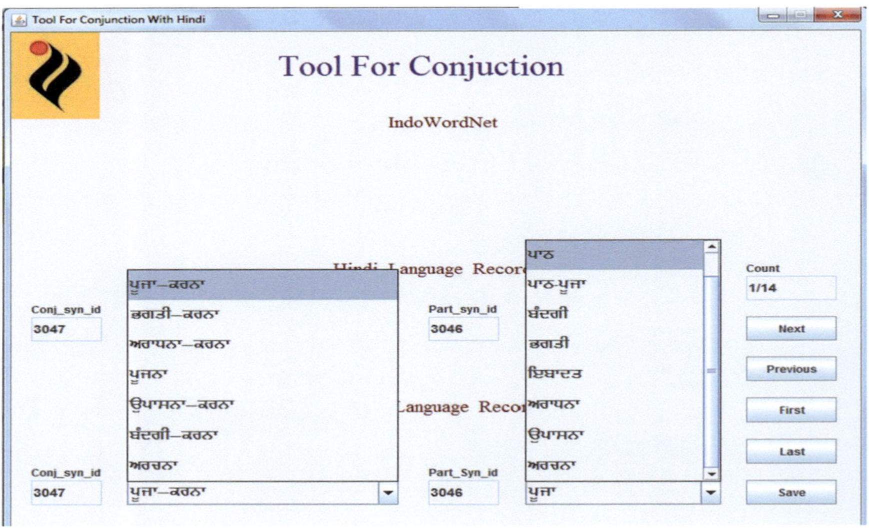

Fig. 5.10 Conjunction creation tool taking Hindi WordNet as basis

5.7.5 Gradation Creation Tool

Gradation is a lexical relation that exists between three word forms. It represents the intermediate concept between two opposite concepts. The snapshot of gradation creation tool taking Hindi WordNet as basis is given in Fig. 5.12.

The snapshot of conjunction creation tool without taking Hindi WordNet as basis is given in Fig. 5.13.

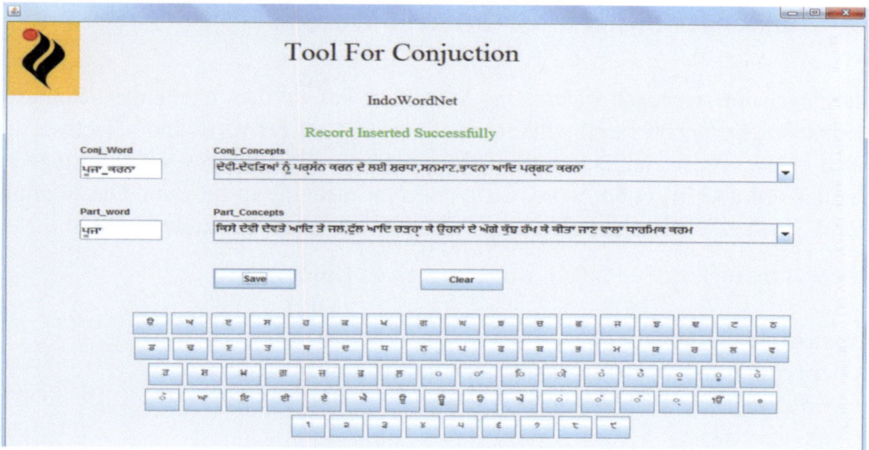

Fig. 5.11 Conjunction creation tool without taking Hindi WordNet as basis

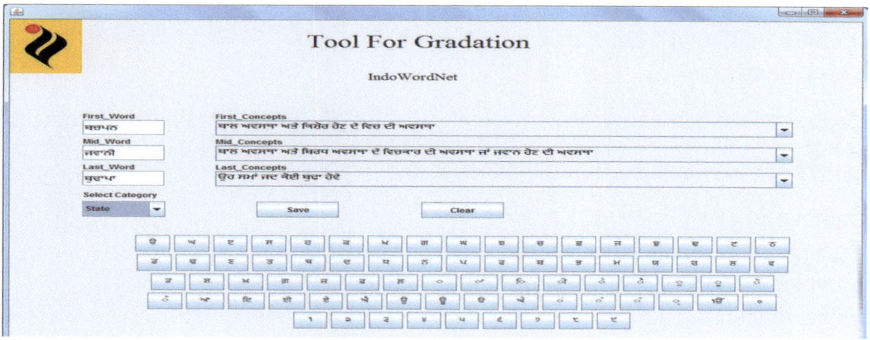

Fig. 5.12 Gradation creation tool taking Hindi Wordnet as basis

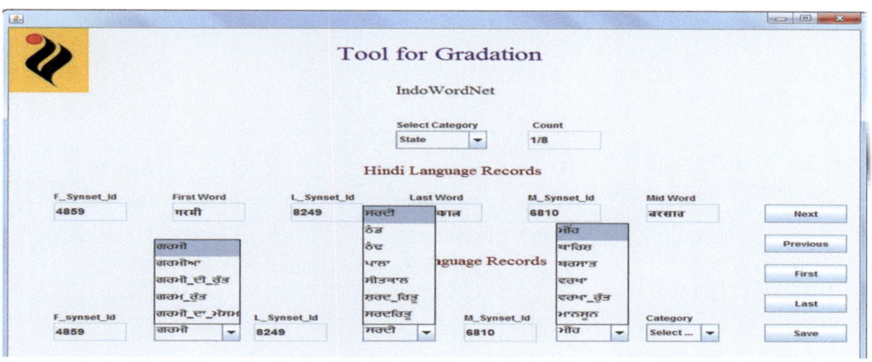

Fig. 5.13 Gradation creation tool without taking Hindi WordNet as basis

5.8 Challenges Faced in Creation of WordNet

The expansion approach of creating WordNets has its own challenges. Some of the challenges that surfaced while creating the synsets for verbs and adjectives are listed below. These challenges are (i) Non-existence of a Punjabi word for a given Hindi Word and (ii) Hindi words with different meaning in Punjabi. The example words for these challenges taken from Hindi WordNet are illustrated below.

(a) Non-existence of a Punjabi word for a given Hindi Word

Example: Id-16469
Concept: ne brtn ko phli baar kaam men laanaa
Example: pujaa ke smy usne ki brtn anvaanse
Synset: anvaansnaa

Here, we don't have an equivalent word for *anvaansnaa* in Punjabi Language.

Example: Id-25639
Concept: sukhi khaansi khaansnaa
Example: aajkl ssurji din-raat dhaanste rhte hain
Synset: dhaansnaa

Here again, we don't have an equivalent word for *dhaansnaa* in Punjabi Language.

(b) Hindi words with different meaning in Punjabi

Example: Id 18497
Concept: thahr-thhrkr pideaa honaa
Example: aadhe ghnte se meraa sr thnk rhaa hai
Synset: thanknaa

In Punjabi, we have a different meaning of word *thanknaa*, this means something odd is going to take place. Table 5.2 consists of verb IDs having non-equivalent Punjabi Words and Table 5.3 consists of adjective IDs having non-equivalent Punjabi Words. These IDs have again been taken from Hindi WordNet.

Table 5.2 Verb IDs having non-equivalent Punjabi words

ID	Synset	ID	Synset
16469	anvaansnaa	18497	thanknaa
27483	taamnaa	27599	kinvn krnaa
26771	khdbdaanaa, khdfdaanaa	23188	abhyaa
20467	plaasnaa	25639	dhaansnaa
18961	carcharaanaa	19755	pitraanaa, pitlaanaa
35383	takaanaa		

Table 5.3 Adjective IDs having non-equivalent Punjabi words

ID	Synset	ID	Synset
20192	pristhaankit	21127	naardiya
21317	talhaa	21978	apasrit
22024	sadshav	22078	apaatradaayi
22152	paatndaar	22302	krishodari, chaamodari, tanumdhyaa, katihinaa
22390	supranak	22774	shaankhik, shaangkhik
23052	abhisikt	23159	abhangai, abhnggai
23193	bhagnapristh	23252	utkhaataa
23306	abhigoptaa	23488	abhisikt
23988	kinvit	24486	savysaachi
25659	khangahaa	25677	aaksepak, aaksepi
26177	abhisekit	26178	abhisyndi, abhisyndi, abhisyndi
26290	kalahntaaritaa, kalahntaaritaa	27905	divaandh, divaandh, divas-andh
28021	abhaum	28022	abhumij, aksitij, abhaum, aprithvij

5.9 Creation of Language-Specific Synsets

Language-specific synsets are the synsets corresponding to the concepts that are available only in a particular language, and they have no conceptual match in other languages. Punjabi language has rich vocabulary for its culture and religion. The most Punjabi language specific words come from Sikh religion.

There are three important regions, namely 'majha,' 'malwa,' and 'doabha' in Punjab. All of these regions have different accent, vocabulary, and pronunciation of words. The vocabulary of these regions is also covered under language-specific synsets.

We have broadly classified language-specific synsets for Punjabi in four categories as discussed below:

(a) **Sikh religion-related concepts**: Punjabi language is much influenced by Sikh religion. For instance, words like 'sikh,' 'langar,' 'hukamnama,' and 'jathedar' are from Sikh religion vocabulary.
(b) **Punjabi culture**: Punjab has its own social cultural rituals, festivals, practices, etc. There are various rituals of Punjab like 'basant panchmi,' 'manghi,' and 'holla Muhalla'. In Sikh community, 'anand karaj' is a marriage ceremony which is followed by Sikh people. Punjab has its own history and mythology like 'puran-bhagat,' the concepts of this form will be specific to Punjabi language.
(c) **Games and Sports**: Many of the terms related to local sports are included in this list. These sports are highly localized such as 'kabadi,' 'kikli,' 'barha dikrhi,' etc.

(d) **Songs, Music, and Dance**: This category refers to folk songs and music such as 'dhola,' 'jugni,' 'jagga,' etc. There are varieties of dances like 'bhagra,' 'sadmi,' 'gidha,' and 'kikli'. It also covers number of tools and musical instruments which are used only in Punjab like 'dhadh,' 'tumbi,' 'algojae,' etc.

5.10 Conclusion

The expansion approach for the development of IndoWordNet has made this development process fast. The semantic relations are borrowed from the source language, Hindi, as they are same for all the languages. Lexical relations are language specific, so they cannot be borrowed from the source language. It has been observed that by using lexical creation tool, the creation of lexical relations has become very fast and easy particularly for Hindi in-family languages, while for languages that do not fall in the same family, the provision of creation of lexical relation without referring to Hindi WordNet has been very useful. The IndoWordNet developed through this initiative will serve as an important tool in field of Natural language processing for Indian languages.

Acknowledgments This work has been carried out under research project titled 'Development of Indradhanush: An Integrated WordNet for Bengali, Gujarati, Kashmiri, Konkani, Oriya, Punjabi and Urdu' under the leadership of IIT Bombay and Goa University. This project is sponsored by MoCIT, Govt. of India. We also acknowledge the contribution of Punjabi University, Patiala team for the development of Punjabi WordNet.

References

Banerjee, S., & Pedersen, T. (2002). an adapted lesk algorithm for word sense disambiguation using WordNet. *3rd International Conference on Intelligent Text Processing and Computational Linguistics* (pp. 1–10). Mexico City.

Bellare, K., Sharma, A. D., Sharma, A. D., Loiwal, N., & Bhattacharyya, P. (2004). Generic Text Summarization Using WordNet. *Language Resources Engineering Conference.* Barcelona.

Bhattacharyya, P. (2010). IndoWordNet. *Lexical Resources Engineering Conference*. Malta.

Gabrilovich, E., & Markovitch, S. (2004). Text categorization with many redundant features: Using aggressive feature selection to make SVMs competitive with C4.5. *21st International Conference on Machine Learning* (pp. 321–328). Canada.

IndoWordNet Database design. (2011). Technical Report by Goa University, Goa.

Khapra, M. M., Chauhan, S., Nair, S., Sharma, A., & Bhattacharyya, P. (2010). Domain specific iterative word sense disambiguation in a multilingual setting. *5th International Conference on Global WordNet*.

Kumar, P., Sharma, R., & Narang, A. (2014). Creation of lexical relations for IndoWordNet. *7th Conference on Global WordNet.* Tartu (Estonia).

Miller, G. A., Beckwith, R., Fellbaum, C., Gross, D., & Miller, K. J. (1990). Introduction to WordNet: An on-line lexical database. *International Journal of Lexicography*, 235–244.

Narang, A., Sharma, R., & Kumar, P. (2013). Development of Punjabi WordNet. *Springer CSI Transactions on ICT* (pp: 349–354).

Rana, P., & Kumar, P. (2015). word sense disambiguation for punjabi language using overlap based approach. In: M. El-Sayed & El-Alfy et al. (Eds.), *Advances in intelligent informatics* (pp. 607–619). Springer International Publishing.

Tufis, D., Cristea, D., & Stamou, S. (2004). Balkanet: Aims, methods, results and perspectives. A general overview. *Romanian Journal of Information, Science and Technology, 7*(1–2), 9–43.

Vossen, P. (Ed.). (1998). *EuroWordNet: A multilingual database with lexical semantic networks*. Dordrecht: Kluwer Academic Publishers.

Chapter 6
Insights on the Konkani WordNet Development Process

Shilpa N. Desai, Shantaram W. Walawalikar, Ramdas N. Karmali and Jyoti D. Pawar

Abstract Konkani is the official language of the state of Goa in India. The Konkani WordNet development activity was possible due to the funding support received from the Department of Electronics and Information Technology (DeitY), New Delhi, and the technical support received from the Indian Institute of Technology (IIT) Bombay, Mumbai. The Konkani WordNet has been developed as part of the Indradhanush WordNet Consortium Project which was funded by DeitY, New Delhi, for developing WordNets of seven Indian languages. In this chapter, we present the journey of the Konkani WordNet development process and its impact on the research activity in Natural Language Processing (NLP) at Goa University. We have also briefly discussed the tools and utilities developed for NLP during the Konkani WordNet creation process.

Keywords WordNet · Multilingual WordNet · Language-specific concepts · Konkani · Concept-based lexical resource · Word sense · Dictionary · Synset

6.1 Origin of Konkani WordNet Development

The start of the Konkani WordNet development activity can be traced to the first IndoWordNet Workshop which was held at Amrita University, Coimbatore, in June 2009. In this workshop, the NLP team from Goa University learnt the synset creation process from IIT Bombay team and understood the challenges involved in the synset creation process. It was realized that this activity was difficult without adequate funding support. Hence, the proposal for Konkani WordNet along with six other Indian languages, namely Bengali, Gujarati, Kashmiri, Konkani, Oriya,

S.N. Desai · S.W. Walawalikar · R.N. Karmali · J.D. Pawar (✉)
Konkani WordNet Team, Goa University, Panaji, India
e-mail: sndesai@gmail.com; goembab@yahoo.co.in; rnk@unigoa.ac.in; jdp@unigoa.ac.in

N.S. Dash et al. (eds.), *The WordNet in Indian Languages*,
DOI 10.1007/978-981-10-1909-8_6

Punjabi, and Urdu, was submitted to DeitY, New Delhi, and funding was obtained for the development of WordNet for seven Indian languages, using the expansion approach with Hindi WordNet as the source WordNet. This WordNet project carried out in consortium mode was named as Indradhanush which means *rainbow* consisting of seven colors cumulatively representing seven Indian language teams working together on this project. The WordNet development activity for some Indian languages, namely Sanskrit, Marathi, Tamil, Telugu, Kannada, Malayalam, Assamese, Manipuri, Nepali, Bodo, had already started as part of other WordNet Project Consortiums.

The first workshop of the Indradhanush WordNet Project Consortium was held in October 2010. The main outcome of this workshop was a plan to classify all the Hindi WordNet synsets into the following categories by each of the Indian languages.

(1) **Universal Synsets**: The concepts that are common to all languages of the world would be placed under this category. This includes concepts such as *sun, moon, earth*.
(2) **Pan-Indian Synsets**: Concepts which are common to India but uncommon elsewhere would be placed under Pan-Indian synset category. This category included concepts such as festival names like *diwali*, food items like *chappati, roti*.
(3) **In-Family Synsets**: Concepts common to a family of languages or group of languages were included in this In-family synset category. This category included concepts such as *navavArI* (a nine-yard saree worn by women in Goa and Maharashtra).
(4) **Rare/Culture-Specific Synsets**: Concepts which occur only specific to a region or place or culture and is not common elsewhere are placed under this category. For example, *motorcycle pilot* is a rare concept present in Goa which refers to a "motorcycle used as means of public transport."

This activity was mainly carried out to select and decide on the common order in which the synsets were to be created by all the Indian languages. It was decided to first create all the universal synsets, followed by Pan-Indian, in-family, and rare/culture specific. The Indradhanush WordNet Project was successfully completed on October 31, 2013. During the project period, several workshops were held, during which the challenges faced by all the languages during the synset creation process were discussed and solutions obtained. The feedback obtained from the members of the Project Review Steering Group (PRSG) also helped in improving the overall process of the WordNet creation activity.

This chapter has been organized as follows. Section 6.2 describes Konkani WordNet as part of IndoWordNet. Section 6.3 gives a brief introduction of the Konkani language for the benefit of all readers. Section 6.4 presents the process followed for Konkani WordNet creation. Section 6.5 discusses the challenges faced during Konkani WordNet development. In Sect. 6.6, the approach used to create Konkani language-specific synsets and the statistics thereof is presented. In Sect. 6.7, the tools developed during the Konkani WordNet development process are presented. Section 6.8 presents the database design implemented and Application Programming Interface (API) developed for IndoWordNet. Applications of Konkani WordNet are presented in Sect. 6.9. In Sect. 6.10, Enhancements to the Konkani WordNet based on the research work carried out in NLP for Konkani are discussed, and Sect. 6.11 concludes the chapter with future work plan.

6.2 Konkani WordNet as Part of IndoWordNet—A Multilingual WordNet

WordNet is an electronic lexical database resource which maintains concepts in a language. A concept is represented as a synset in the WordNet and is made up of synonym words that describe the concept, a gloss that explains the concept and example sentences which illustrate the use of the concept.

Example (Synset)
The synset for *sUrya* (sun) in Konkani is as follows:

Pos category	:	Noun
Synonym words	:	sUrya (sun),[1] ravI (sun), arUNa (sun), bhAskara (sun), dinakara (sun), Aditya (sun), divAkara (sun), bhAnU (sun), saura (sun)
Gloss/concept definition	:	JAkA lAgUn sagalyA giryAMka garmI AnI ujavAD meLaTa aso girAvaLIMtalo sagalyAMta vhaDa AnI jvalaMta piMD (The largest bright star in the solar system which provides heat and light to all planets)
Example sentences	:	1. surya sourya ujeche eka vhad sadhan (The sun is one of the big source of solar energy)
		2. udeMtetalyAna sUrya yetA to paLovana kaLokha dhaMvana gelo (The darkness was dispelled by the arrival of the sun)

[1]A word in Konkani language is followed by transliteration in Roman script that resembles ITRANS (http://www.aczoom.com/itrans/html/tblall/tblall.html) and translation in English in brackets

WordNet is heavily used by researchers in the area of computational linguistics, text processing and many other related areas. Multilingual WordNet is a collection of WordNets linked to each other using a common identifier for a concept (Bhattacharyya et al. 2010). Multilingual WordNet named IndoWordNet has been built for Indian languages to aid in multilingual machine translation, cross-lingual information retrieval and to promote tourism, farming, education, and other related activities. This multilingual WordNet has been developed using "expansion approach". This approach uses one language WordNet as the source WordNet and concepts covered in this source language are translated into other languages. The Indradhanush WordNet used the Hindi WordNet developed by Indian Institute of Technology Bombay (IITB) as a source WordNet (Narayan et al. 2002). The Offline Synset Creation and Linking Tool developed at IITB was used for creating synset in the languages such as Konkani covered under Indradhanush Project. The Konkani WordNet currently has approximately 34K synsets.

6.3 The Konkani Language

Konkani is the official language of the State of Goa. Konkani is an Indo-European (Indo-Aryan) language derived from Sanskrit through Prakrit and is influenced and enriched by various other languages such as Marathi, Kannada, Malayalam, Hindi, Portuguese, and English. Though Devanagari script is recognized as official script of Konkani, it is also written in Roman and Kannada scripts. Konkani is an inflectional language, with two numbers, namely *singular* and *plural,*; three grammatical genders, namely *feminine, masculine*, and *neuter*; and two cases for nouns, namely *direct* and *oblique* (Sardesai 1986). Konkani nouns and pronouns inflect for number and case; verbs are inflected for person, number, gender, tense, and aspect (Walawalikar 2010). Konkani verbs also have a negation inflection system (Almeida 2008; Borkar 1986; Shennoi 1949). Adjectives in Konkani are inflected for number and gender.

Any language is influenced by demography and past history of the place where it is used. Goa is ensconced between Maharashtra and Karnataka on the west coast of India. It is separated from the rest of the country by the Western Ghats. The state is ruled by various rulers over the centuries, right from the Kadambas, Shakas to Maratha and Portuguese, all of whom have used their native tongues as the language of the administration. The culture and vocabulary of Konkani has been greatly influenced by these sociocultural and sociopolitical events, as a result of which most of the words have undergone transformation to blend and mutate with the local linguistic climate over the centuries.

6.4 Konkani WordNet (KWN) Creation Process

WordNets can be built using the merge approach or the expansion approach (Vossen 1998). The merge approach is time-consuming and makes use of an exhaustive dictionary or a collection of dictionaries in the language to create the WordNet. The other approach used for WordNet creation is the expansion approach. Expansion approach makes use of an already existing WordNet as the source WordNet. A lexicographer carefully studies each synset entry from the source WordNet to understand the underlying concept. The concept is then translated into the language for which the WordNet is being developed. The language for which the WordNet is being created is referred to as the target language. The synsets are constructed for the target language following the three principles of minimality, coverage, and replaceability (Bhattacharyya 2010). The advantages of using expansion approach for WordNet creation are

(a) Automatic linking to other WordNets based on the concept thus creating a multilingual WordNet and
(b) The position in ontology and the semantic relations for concepts are directly borrowed from the source WordNet.

The Konkani WordNet is a part of the IndoWordNet and has been developed using the expansion approach. The Hindi WordNet developed by Indian Institute of Technology Bombay, Mumbai, was used as the source WordNet. The Hindi WordNet, used as the source WordNet, currently has around 36321 synsets of which around 22826 synsets are linked with synsets of the Princeton WordNet. The Offline Synset Creation and Linking Tool was used for creating synset in Konkani and linking them to the Hindi synsets. The following steps were followed to create synsets in Konkani:

Step 1 Each synset entry from the source WordNet was accessed through the tool by the junior lexicographer, it was carefully studied, and the corresponding synset was created for Konkani.

Step 2 Synonym words for that particular synset were chosen from the lexical stock of Konkani following the three principles of minimality, coverage, and replaceability (Bhattacharyya 2010).

Step 3 The concept definition or gloss and examples were translated into Konkani from Hindi. Thus, the Hindi WordNet and Konkani WordNet have identical glosses. Examples were also maintained identical as far as possible. In certain cases where translation of examples to Konkani was found inappropriate, different appropriate examples were used.

Step 4 The Konkani synset created was validated by a senior lexicographer by checking for spelling mistakes, concept mismatch, and example relevance with respect to Konkani language.

Till date approximately 34K Konkani synsets have been created and linked to Hindi WordNet and the act of linking other synsets is in progress with a goal for covering the entire list of synsets. The number of unique words so far generated stands around 40821. These synsets are classified according to the regular scheme of lexical classes into four major part of speech: nouns, verbs, adverbs, and adjectives.

6.5 Challenges Faced During Konkani WordNet Development

This section presents the various challenges faced during the synset creation process. These challenges fall under the following two heads:

- Discrepancies and issues in source WordNet
- Challenges due to differences in source and target language

6.5.1 Discrepancies and Issues in Source WordNet

The use of expansion approach to create the Konkani WordNet brought forth a few discrepancies and issues in the source WordNet-Hindi. These discrepancies and issues were reported to the source WordNet maintenance team who immediately fixed the discrepancies and issues after deliberations in workshops held to sort out WordNet creation problems faced. The expansion approach provided a rigorous testing platform for the source WordNet which lead to the overall improvement in the quality of the source WordNet. The target WordNets like Konkani benefitted from this exercise and were able to avoid such discrepancies. Some of the discrepancies and issues observed in the source WordNet during the creation of the Konkani WordNet, which were later resolved, are presented below.

6.5.1.1 Concept/Gloss Definition Unclear

Discrepancy details: The English sense of the below synset was "*appropriate*." However, it did not agree with the concept definition/gloss of the synset.
Example:

Id No	:	2923
Concept	:	pUrvApara yA AsapAsa kI bAtoM ke vicAra se athavA aura kisI prakAra se ThIka baiThane yA mela raKane vAlA (suitable for a particular person or place or condition, etc.)
Example	:	maMtrIjI ke saMgata uttara se patrakAra cupa ho gaye (The reporters were silenced by the Ministers appropriate response.)
Synset	:	saMgata, yogya (appropriate)

Discrepancy details: Concept did not represent the appropriate meaning of the synset.
Example:

Id No	:	5150
Concept	:	uMgaliyAM Adi hilAkara maTakanA (To walk with a lofty proud gait, often in an attempt to impress others)
Synset	:	itarAnA, camakanA, aMgarAnA (strut)

6.5.1.2 Concept/Example/Synset Mismatch

Discrepancy details: Concept not properly narrated and the example sentence contains the phrase "(A~MKe PADxanA)" which does not make justice to the sense of synset "फाड़ना (PADxanA)."
Example:

Id No	:	5255
Category	:	Verb
Concept	:	saMdhi yA joDx PailAkar acCI taraha se KolanA
Example	:	ramA kI aviSvasanIya bAta sunakara usane AMKe PADxI
Synset	:	PADxanA, visPArita karanA

Discrepancy details: Concept was about "The chill that exists in the surroundings at morning and evening time." The synset was an adverb which depicts the motion. The example sentence narrated movement and temperament. The concept and example did not match to each other.
Example:

Id No	:	19130
Category	:	Adverb
Concept	:	jaba mausama meM ThaMDApana ho viSeShakara subaha yA SAma ke samaya para
Example	:	maiM ThaMDe-ThaMDe calA jAtA hUM
Synset	:	ThaMDe-ThaMDe, ThaMDe ThaMDe, ThaMDhe-ThaMDhe, ThaMDhe ThaMDhe (Chill)

Discrepancy details: Concept should have been for the English sense opening rather than the concept given.
Example:

Id No	:	35699
Category	:	Adjective
Concept	:	jo guNoM, kAranAmoM Adi ke kAraN salAma karane yogya ho
Example	:	sacina BArata ke salAmI ballebAza haiM (Sachin is the opening batsman for India)
Synset	:	salAmI (opening)

6.5.1.3 Example Sentences in Synset Found Unsuitable

Discrepancy details: Some example sentences were perceived to be of unsuitable nature or had negative expressions, which could have been avoided.

6.5.1.4 Recursive Definition of Concepts

Discrepancy details: Some concepts were recursive in nature wherein the synset itself has been used to explicate the concept.

6.5.1.5 Factual Errors

Discrepancy details: Statements were factually incorrect. Concept for Saturn is stated as the seventh planet of solar system which is incorrect as Saturn is the sixth planet of our solar system.

Example:

Id No	:	228
Category	:	Noun
Concept	:	saura jagat kA sAtavAM graha (Seventh planet in the solar system)
Synset	:	Sani (Saturn)

6.5.2 Challenges Due to Differences in Source and Target Language

The other types of challenges faced in Konkani WordNet creation were due to the differences in the source language Hindi and the target language Konkani as both these languages are used in different geographical areas and are influenced by the culture followed in that area. Some of the challenges faced are as presented below:

6.5.2.1 Linking Culture-Specific Concepts

Local customs and culture has a crucial role to play in the WordNet creation. Culture-specific concepts from Hindi WordNet that do not have a parallel in Konkani provide a unique challenge during linkage process. For example, in Hindi region *capAtI* vendor possibly comes door to door selling his *chapatis* (a thinly made bread-like eatable prepared from wheat flour). Although Konkani people are not familiar with this concept, they have a similar concept of a vendor popularly known as *padera* "bread seller" who visits residential areas.

6.5.2.2 Linking Concept/Synset Partly Specific to Konkani

Certain concepts in Hindi are more general and corresponding concepts in Konkani are more specific. For example, in Konkani there is a specific word *muT-gandh* for "miTTi kaa gandh." Hence, the synset example given below required to be split into two separate synsets.

Id No	:	10272
Category	:	Adjective
Concept	:	miTTI para varShA kA pahalA pAnI paDxane yA Bune hue cane, besana Adi se nikalane vAlI (sugaMdha)
Example	:	BAMDx ke pAsa pahu~Mcate hI sauMdhI mahaka Ane lagI
Synset	:	soMdhA, sauMdhA

6.5.2.3 Change in Part of Speech of the Synset

Certain concepts in Hindi have a different part-of-speech (POS) category from the corresponding concept in Konkani. For example, the POS for the word *kala* "tomorrow" is noun in Hindi, while in the Konkani translation the same word occurs as an adjective.

Id No	:	632
Category	:	Noun
Example	:	yaha leKa kala ke samAcAra patra meM nikalegA

6.5.2.4 Coverage of Synsets

Inclusion of metaphorical usage or uncommon usage of words to satisfy coverage (Bhattacharyya 2010) criterion of synset creation. For example, words like *ravi, Aditya* which mean *sun* are mostly used in poetry but are not used to refer to sun in literature or parlance. There are many such words which are used for the sun in Puranas (ancient literature). A challenge is whether to include all such words.

6.5.2.5 Linking Target Language Concepts

Inclusion of target Konkani language concepts which are not present in the source Hindi WordNet. For instance, the concept of a *nine-yard saree* (navavArI). Synset for this concept was not present in source WordNet. It was later decided that each target language will create a repository of such concepts for their language and appropriate synsets would be created later.

6.5.2.6 Coining New Words

For concepts that did not have a word in Konkani, the challenge faced was choice between transliteration of concept and coining new word or phrase for the concept. For example, the Hindi synset expresses certain concepts in one word but in Konkani there is no single-word unit like for *aByaMjanIya*. Therefore, a phrase *mAlISa karapA sArakeM* is required to express the same. These challenges have been discussed with examples in Walawalikar et al. (2010).

6.6 Konkani Language-Specific Synsets (KLSS)

Having gone through the experience of creating synsets from source to target language, it was understood that the task of creating the Language Specific Synset (LSS) for Konkani previously referred to as rare/culture-specific had to be carried out to make the Konkani WordNet a complete concept repository for Konkani. The approach adopted to create Konkani language-specific synset (KLSS) is presented next.

6.6.1 Approach Used for Identifying KLSS

Finding concepts specific to a particular language was not an easy task. Finding out KLSSs is an ongoing process. Multiple revisions may be necessary before it can be said with certainty that most language-specific concepts have been identified. The approach that was used to identify concepts specific to Konkani had the following steps:

- Collection of candidate language-specific words/concepts from multiple sources.
- Verification of language-specific nature of the words/concepts.
- Categorization of the identified concepts.

6.6.1.1 Collection of Candidate Language-Specific Words/Concepts From Multiple Sources

The lexicographer identified various sources to obtain the language-specific concepts. Those concepts which the lexicographer felt were not present in any other language were picked from the identified sources (Mahale 1992). The sources used to identify the concepts were as follows

- Konkani dictionary (Ghanekar 1999).
- Interactions with language experts.
- Konkani encyclopedia (Halankar et al. 1991).
- Ongoing synset linkage experience.
- Search words belonging to per-identified domains.

The method used for finding unique concepts in each of the above stated resources for Konkani was as follows:

- The Konkani dictionary that was referred to was the *Konkani Abyaskosha*. The lexicographer searched through the dictionary in alphabetical order and identified the words that could be claimed to be specific for Konkani. The lexicographer then mapped the words to the concepts which he/she felt were language-specific.
- The language experts and native speakers of Konkani were asked to come up with concepts which they felt to be specific to Konkani. A search at Ancestral Goa[1]

[1]Ancestral Goa is a museum-like landscape area, in South Goa, wherein collection of ancestral instruments/articles is preserved and a full size human folk are depicted doing their old time village routines. This is also known as Big Foot in Goa.

was also made on June 1, 2011, to identify all region-specific and historically important concepts.

- The lexicographer also consulted all four volumes of the Konkani Encyclopedia to find out the Konkani language-specific concepts.
- Sometimes the then-ongoing synset linkage experience helped to come up with concepts unique to Konkani. During the linkage process, it was noted that while a concept in the source language is a general concept, in Konkani it was more specific and, therefore, may be considered as "language-specific." For example, Konkani has many words to express finer differences and types of odors. Such concepts were then listed in the KLSS.
- Interactions with language experts brought forward the idea that many language-specific concepts actually belonged to some specific domains, such as, cuisine, religion, adornments, and festivals. This prompted to look at specific categories as potential search areas for language-specific concepts. Thus, recipe books, religious literature, and regional novels were useful sources for language-specific concepts.

6.6.1.2 Verification of Language-Specific Nature of Concept

The candidate language-specific concepts collected in the first step had to be verified as unique to the Konkani language. This was done in the following ways:

- Check if the concept was absent in the source language WordNet.
- Each and every concept, which was identified as specific to Konkani language, was discussed with both Konkani and Hindi experts to confirm its absence in the source language.
- Certain concepts not found in the source language could be shared with other regional language speakers. To avoid such overlap, the native speakers of other languages were consulted to the extent possible. Thus, common concepts were filtered out and put in the list of shared concepts. For example, after verification across languages, it was observed that unique words referring to some parts of coconut tree were available only in Konkani and Malayalam.

Such interactions were of limited nature constrained by availability of native speakers of other languages. For KLSS, the languages that were considered include Marathi, Gujarati, Kannada, and Malayalam.

6.6.1.3 Categorization of Language-Specific Concepts

The language-specific concepts were then classified into following two types

- Unique Concept: Concept unique to Konkani language.
- Unique Word: A specific word being used in Konkani for which a phrase has to be used in other language.

Table 6.1 Classification of KLSS based on the domains of extraction

Category	Count	Examples
Cuisine	59	huddameWI, pAWolYI
Agriculture and plant life	32	KarAdI, KAjana, cuttI
Dance	26	XAlo, MAMdo
Festivals	24	Sigamo, sAMjAMva
Culture and traditions	23	vajeM, gAvado, xivaja
Religion	16	sAMwerI, bewAlYa, sAsAya
Household items	14	kolYamUiYa, kolYamI
Clothes and adornments	9	AtI, xeMTaiI
Borrowed words	9	kArrera, kAminAMva
Professions	6	Pexo, pAyalata
Others	55	xiPalYo, ciro, wAbUla

6.6.2 KLSS Statistics

The work of identifying KLSS was carried on for nearly three months, and nearly 700 KLSSs were selected. After cross-lingual verification, the list was reduced to 350 words. Out of these, word concept has been defined, and synsets were created for only 283 words. Of these, 56 belong to the class of Unique Words and the rest belongs to the class of Unique Concepts. The part-of-speech distribution of the KLSS was as follows:

a. Nouns: 255,
b. Adjectives: 15,
c. Verbs: 12,
d. Adverbs: 1.

Identified synsets were classified based on the categories in which they occur. Table 6.1 tabulates the categories identified from the synsets created.

6.7 Tools Developed During the Konkani WordNet Development Process

In order to address some of the challenges faced by the linguists and to speed up the WordNet Development process, initiative was taken by the computer scientists to develop several tools, some of which are listed below.

6.7.1 WordNet Web site Development Using Content Management System (CMS)

A Content Management System (CMS) for WordNet Web site development was designed to speed up the WordNet Web site development and deployment activity. The details of the WordNet CMS can be found in Prabhugaonkar et al. (2012b). This WordNet CMS has been used for WordNet Web site development of majority of the Indian languages.

6.7.2 Concept Space Synset Management Tool (CSS)

After using the expansion approach, which speeded up the synset creation task, it was decided to focus on the creation of language-specific synsets. The CSS tool was developed to assist creation of language-specific concepts/synsets and manage their linkages to other Indian language WordNets. The details of the CSS management tool are published in Nagvekar et al. (2014). The CSS tool has provision to store additional metadata about the concepts/synsets stored in the WordNet. The Web site for Konkani WordNet can be accessed through the Internet by any user. Figure 6.1 is a screenshot of the Konkani WordNet Web site developed.

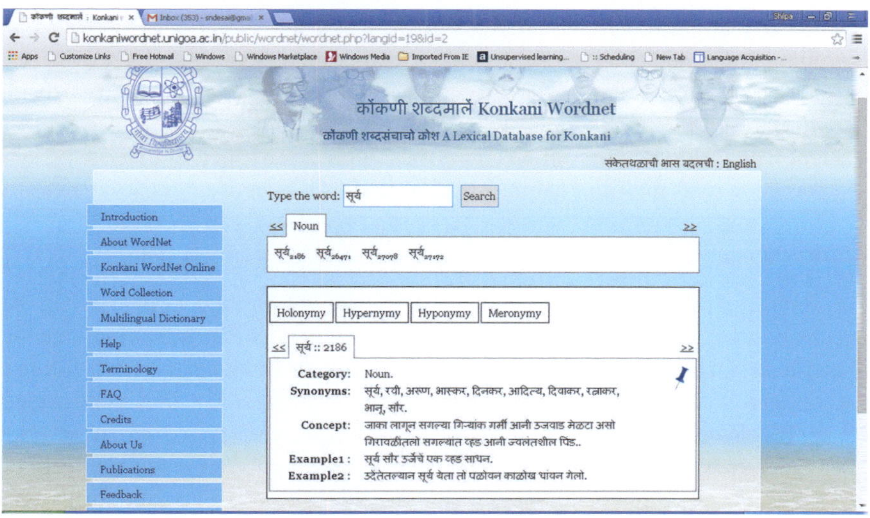

Fig. 6.1 Screenshot of Konkani WordNet Web site

6.8 Database Design and Application Programming Interface (IWAPI) for IndoWordNet

The IndoWordNet is a multilingual WordNet which links WordNets of different Indian languages on a common identification number given to each concept. The IndoWordNet database is designed to maintain the data for IndoWordNet in two databases. The common data such as semantic relations and ontology details for all languages is maintained in a common database called WordNet-Master. The WordNet-Master maintains the data shared by all the languages. This database maintains tables which borrow the relations from the source WordNet (Hindi WordNet). The WordNet-Master includes tables for semantic relations. It includes all ontology related tables in English. The synset data for a language are maintained in a separate database for each language called WordNet <language-name>, e.g., WordNet-Konkani, WordNet-Hindi, and WordNet-Marathi for Konkani, Hindi, and Marathi languages, respectively. Some of the salient features of using IndoWordNet Database design for storing synset data are as follows:

- Centralized database for common concepts and language databases for language concepts.
- Incorporates both merge approach and expansion approach data
- Design provides for developing a centrally controlled system for issuing Ids in case of concepts specific to a language or language group.
- Open, scalable, normalized, and modular design.
- Maintains language-specific relations in the WordNets.
- Achieves maximal compatibility across the different resources.
- Can be used for building the WordNets relatively independently (re-) using existing resources.
- Supports development of online and offline applications such as dictionary, synset creation tool, multilingual information retrieval. Speeds up retrieval and processing time.
- Stores semantic, lexical relations, ontological details, and meta-data.

The details of the database design are presented in Prabhu et al. (2012). An object-oriented Application Programming Interface (API) was implemented to facilitate easy and rapid development of tools and other software resources that require WordNet access and manipulation functionality. The main objective of IndoWordNet Application Programming Interface (IWAPI) is to provide access to the WordNet resource independent of the underlying storage technology. The current implementation manipulates data stored in a relational database. Furthermore, the IWAPI also supports parallel access and manipulation of WordNets in multiple languages. The details of the IWAPI are presented in Prabhugaonkar et al. (2012a, b).

6.9 Main Applications of the Konkani WordNet

Some of the main applications of the Konkani WordNet are listed below:

6.9.1 Konkani Language Learning in Schools and Colleges

The Konkani WordNet acts like a dictionary cum thesaurus and can be used by Konkani students and teachers for reference. The language learning can be made interesting by designing word puzzles using the WordNet Synsets. This can help in improving the language vocabulary too in an innovative manner.

6.9.2 Multilingual Dictionary Creation

The Konkani WordNet can be used for creating a multilingual dictionary. A multilingual dictionary will help human translators with suggestions of appropriate words.

6.9.3 NLP Research in Konkani

The WordNet is a crucial resource for building NLP applications for Konkani and has been extensively used for NLP research in Konkani. The WordNet has been used to build morphological lexicons for Konkani by automatically selecting paradigms for words in Konkani WordNet (Desai et al. 2012, 2014a), which has aided the development of Morphological Analyzer tool for Konkani. Konkani WordNet has also been used to learn derivational suffixes and derivational paradigms in Konkani using unsupervised morphology learning techniques (Desai et al. 2014b).

6.10 Enhancement to the Konkani WordNet

The Konkani WordNet was created using the expansion approach; hence, the coverage was found to be low. The sense-marking activity was carried out using the Konkani Text Corpus to find the senses found in the Konkani WordNet.

Sense-marking was undertaken to find the coverage of the WordNet and add missing synsets. This task of sense-marking undertaken lead to the improvement in the quality of the WordNet in the following ways:

- Sense-marked corpus created lead to increase the example sentences in the WordNet.

- Identification and correction of spelling errors, category mismatch, and incomplete gloss.
- Spelling variations were added to WordNet.
- Concepts, specific to Goa and Konkani language occurring in the corpus to be sense marked, were added to the WordNet.
- The coverage of synsets was improved by adding false negatives, i.e., missing senses of words.
- The quality of synset was improved by removing false positives, namely irrelevant words that were erroneously included in the synset.

The details of the sense-marking activity and its impact on WordNet coverage and quality are presented in Prabugaonkar et al. (2014).

Grammatical Gender identification: Knowledge of grammatical gender is essential for languages like Konkani, which have an agreement system with other aspects of the language. Augmenting the Konkani WordNet with grammatical gender will increase the usefulness of the WordNet. Konkani has three grammatical genders, namely *masculine*, *feminine*, and *neuter*. Since the source WordNet-Hindi has only two grammatical genders, namely *masculine and feminine*, this grammatical property of nouns could not be directly borrowed from the source language-like semantic relation. Provision to augment the Konkani WordNet with grammatical gender has been made by making use of morphological and word features of nouns in the WordNet. The details of the automatic grammatical gender identification process are presented in Desai et al. (2015).

6.11 Conclusion and Future Work

The use of expansion approach and the funding for the project helped in creating a Konkani WordNet consisting of approximately 34-K synsets in short span of three years. In order to improve the quality by public feedback, the Konkani WordNet has been made available online at http://konkaniwordnet.unigoa.ac.in/public/wordnet/wordnet.php so that Konkani speakers use the same and report errors and suggest improvements to the WordNet. In order to reach maximum users, development of a mobile-based interface for WordNet has been taken up. The future plan is to improve the user interface and extend the WordNet to store more features so as to help in improving the efficiency of word sense disambiguation algorithms to help in main applications such as machine translation.

Acknowledgment The authors wish to express their sincere gratitude to Dr. Chandralekha D'Souza, Shri Damodar Ghanekar, Shri Sushant Naik, and Ms. Kapila Dessai for their invaluable inputs during identification and verification of KLSS. We also wish to express our gratitude to the entire NLP team of Goa University and Indian Institute of Technology Bombay (IITB) for providing the tools and assisting in the process of Konkani WordNet Creation. We thank Goa University for providing infrastructure for this project. We are grateful to the Department of Electronics and Information TechnologY (DeitY), New Delhi, for funding the Indradhanush WordNet Project, without their financial support this work would not have been possible.

References

Almeida, M. (2008). *A Description of Konkani*. Panaji: Thomas Stephens Konkani Kendra. 1989. Asmitai Pratishthan. *Dalgado on Konkani*.

Bhattacharyya, P. (2010). IndoWordNet, Lexical Resources Engineering Conference 2010 (LREC 2010), Malta, May, 2010.

Bhattacharyya, P., Fellbaum, C., & Vossen, P. (2010). Principles, constructions and applications of multilingual WordNets. *5th Global WordNet Conference, Mumbai*.

Borkar, S. J. (1986). *Konkani Vyakaran*. Margao: Konkani Bhasha Mandal.

Desai, S., Pawar, J., & Bhattacharyya, P. (2012). Automated paradigm selection for FSA based Konkani verb morphological analyzer. *Proceedings of COLING 2012: Demonstration Papers, Mumbai, India, 2012* (pp. 103–110). http://aclweb.org/anthology/C12-3013.

Desai, S., Desai, N., Pawar, J., & Bhattacharyya, P. (2014a). *Proceedings of the 11th International Conference on Natural Language Processing, chapter AutoParSe: An Automatic Paradigm Selector for Nouns in Konkani, Goa, India* (pp. 154–162).

Desai, S., Pawar, J., & Bhattacharyya, P. (2014b). *Proceedings of the Fifth Workshop on South and Southeast Asian Natural Language Processing, chapter A Framework for Learning Morphology using Suffix Association Matrix, Dublin, Ireland* (pp. 28–36).

Desai, S., Pawar, J., & Bhattacharyya, P. (2015). *Proceedings of the 16th International Conference on Intelligent Text Processing and Computational Linguistics, chapter Staged Approach for Grammatical Gender Identification of Nouns using Association Rule Mining and Classification. Cairo, Egypt*.

Ghanekar, D. (1999). *Konkani Sachitra Astangi Abhyaskosha*. Panaji: Rajhauns Vitaran.

Halankar, T., Sardessai, M. (1991). *Konkani Biswakosha*. 4 volumes. Goa University.

Mahale, K. (1992). *Konkani Utrabol*. Panaji: Goa Konkani Akademi.

Nagvenkar, A., Prabhugaonkar, N., Prabhu, V., Karmali, R., & Pawar, J. (2014). *Proceedings of the Seventh Global Wordnet Conference, chapter Concept Space Synset Manager Tool, Tartu, Estonia* (pp. 86–94). http://aclweb.org/anthology/W14-0112.

Narayan, D., Chakrabarty, D., Pande, P., & Bhattacharyya, P. (2002). An experience in building the Indo WordNet—a WordNet for Hindi. *Proceedings of the First International Conference on Global WordNet, Mysore, India*, January, 2002.

Prabhu, V., Desai, S., Redkar, H., Prabhugaonkar, N., Nagvenkar, A., & Karmali, R. (2012). *Proceedings of the 3rd Workshop on South and Southeast Asian Natural Language Processing, chapter An Efficient Database Design for IndoWordNet Development Using Hybrid Approach* (pp. 229–236). Mumbai, India: The COLING 2012 Organizing Committee. http://aclweb.org/anthology/W12-5021.

Prabhugaonkar, N., & Pawar, J. (2014). *Proceedings of the Seventh Global Wordnet Conference, chapter Use of Sense Marking for Improving WordNet Coverage, Tartu, Estonia* (pp. 95–99). http://aclweb.org/anthology/W14-0113.

Prabhugaonkar, N., Nagvenkar, A., & Karmali, R. (2012a). *Proceedings of the 3rd Workshop on South and Southeast Asian Natural Language Processing, chapter IndoWordNet Application Programming Interfaces* (pp. 237–244). Mumbai, India: The COLING 2012 Organizing Committee. http://aclweb.org/anthology/W12-5022.

Prabhugaonkar, N., Nagvenkar, A., Prabhu, V., & Karmali, R. (2012b). Wordnet website development and deployment using content management approach. In *Proceedings of COLING 2012: Demonstration Papers, Mumbai, India* (pp. 361–368). http://aclweb.org/anthology/C12-3045.

Sardesai, M. (1986). Some aspects of Konkani grammar. Department of Linguistics, Deccan College, Pune.

Shennoi, G. (1949). *Konkanichi Vyakarani Bandavol*. Gomantak Chhapkhano Girgaum Mumbai.

Vossen, P. (1998). *EuroWordNet: A Multilingual Database with Lexical Semantic Networks*. Kluwer Academic Publishers: Dordrecht.

Walawalikar, S., Desai, S., Karmali, R., Naik, S., Ghanekar, D., D'Souza, C., et al. (2010). Experiences in building the konkani wordnet using the expansion approach. In *Proceedings of the 5th Global WordNet Conference, Mumbai*. http://www.cfilt.iitb.ac.in/gwc2010/pdfs/54_Konkani_WordNet_Walawalikar.pdf.

Chapter 7
Malayalam WordNet

S. Rajendran and K.P. Soman

Abstract Building of Malayalam has been initiated in Amrita Vishwa Vidyapeetham, Coimbatore, in December 2011, as a part of the project entitled 'Development of Dravidian WordNet: An Integrated WordNet for Telugu, Tamil, Kannada and Malayalam' funded by Department of Information Technology, MCIT, Govt. of India. The main objective of the project is to build WordNets for Dravidian languages by making use of the already built Hindi WordNet under the project scheme IndoWordNet. Hindi WordNet has been built based on Princeton English WordNet which is a component of EuroWordNet. The main objective of EuroWordNet is to develop an extensive and high-quality multilingual database with WordNets for several languages (mainly European languages such as French, German, Czech and Italian) in a cost-effective manner. On the similar line, IndoWordNet is being built for Indian languages. Malayalam WordNet is a component of Dravidian WordNet which in turn is the component of IndoWordNet. Malayalam WordNet is an online lexical database. It is useful for many applications of natural language processing.

7.1 Introduction

Malayalam WordNet aims to capture the network of lexical or semantic relations between lexical items or words in Malayalam. As we know, lexical items are related to one another in the hierarchical dimension as taxonomies (which show

S. Rajendran (✉) · K.P. Soman
Department of Computational Engineering and Networking,
Amrita Vishwa Vidyapeetham, Coimbatore, Tamil Nadu, India
e-mail: rnk@unigoa.ac.in

N.S. Dash et al. (eds.), *The WordNet in Indian Languages*,
DOI 10.1007/978-981-10-1909-8_7

hyponymy–hypernymy and meronymy–holonymy relationship) and non-hierarchical dimension as opposites (which include complementaries, antonyms, antipodals, counterparts, reversives and converses) and synonyms (Lyons 1977; Cruse 1986). Also words are related to one another due to their derivational as well as collocational meaning. Componential analysis which studies meanings of lexical items in terms of meaning components or features can help us to capture the above-mentioned network of relations in a more systematic way (Nida 1975a).

A database has to be created depicting the lexical items and their meaning relations such as hyponymy–hypernymy (subordination–superordination relationship), meronymy–holonymy (part–whole relationship), synonymy and lexical opposition and the formal relations such as derivation and collocation. The network of relations exist between the lexical items are captured in the WordNet. Such a study can be made use of for various lexical studies as well as application-oriented studies like machine translation (in which word disambiguation is a crucial issue), and machine-oriented language learning and teaching.

7.2 Strategy of the WordNet

According to Miller et al. (1990) ‘WordNet is an online lexical reference system whose design is inspired by current psycholinguistic theories of human lexical memory’. The organization or WordNet is based on the presumption that there is a mental dictionary or thesaurus in which the words are organized under conceptual fields or semantic domains. The WordNet aims at organizing lexical information in terms of word meanings or concepts rather than word forms. WordNet in this sense resembles a thesaurus more than a dictionary. A thesaurus in its widest contemporary sense is a classification of words by concepts, topics, or subjects. But the WordNet is much more efficient and versatile than the thesaurus whether it is in paper form or available in electronic form. In one sense, WordNet is an online thesaurus. But its efficiency in bringing out the lexical relations exalts it from thesaurus. The present WordNet of Malayalam is aimed to be built on the foundation offered by natural language processing (NLP) taking into account its application in the fields language teaching and language learning, lexicography, translation, both machine and human, and artificial intelligence (AI) knowledge representation. The ideas propounded by Miller (1991) and Miller et al. (1990) are profusely used in the preparation of WordNet for Malayalam.

WordNet resembles a thesaurus in its broad framework. Its building blocks are synsets; each synset consists of all the words that express a given concept. This facilitates the user of a WordNet to recall the words expressing this concept knowing any one of the words which has lexicalized the same concept. But WordNet is not a list of concepts in the form of synsets. The relations such as hyponymy, meronymy, and entailment link the synsets to one another.

WordNet resembles a traditional dictionary in some respects. For instance, one can find definitions and sample sentences in WordNet for most of its synsets.

Information about morphologically related words also finds its place in WordNet. The goals of WordNet resemble those of a standard dictionary, and the semantics of WordNet is based on the notion of sense that the lexicographers have traditionally used in writing dictionaries. WordNet differs from the dictionaries in their organization. WordNet does not give pronunciation, derivation morphology, etymology, usage notes, or pictorial illustrations. However, WordNet depicts the semantic relation between word senses more transparently and elegantly.

WordNet relies on two commonly accepted relations: the conceptual–semantic relations which link concepts and the lexical relations which link individual words. The mental lexicon tends to build semantic networks with conceptual–semantic relations, whereas those who are focusing on lexical aspects use primarily lexical, word–word relations. Thus, WordNet is organized by lexical and semantic relations. Since a semantic relation is a relation between meanings, and since meanings can be represented by synsets, it is natural to think of semantic relations as pointers between synsets. It is characteristic of semantic relations as pointers between synsets. WordNet does not contain syntagmatic relations linking words from different syntactic categories. The four major syntactic categories (noun, verb, adjective, and adverb) are treated separately. Nouns are organized in lexical memory as topical hierarchies. Verbs are organized by a variety of entailment relations. Adjectives and adverbs are organized as N-dimensional hyperspaces (Miller et al. 1990). The basic semantic relation in WordNet is synonymy. Sets of synonyms (synsets) form the basic building blocks. The notion of synonymy used in WordNet does not entail interchangeability in all contexts. A synset has only a single gloss.

7.3 Nouns in WordNet

Nouns are organized in a lexical inheritance system. A typical definition of a noun contains a superordinate term followed by certain distinguishing features. The relation of subordination (or class inclusion or subsumption), which is called hyponymy, organizes nouns into a lexical hierarchy. The superordinate relation generates a hierarchical semantic organization of nouns. Synset which contains a group of synonyms representing a concept is the building blocks of noun WordNet. Synonymy is a lexical relation that holds between word forms, whereas the semantic relation holds between lexicalized concepts.

7.3.1 Hyponymy and Hypernymy

Hyponymy is the relationship that exists between specific and general lexical items, such that the former is included in the latter. The relation that is reverse to hyponymy is hypernymy. The set of items that are hyponyms of same superordinate term or hypernym are co-hyponyms (or coordinates). The hyponymy–hypernymy relation is variously termed as subordination–superordination, subset-superset, etc. The relationship existing between *paSu* 'cow' and *mRIgaM* 'animal' and *eruma* 'buffalo' and *mRIgaM* 'animal' is hyponymy and *paSu* and eruma are co-hyponyms. *mRIgaM* is the hypernym of *paSu* and *eruma.* Hyponymy is unilateral and asymmetrical.

avaL~ talayil~ mullapuuv cuuTiyirikkunnu
she head_LOC flower keep_PRES_she
'She is wearing jasmine on her head'

.

avaL~ talayil~ puu cuuTiyirikkunnu
she head_LOC flower keep_PRES_she
'She is wearing flower on her head'
avaL~ talayil~ puu cuuTiyirikkunnu
she head_LOC flower keep_PRES_she
'She is wearing flower on her head'

.

**avaL~ talayil~ mullapuuv cuuTiyirikkunnu*
she head_LOC jasmine keep_PRES_she
'She is wearing jasmine on her head'

Since the hyponymy relation is unilateral and symmetrical, the sentence with '*' marker is a wrong claim. Hyponymy shows transitive relation as shown below.

mRIgaM 'animal' · *sastani* 'mammal'
sastani 'mammal' · paSu 'cow'
mRIgaM 'animal' · *sastani* 'mammal' · *paSu* 'cow'

7.3.2 Lexical Hierarchy

The conventional dictionaries make use of the hyponymic relations between nouns to represent the meaning. The following illustration depicts it clearly.

tatta 'parrot'
ushNa meekhalayil~ kaaNappeTunna bhaMgiyuLLa paccaniRattooTu kuuTiyatuM kaTTiyuLLa taazhooTTu vaLanjnja cuNTukaL~ uLLatuM paruparutta uLLatumaaya oruyinaM pakshiyaaN.ii var~ggattil~ppeTunna cilayinaM tattakaL~kk manushyassvaraM anukarikkaanuLLa kazhivuNT.
'A mainly tropical bird, typically brightly coloured, with a strong downcurved hooked bill and raucous voice, some kind of which are able to mimic human speech'.

pakshi 'bird'—*ushNa raktamuLLatuM muTTayiTunnatuM tuuvalukaL~ uLLatuM muN~ kaikaL~ ciRakukaLaayi ruupaantarappeTTiTTuLLatuM maaya oru jantu var~ggaM.(jiivi).*
'bird—a warm-blooded egg-laying animal having feathers and forelimbs modified as wings'.

jantu '*animal*'—*svantamaayi SvasikkaanuM calikkaanuM kazhivuLLatuM, njaaneendriyangngaL~ uLLatuM selluloosillaatta kooSangngaL~ uLLatumaaya jiivi.*
'animal—an organism capable of breathing and voluntary movement and possessing sense organs and cells with non-cellulose walls'
jiivi 'organism'—*jiivikkunnava*
'organism—a living entity'

Each hypernymic relation can be represented by a corresponding hyponymic relation that points in the opposite direction. A lexical hierarchy emerges from this manner of representing hyponymy and hypernymy relations. Knowledge representations by computer scientist make use of the hierarchies of these sorts widely. The nouns in WordNet depict a lexical inheritance system. Systematic effort has been made in the WordNet to connect hyponyms with their hypernyms (and vice versa).

WordNet presupposes a linguistic knowledge of anaphoric relations; an anaphor can be a hypernym of its antecedent. Each hypernym leads on to a more generic hypernym. Hypernym cannot be represented as a simple relation between word forms. Hypernymy is a relation between lexicalized concepts. It is represented in WordNet by a pointer between the appropriate synsets. A lexical hierarchy can be reconstituted by a series of synsets which are related by means of hypernymy.

{*tatta, kiiraM*} 'parrot' @ · · {*pakshi, paRava*} 'bird' @ · {*jantu*} 'organism' @ · {*jiivi, jiivanuLLava, jiivikkunnava, jantujaalangngaL~*} 'living being'

The hyonymy–hypernymy relation can be read as 'IS-A' and 'IS-A-KIND-OF'; For example, *tatta oru pakshi* 'Parrot is a bird' or *tatta oru taraM pakshiyaaN* 'Parrot is a kind of bird'.

7.3.3 Unique Beginners

The hierarchical structuring of nouns can be assumed to be contained in a single hierarchy. Instead, WordNet divides the nouns into several hierarchies, each with a different unique beginner. The semantic fields or domains (Lehrer 1974) which contain their own stock of vocabulary can be equated with these multiple hierarchies. Unique beginner corresponds roughly to a primitive semantic component in a compositional theory of lexical semantics. There is a list of 25 unique beginners for noun source files of EuroWordNet (Vossen 1998).

{act, activity}	{natural object}
{animal, fauna}	{natural phenomenon}
{artifact}	{person, human being}
{attribute}	{plant, flora}
{body}	{possession}
{cognition, knowledge}	{process}

{communication}	{quantity, amount}
{event, happening}	{relation}
{feeling, emotion}	{shape}
{food}	{state}
{group, grouping}	{substance}
{location}	{time}
{motivation, motive}	.

This way of representing lexical items depicts the ontological structures which captures the lexical inheritance of one item from the other as shown under the title 'lexical inheritance'.

7.3.4 Distinguishing Features

The hyponymy relation generates the overall structure of noun hierarchies. But the details given by the features distinguish one concept from another. For example, *tatta mikkavaaRuM pacca niRavuM kaTTiyuLLa taazhooTT vaLanjnja cuNTukaLuM raNT ciRakuaLuM uLLa paruparutta SabddamuNTaakkunnatuM paRakkunnatuM aaya oru pakshiyaaN* 'parrot' is a bird that is mostly green in colour and with two wings and raucous voice. It may be possible to associate parrot with at least three different kinds of distinguishing features:

1. Attributes: *pacca niRaM* 'green colour'
2. Parts: *kaTTiyuLLa taazhooTT vaLanjnja cuNTukaL~* 'strong downcurved hooked bill', *raNT ciRakukaL* 'two wings'
3. Functions: *paruparutta SabddamuNTaakkuM* 'raucous voice', *paRakkuM* 'flies'

7.3.5 Attributes and Modification

Values of attributes are expressed by adjectives. For example, size and colour are attributes of parrot: the usual colour of parrot can be expressed by the adjective *pacca* 'green'. The attributes associated with a noun are reflected in the adjectives that can normally modify it.

7.3.6 Function and Predication

It seems natural to say that the function of a pencil is to write or the function of knife is to cut, but to say that the function of a parrot is to fly or to sing seems a bit forced. Nominal concepts can play various semantic roles as arguments of the verbs that they co-occur with in a sentence.

katti ‘knife—*muRikkuka* ‘cut’
kuzhi ‘hole’—*kuzhikkuka* ‘dig’
citraM ‘picture—*varaykkuka* ‘draw’
peTTi ‘box’—*piTikkuka* ‘ hold’

There are also linguistic reasons to assume that a thing’s function is a feature of its meaning. It should be remembered in this context that Pustejovksy who advocates for generative lexicon (Pustejovksy 1995, p. 76, 2001, p. 56) assumes that word meaning is structured on the basis of four generative factors, or qualia roles, that capture how humans understand objects and relations in the world and provide the minimal explanation for the linguistic behaviour of lexical items.

CONSTITUTIVE: the relation between an object and its constituent parts
FORMAL: the basic category that distinguishes the object within a larger domain
TELIC: the object’s purpose and function
AGENTIVE: factors involved in the object’s origin or ‘coming into being’

Pustovsky’s qualia roles have to be remembered while making definitions for synsets in WordNet.

7.3.7 Meronymy and Holonymy

Meronymy is the part–whole relation between nouns which is generally considered to be a semantic relation. Meronymy is comparable to synonymy, antonymy, and hyponymy which are the different kinds of relations captured in the WordNet. Reverse of meronymy is holonymy. If X is a meronymy of Y, then Y is said to be a holonym of X (X = meronym; Y = holonym). Many concrete objects like bodies and artefacts are defined by meronymy–holonymy relation. Meronyms are distinguishing features that hyponyms can inherit. Consequently, meronymy and hyponymy are intertwined in complex ways. For example, if *cuNT* ‘beak’ and *ciRak* ‘wing’ are meronyms of bird, and if parrot is a hyponym of bird, then by inheritance, beak and wing must also be meronyms of *parrot*. The fact that parts are hyponyms as well as meronyms complicates the relations between meronymy and hyponymy. For example, {*cuNT, kokk* ‘beak’} is not only a meronym of {*pakshi* ‘bird’}, it is a hyponym of {*taaTi* ‘jaw’}, which in turn is a meronym of {*talayocT* ‘skull’} and a hyponym of {*asthi* ‘skeletal_structure’}. It has been said that distinguishing features are introduced into noun hierarchies primarily at the level of basic concepts; some claims have been made that meronym is particularly important for defining basic concepts. Meronymy is often compared to hyponymy: both are asymmetrical and transitive, and both can relate terms hierarchically. In many instances, transitivity seems to be limited. For example, *piTi* ‘handle’ is a meronym of *katak* ‘door’ and ‘door’ is a meronym of *viiT* ‘house’, yet is sound odd to say *viiTin piTiyuNT* ‘The house has a handle’ or *viiTinte oru bhaagamaaN piTi* ‘The handle is a part of the house’.

7.3.8 Antonymy

Antonymy is lexical in nature and is founded on linguistic as well as psycholinguistic principles. Normally the word association test brings together antonymous words.

vijayaM 'victory'—tool~vi 'defeat'
santooshaM—'happiness'—*asantushTi* 'unhappiness'

Though semantic opposition is not a fundamental organizing relation between nouns, it is captured in WordNet for its own merits.

{[*purushan~* 'man', *strii* 'woman', !], *vyakti* 'person', @…(*purushavyakti* 'a male person')}
{[strii 'woman', *purushan~* 'man', !], *vyakti* 'person', @…(*striivyakti* 'a female person')}

Antonymy is a lexical relation between words, rather than a semantic relation between concepts. The three kinds of semantic relations—hyponymy, meronymy, and antonymy—depicts nouns as an interconnected network.

7.3.9 Binary Opposition

Antonymy, which is often considered opposite to synonymy, relies on the lexical relation, incompatibility. The table gives the typology of binary opposition (Lyons 1977, vol. 1). There are many kinds of oppositions between words and antonymy is one among the opposite relations. The different types of opposition relations are listed below:

Type	Example
Antonymy	*valut* 'big one': *ceRut* 'small one'
Complementarity: Complementarity is a contrastive relation between two lexemes which exhaustively divide some conceptual domain into two mutually exclusive compartments, so that what does not fall into one of the compartments must necessarily fall into the other. There is no 'no-man's land', no neutral ground, no possibility of a third term lying between them	*pakal~* 'day': *raatri* 'night', *satyaM* 'true': *asatyaM* 'false', *jayaM* 'pass': *tool~vi* 'fail'
Converseness: The pairs which express a relationship between two entities by specifying the direction of one relative to the other along some axes	*bhar~ttaav* 'husband' versus *bhaarya* 'wife'

(continued)

(continued)

Type	Example
Privative opposition: It is a contrastive relation between two lexemes, one of which denotes some positive property and other of which denotes the absence of that property	*budhisaali* 'clever' versus *maNTan* 'fool'
Equipollent opposition: An equipollent opposition is a relation in which each of the contrasting lexemes denotes a positive property	*aaN* 'male person' versus *peNN* 'female person'
Reciprocal social roles	*bhishvaguran~* 'doctor': *roogi* 'patient', teacher': student, *muta-laaLi* 'boss': *tozhilaaLi* 'servant'
Kinship opposition	*acchan~* 'father': *makan~* 'son' *amma* 'mother': *makaL~* 'daughter'
Temporal opposition: shows converseness temporally	*mun~p* 'before': pin~p 'after'
Spatial opposition: shows converseness spatially	*mukaLil* ~'above': *taazhe* 'below'
Orthogonal opposition or perpendicular opposition	*vaTakk* 'north': *kizhakk* 'east' and *paTinjnjaaR* 'west' *kizhakk* 'east': *tekk* 'south' and *vaTakk* 'north'
Antipodal opposition or diametrical opposition	*vaTakk* 'north': *tekk* 'south' *kizhakk* 'east: *paTinjnjaaR* 'west'

Most of the spatio-temporal postpositions and spatio-temporal adverbs are together considered as spatio-temporal nouns in the present WordNet.

7.3.10 Multi-member Opposition

There are different types of multi-member sets in a language whose lexical relations can be described as incompatible denoting non-binary contrasts as opposed to binary contrasts. Various kinds of ordering are found in multi-member sets of incompatibles, and such sets may be serially or cyclically ordered (Cruse 1986). The constituents of a serial or cycle may be fixed or overlapping. The fixedly ordered items form a rank. The overlapping items may form a scale.

SERIAL

onn'one'
↓
raNT 'two'
↓
muunn 'three'
↓
naal 'four'
↓
anjc 'five'

Cycle

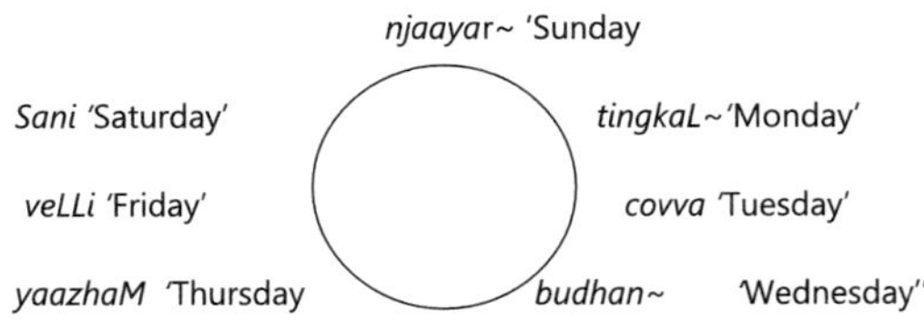

SCALE

SreeshThaM 'excellent'
↓
nallat 'good'
↓
tRIptikaraM 'satisfactory'
↓
mooSaM 'bad'
↓
vaLareemooSaM 'very bad'

RANK

keeNal~ 'Colonel'
↓
lephRRanenRR keeNal~ 'Lieutenant colonel'
↓
meejar~ 'Major'
↓
kyaapRRan~ ' Captain'
↓
lephRRanenRR 'Lieutenant'

7.3.11 Summing up of Relations in Nouns

The different types of lexical/semantic relations exhibited in Malayalam WordNet are listed in the following table:

Relations	Subtypes	Example
Synonymy	–	*pustakaM to* 'book' *bukk* 'book'
Hypernymy–hyponymy	–	*mRIgaM* 'animal' to *sastani* 'mammal'
Hyponym–hypernymy	–	*paSu* 'cow' to *sastani* 'mammal'

(continued)

(continued)

Relations	Subtypes	Example
Holonymy–meronymy	From wholes to parts	*meeSa* ‘table’ to *kaal~* ‘leg’
	From groups to their members	*vakupp* ‘department’ to *aacaaryan~* ‘professor’
Meronymy–holonymy	From parts to wholes	*cakraM* ‘wheel’ to *cumaTu-vaNTi* ‘cart’
	From members to their groups	*seenaapati (paTattalavan~)* ‘captain’ to *seena* ‘army’
Opposition	Antonymy (gradable opposites)	*nallavyakti (nallavan~)* ‘good person’ to *vRIttikeTTavan~* ‘bad person’
	Complementarity (an item complements another item)	*aaN~* ’male’ to *peNN* ‘female’
	Privative opposition (presence of a feature implies the absence of another)	*budhisaali* ‘clever’ versus *maN-Tan~* ‘fool’
	Converse opposition: Spatial opposites showing converseness	*miite (mukaLil~)* ‘above’ versus *taazhe* ‘below’
	Converse opposition: Temporal opposites showing converseness.	*mun~p* ‘before’ to *pin~p* ‘after’
	Equipollent opposition (both the items have positive features)	*aaN~* ‘male’ to *peNN* ‘female
	Reciprocal social roles	*bhishvaguran~* ‘doctor’ to *roogi* ‘patient’
	Kinship opposition	*acchan~* ‘father’ to *makan~* ‘son’; *amma* ‘mother’ to *makaL~* ‘daughter’
	Orthogonal opposition or perpendicular opposition	*vaTakk* ‘north’ to *kizhakk* ‘east’ and *paTinjnjaaR* ‘west’ *kizhakk* ‘east’ to *tekk* ‘south’ and *vaTakk* ‘north’
	Antipodal opposition or diagonally opposite relation	*vaTakk* ‘north’ to *tekk* ‘south’
Multiple opposites	Serial	*onn* ‘one’, *raNT* ‘two’, *muunn* ‘three’, *naal* ‘four’, and so on.
	Cycle	*njaayar~* ‘Sunday’ to *tingkaL~* ‘Monday’to *covva* ‘Tuesday’ to *budhan~* ‘Wednesday’ to *vyaazhaM* ‘Thursday’ to *veLLi* ‘Friday’ *Sani* ‘Saturday’

7.4 Adjectives in WordNet

Adjective is the syntactic category which is associated with noun modification. The sole function of adjectives is modification of nouns. But noun, verb, and prepositional phrases do not have the sole responsibility of modifying. Adjectives are organized in WordNet is a unique way which differs from the organization of the other major syntactic categories, noun and verb. WordNet contains:

(1) Descriptive adjectives (Ex. *valiya* 'big', *taatparyamuLLa* 'interesting', *saadhyamuLLa* 'possible')
(2) Relational adjectives (Ex. *adhyakshata* presidential, *kaar~shika* 'agriculatural', *saMgiita* 'musical', *dvanta* 'dental')
(3) Reference-modifying adjectives (Ex. *mun~patte* former, *aaroopitamaaya* alleged)

(a) Descriptive adjectives:
'A descriptive adjective is one that ascribes a value of an attribute to a noun. That is to say, x is Adj presupposes that there is an attribute A such that A(x) = Adj'. (Gross and Miller 1990)

at *nalla bhaaramuLLa cumaTaaN* 'that luggage is heavy'

The above sentence presupposes that there is attribute *bhaaraM* 'WEIGHT' such that *bhaaraM* 'WEIGHT' *(cumaT* 'luggage') = *bhaaraM* 'heavy'. In the same way, *taazhnna* 'low' and *uyar~nna* 'high' are values of *uyaraM* 'HEIGHT'. The WordNet has to link the descriptive adjectives with the appropriate attributes. The descriptive adjectives require a semantic organization which differs drastically from that of nouns. The hyponymic relation that builds nominal hierarchies is not available for adjectives. It is not possible to say that one adjective 'is a kind of' some other adjectives. As we propose to keep the referential meanings representing abstract nouns, adjectives, and adverbs under the semantic domain 'abstracts', the adjectives will naturally fall under their related abstract nouns. For example, the adjectives *viitiyuLLa* 'wide' and *iTungngiya* 'narrow' are kept under the semantic domain 'dimension' in which the attribute *viiti* 'width' is kept. Relating descriptive adjectives with the particular noun they pertain to is known by the term pertainymy.

(b) Colour adjectives:
Colour adjectives are the intensely studied ones and are organized differently in WordNet. Colour adjectives can function as nouns as well as adjectives in Malayalam. They can be graded, nominalized and conjoined with descriptive adjectives. But the pattern of direct and indirect antonymy that is observed for other descriptive adjectives does not hold good for colour adjectives. Formation of colour terms is a productive process in Malayalam. New colour terms are coined by the Malayalam speakers to denote different shades of colours (e.g. *ilapacca* 'leaf-like green', *tattapacca* 'parrot like green', *raktacuvapp* 'blood red'). The colours of a spectrum can be visualized as a cycle as shown below.

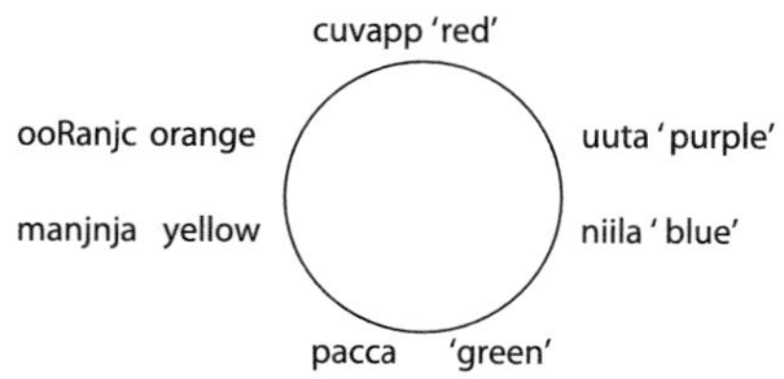

Colours can be graded between *veLLa* 'white' and *kaRupp* 'black'. They can be graded by the attribute *iLaM* 'light' (e.g. *iLaM pacca* 'light green', *iLaM cuvapp* 'light red) and *kaTuM* '*dark*' (*kaTum pacca* 'dark green', *kaTum cuvapp* ' dark red').

(c) Quantifiers:
Quantifiers are listed under determiners by some linguist. According to Lyons (Lyons 1977, vol.2, p. 455), quantifier tells us how many entities or how much substance is being referred to. WordNet, therefore, distinguishes quantifiers from determiners. In Malayalam, the words such as the following can be classified under quantifiers: *ellaa/sakala* 'all', *aneekaM/pala* 'many', *atikaM/orupaaT* 'much'. *kuRacc/cila/mikka* 'some', *parimitaM/curukkaM/kuRe* 'few', *raNTu* 'both'. In many respects quantifiers resemble descriptive adjectives. Like adjectives, many quantifiers are gradable (e.g. *vaLare kuRacc aaLukaL~* 'very few persons', *vaLare atikaM aaLukaL~* 'very many persons').

(d) Participial adjectives:
The adjectival participle forms of verbs function as adjectives in Malayalam. For example, the adjectival participle forms such as *viramicca* 'retired' (*viramicca paNDitan~*'retired professor'), *tiLappicca* 'boiled' (*tiLappicca veLLaM* 'boiled water'), *vivaahaM kazhiyaatta* (*vivaahaM kazhiyaatta peNN* 'unmarried woman'), *vivaahaM kazhinjnja* (*vivaahaM kazhinjnja peNN* 'married woman'), *veer~pirinjnja* (*veer~pirinjnja dampati* 'divorced couple') can function as adjectives. The adjectivalizers (or adjectival suffixes) such as *aaya* and *uLLa* are basically the adjectival participle forms of the verbs *aakuka* 'become' and *uL* 'be', respectively. They form adjectives when suffixed to nouns (e.g. *miTukkan~*' clever male person' + *aaya* > *miTukkanaaya* 'clever' *sundari* 'beautiful female person' + *aaya* > *sundariyaaya* 'beautiful', *azhak* 'beauty' + *uLLa* > *azhakuLLa* 'beautiful', *kaTTi* 'thickness' + *uLLa kaTTiyuLLa* 'thick').

7.4.1 Antonymy in Adjectives

Antonymy is the basic semantic relation that exists among descriptive adjectives. The word association tests reveal the importance of antonymy in adjectives. As the function of descriptive adjectives is to express values of attributes, and that nearly all attributes are bipolar, antonymy becomes important in the organization of descriptive adjectives. Antonymous adjectives express opposing values of an attribute. For example, the antonym of *bhaaramuLLa* 'heavy' is *bhaaraM kuRanjnja* 'light' that expresses a value at the opposite pole of the *bhaaraM* WEIGHT attribute. This binary opposition is to be represented in Malayalam WordNet.

7.4.2 Gradation and Non-gradation in Adjectives

Distinction is drawn between gradable and non-gradable adjectives. The first is referred as antonyms and the second one as complementaries by Lyons. The essence of a pair of complementaries is that between them they exhaustively divide some conceptual domain into two exclusive compartments, so that what does not fall into one of the compartments must necessarily fall into the other. There is no 'no-man's land', no neutral ground, no possibility of a third term lying between them. It has been claimed that complementary adjectives are not normally gradable, that is to say, they are odd in the comparative or superlative degree or when modified by intensifiers such as *tiivramaaya* 'extremely', *mitamaaya* 'moderately' and *neeriya* 'slightly'. Antonymy is expressed by pairs such as *niiNTa* 'long'/*kuRukiya*' short', *veegattil~* 'fast'/*patukke* 'slow', *laLitamaaya* 'easy'/*kaThinamaaya* 'difficult', *nalla* 'good'/*mooSamaaya* 'bad', *cuuTuLLa* 'hot'/*kuLiruLLa* 'cold'. They are fully gradable. The members of a pair denote degree of some variable properties such as length, speed, weight, accuracy.

The terms of a pair do not strictly bisect a domain: there is a range of values of the variable property, lying between those covered by the opposed terms, which cannot be properly referred to by either term. The complementaries and antonyms of Lyon are otherwise called as contradictory and contrary terms, respectively. Two propositions are said to be contradictory if the truth of one implies the falsity of the other and are said to be contrary if only one proposition can be true but both can be false. For example, *jiivanuLLa* 'living' and *jiivanillaatta* 'non-living' are contradictory terms as at *jiivanuLLa jantu* 'it is a living creature' necessarily implies at *jiivanillaatta jantu* 'it is not a non-living creature'. But *taTicca* 'fat' and *melinjnja* 'thin' are contrary terms because *maala taTicca peNN kuTTiyaaN* 'Mala is a fat girl' and *maala melinjnja peNN kuTTiyaaN* 'Mala a thin girl' cannot both be true, although both can be false if maalaa 'Mala' is of average weight.

Contraries are gradable adjectives, whereas contradictions are not. Gradation must also be considered as a semantic relation to organize adjectives. The following data will exemplify the gradation found among adjectives:

nalla cuuTuLLa	'very hot'
cuuTuLLa	'hot'
iLaM cuuTuLLa	'warm'
taNutta	'cold'

WordNet has to account for the gradation found among adjectives.

7.4.3 Similarity in Adjective

The adjectives lacking antonyms are similar in meaning to adjectives that do have antonyms. Adjectives are organized in clusters of synsets associated by semantic similarity to a focal adjective that relates the cluster to a contrasting cluster at the opposite pole of the attribute. In WordNet, direct antonyms are represented by antonymy pointer!; indirect antonyms are inherited through similarity, which is indicated by the similarity pointer and meaning 'IS SIMILAR TO'. The following figure illustrates this.

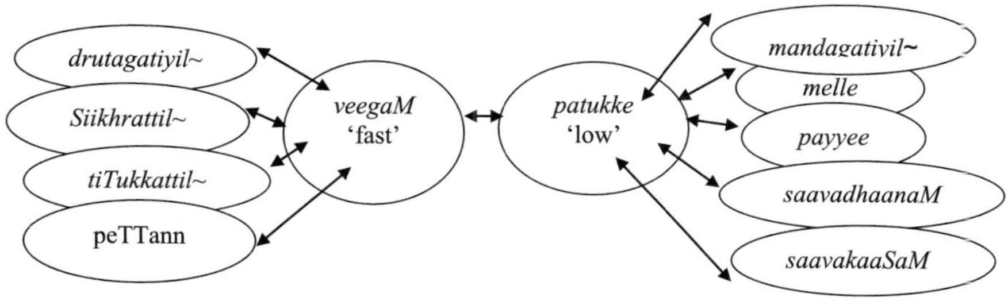

In the figure, *veegam* 'fast' and *patukke* 'slow' are direct antonyms; others are related to the directly antonymous words by 'similarity'. Overwhelmingly, association data and co-occurrence data indicate that *valiya* 'big' and *ceRiya* 'little' are considered as a pair and *uyar~nna* 'high' and *taazhnna* 'low' are considered as a pair. These pairs demonstrate that antonymy is a semantic relation between words rather than concepts. Polysemy is found among adjectives as a limited number of adjectives are used to attribute a considerable number of nouns.

7.4.4 Markedness in Adjectives

Binary oppositions frequently have a marked term and an unmarked term. That is, the terms are not entirely of equivalent weights, but one (the unmarked one) is neutral or positive in contrast to the other. Marked/unmarked distinction is found in polar oppositions such as *uyar~nna* 'high'/*taazhnna* 'low, *praayamuLLa* 'old'/*yauvanamaaya* 'young', *niiLamuLLa* 'long'/*kuRukiya* 'short', *visthaaranuLLa* 'wide/*iTungngiya* 'narrow'. We measure things by *uyaraM* 'height' rather than *uyaraM kuRanjnja* 'shortness'.

While asking questions about 'height', we say *at yatra uyaramuLLa tuuNaaN* 'How high that pillar is?' rather than *at yatra uyaramkuRanjnja tuuNaaN* 'How short that pillar is?'. A question 'How short is X?' is felt to contain the assumption that X is short, while no equivalent assumption is present in 'How high is X?' That is, if the two antonyms contrast with reference to a scale of measurement, the unmarked one is capable of referring to a point on that scale, thereby neutralizing the contrast. Thus, the primary member, *uyaramuLLa* 'high', is the unmarked term; the secondary member, *uyaraM kuRanjnja* 'short', is the marked one. They are related to the attribute noun *uyaraM* 'height'. WordNet has to capture the relation between marked and unmarked terms and their cross reference to their variable property.

Binary oppositions frequently have a marked term and an unmarked term. That is, the terms are not entirely of equivalent weights, but one (the unmarked one) is neutral or positive in contrast to the other. Marked/unmarked distinction is found in polar oppositions such as

uyaraM: taazhcca 'high': 'low', *vayassaaya: ceRuppamaaya* 'old': 'young',
niiLamuLLa: kuRukiya 'long: short', *visthaaramuLLa: iTungngiya* 'wide': 'narrow'

7.4.5 Polysemy and Selectional Preferences

Polysemy is found among adjectives as a limited number of adjectives are used to attribute a considerable number of nouns. For example, the use of *nalla* in the following phrases illustrates the polysemous nature of it. The semantic interpretation of adjectives depends on the head noun they modify. Many adjectives take on different meanings when they modify different nouns. The following example will exemplify this statement.

nalla samayaM 'good time'
nalla naaNayaM 'good coin'
nalla suhRItt 'good friend'
nalla cerupp 'good chappal'

Adjectives are choosy about the nouns they modify. The general rule is that if the referent denoted a noun does not have the attribute whose value is expressed by the adjective, then the adjective–noun combination requires a figurative or idiomatic interpretation (Gross and Miller 1990). For example, a road can be long because roads have LENGTH as an attribute, but stories do not have LENGTH, so *niiNTa* 'long' does not admit literal readings. The selectional preferences of adjectives should be captured in the WordNet by organizing the adjectives under abstracts.

7.5 Adverbs in WordNet

Adverbs may be morphologically complex or simple in Malayalam. Among those that are morphologically complex, some can readily be considered the result of a derivational process that is still productive, and some the result of a process that is no longer so. The most productive process by which adverbs are derived from nouns (and occasionally from adjectives) by the suffixation of *–aayi* (e.g.

bhaMgiyaayi 'beautifully', *gaMbhiiramaayi* 'grand manner', *taazhmayaayi* 'humbly', *viSadamaayi* 'in detail', *aadyamaayi* 'for the first time').

Semantically adverbs can be classified into three broad categories: spatial adverbs (*aviTe* 'here', *eviTe* 'where'), temporal adverbs (*ippoL* ~ 'now', *eppooL* ~ 'when', *inn* 'today', *innalee* 'yesterday'), and manner adverbs (*patukke* 'slowly', *uRakke' loudly', veegam* 'quickly').

In Malayalam WordNet, adverbs derived from nouns are linked to their nominal senses by means of a pointer meaning 'DERIVED FORM'. The semantic organization of adverbs is simple and straightforward. There is no tree structure, as for nouns and verbs; nor is there a cluster structure as for adjectives. Synonymy and sometimes antonymy are recognized. All adverbs are listed individually in a single adverb file in WordNet.

7.6 Verbs in WordNet

Verbs are arguably most important lexical and syntactic category of a language. The verb provides the relational and semantic framework for its sentence. Its predicate-argument structure (or subcategorization frame) specifies the possible syntactic structures of the sentence in which it can occur.

7.6.1 Organization of Verbs in WordNet

In EuroWordNet, verbs are grouped under 15 semantic domains (Vossen 1998)

1. Verbs of bodily functions and care (e.g. sweat, shiver, faint)
2. Verbs of change (e.g. change)
3. Verbs of communication (e.g. stammer, appeal, bet, teach, creak)
4. Competition verbs (e.g. fight)
5. Consumption verbs (e.g. drink)
6. Contact verbs (e.g. hit, scrub, wipe)
7. Cognition verbs (e.g. infer, guess, assume)
8. Creation verbs (e.g. engrave, print)
9. Motion verbs (e.g. gallop, race, fly, swim)
10. Emotion or psych verbs (e.g. amuse, charm)
11. Stative verbs (e.g. surround, cross)
12. Perception verbs (e.g. watch, spy)
13. Verbs of possession (e.g. have, rob, bestow, auction)
14. Verbs of social interaction (e.g. impeach, franchise, excommunicate)
15. Weather verbs (e.g. rain, thunder, snow, hail).

7.6.2 Unique Beginners

The verbs are divided into certain number of semantic domains so as to organize them in the verb lexicon. It is difficult to think of a single root verb or 'unique beginner' that could head the entire verb lexicon. The above-mentioned semantic domains act as unique beginners for verbs in the present WordNet.

7.6.3 Polysemy in Verbs

The verbs are fewer in number than nouns in Malayalam, and at the same time, verbs are more polysemous in nature than nouns. The semantic flexibility of verbs makes the lexical analysis of verbs difficult. The polysemous nature of the verbs suggests that verb meanings are more flexible than noun meanings. Verbs change their meaning depending on the kinds of noun arguments with which they co-occur, whereas the meanings of nouns tend to be more stable in the presence of different verbs.

7.6.4 Componential Features of Verbs

Verbs can be paraphrased in terms of finer semantic features. The decompositional nature of verbs has been exploited for the interpretation of verbs denoting complex events in terms of verbs denoting simple events. For example, the verb *kolluka* 'kill' can be decomposed into 'cause not to become alive'. The verb *eRiyuka* 'throw' can be decomposed into 'cause an object to move away from one's possession by force'. The decompositional nature of verbs reveals the entailment relation existing between verbs. For example, the entailment of simple verb under causative verb (ex. *ooTuka* 'run' vs. *ooTikkuka* 'cause to run') is understood by the decompositional nature of verbs. The decompositional features of verbs can be captured by the componential analysis of verbs into finer semantic components (Leech 1974). All types of lexical relations such as synonymy, entailment, hyponymy, and troponymy and sentential properties such as presupposition, inconsistency, tautology, contradiction, and semantic anomaly can be mapped clearly if verbs are decomposed into componential features.

7.6.5 Synonymy Among Verbs

Synonymy is a rare phenomenon in verbal domain. Verbal domain exhibits only a few truly synonymous verbs. Take, for example, the words *kazhikkuka* 'eat' and *tinnuka* "eat'. *avan~ cooRukazhikkunnu* 'He is eating the meals' can entail *avan~ cooRukazhikkunnu* 'He is eating the meals. The relation existing between *kazhikkuka* and *tinnuka* is synonymy and *kazhikkuka* and *tinnuka* are synonyms, at least in this context. Truly synonymous verbs are difficult to find and mostly quasi-synonymous verbs are found in Malayalam. The existence of a simple and a parallel compound form (noun + verbalizer) causes synonymy (quasi-synonymy) in verbal system of Malayalam.

kolluka 'kill' and *kolaceyyuka* 'murder'
anveeshikkuka 'enquire' and *vicaaraNaceyyuka* 'investigate'

The synonymous expressions of many verbs show that they are manner elaborations of more basic verbs. For example, *vitaraNaM ceyyuka* 'distribute' can be considered as an elaboration of the basic verb *koTukkuka* 'give'. The more effective way of depicting the lexical and semantic relations among verbs is to establish these relations in terms of different senses of each verb.

7.6.6 Lexical Entailment and Meronymy

Lexical entailment refers to the relation that holds between two verbs *V1* and *V2* when the statement *Someone V1* entails *Someone V2* (Miller 1991, p. 233). For example, *kuur~kkaM valikkuka* 'snore' lexically entails *uRangnguka* 'sleep', because the sentence *avan~kuur~kkaM valikkunnu* 'he is snoring' implies *avan uRangngunnu* 'he is sleeping'; the second sentence is true if the first one is true. Lexical entailment is a unilateral relation: if a verb V1 entails another verb V2, then it cannot be that case that V2 entails V1. For example, *uRangnguka* need not entail *svapnaM kaaNuka.*

The entailment relation between verbs discussed above is similar to meronymy found between nouns, but meronymy is more suitable to nouns than to verbs. Fellbaum and Miller (1990) argues that, first, verbs cannot be taken as parts in the same way as nouns, because the parts of verbs are not analogous to the parts of nouns. Most nouns and noun parts have distinct, delimited referents. The referents of verbs, on the other hand, do not have the kind of distinct parts that characterize objects, groups, or substances. Componential analyses have shown that verbs cannot be broken into referents denoted solely by verbs. It is true that some activities can be broken down into sequentially ordered subactivities, say, for example, *paacakaM ceyyuka* 'cook' is a complex activity involving a number of subactivities. Consider the relation between the verbs *vaangnguka* 'buy' and *koTukkuka* 'pay'.

Although neither activity is a discrete part of the other, the two are connected in that when you buy something, somebody gives it to you. Neither activity can be considered as a subactivity of the other. Consider the relations among the activities denoted by the verbs *kuur~kkaM valikkuka* 'snore', *svapnaM kaaNuka* 'dream', and *uRangnguka* 'sleep'. Snoring or dreaming can be part of sleeping, in the sense that the two activities are, at least, partially, temporally co-extensive; the time that you spend for snoring or dreaming is a proper part of the time you spend for sleeping. And it is true that when you stop sleeping you also necessarily stop snoring or dreaming. The relation between pairs like *vaangnguka* 'buy' and *koTukkuka* pay' and *kuur~kkaM valikkuka* 'snore' and *uRangnguka* 'sleep' are due to the temporal relations between the members of each pair. The activities can be simultaneous (as in the case of *vaangnguka* 'buy' and *koTukkuka 'pay'* or one can include the other (as in the case of *kuur~kkaM valikkuka* 'snore' and *uRangnguka* 'sleep').

7.6.7 Hyponymy Among Verbs

Some verbs seem more generic than others. For example, *koTukkuka* 'give' describes a wider range of activities than *vitaraNaM ceyyuka* 'distribute'. The hyponymous relation of the kind found in nouns cannot be realized in verbs. The sentence frame, *An x is a y*, which is used to establish hyponymous relation between nouns, is not suitable for verbs, because it requires that *x* and *y* be nouns. The scrutiny of hyponyms and their superordinates reveals that lexicalization involves different kinds of semantic expansions across different semantic domains. The analysis of verbs of motion in Malayalam reveals the fact that the semantic component such as +DIRECTION (e.g. *kayaRuka* 'climb up' vs. *iRangnguka* 'climb down'), +MANNER (e.g. *vazhuti viizhuka* 'slip down' vs. *viizhuka* 'fall') + CAUSE (e.g. *ooTuka* 'run' vs. *ooTikkuka* 'cause to run', +SPEED (e.g. *izhayuka* 'crawl' vs. *ooTuka* 'run) added to the common semantic component +MOVE establish co-hyponymous relation found among verbs of motion. Miller (1991) makes use of the term troponymy to establish this type of relation existing between verbs. 'When two verbs can be substituted into the sentence frame To V1 is to V2 in a certain manner, then V1 is a troponym of V2' (Miller 1991, p. 228). For example, *muTantuka*'to walk unevenly' is a troponym of *naTakkuka* 'walk' as the former entails the latter.

7.6.8 Troponymy and Entailment

Troponymy is a particular kind of entailment in that every troponym *V1* of a more general verb V2 also entails V2 (Miller 1991). Consider, for example, the pair *muTantuka* 'limp' and *naTakkuka* 'walk'. The verbs in this pair are related by troponymy: *muTantuka* is also *naTakkuka* in a certain manner. So *muTantuka* is a troponym of *naTakkuka.* The verbs are also in entailment relation: the statement *avan~ muTantunnu* 'he is limping' entails *avan~naTakkunnu* 'he is walking'.

In contrast with pairs like *muTantuka* 'limp' *and naTakkuka* 'walk', a verb like *kuur~kkaM valikkuka* 'snore' entails and is included in *uRangnguka* 'sleep', but is not a troponym of *uRangnguka.* Similarly *vaangnguka* 'buy' entails *koTukkuka* 'give', but is not a troponym of *koTukkuka* 'give'. The verbs in the pairs like *kuur~kkaM valikkuka* snore' and *uRangnguka* 'sleep' are related only by entailment and proper temporal inclusion. It can be generalized that the verbs related by entailment and proper temporal inclusion cannot be related by troponymy. If the activities denoted by two verbs are temporally co-extensive, they can be linked by troponymy. Troponymy represents a special kind of entailment. The following tree diagram adopted from Fellbaum (1990) depicts the two categories of lexical entailment that have been identified so far:

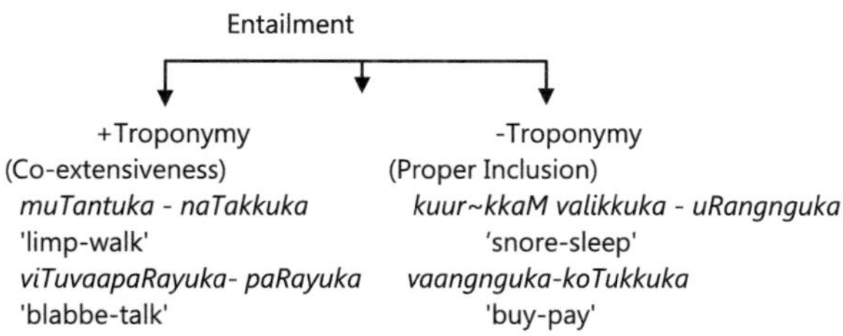

Troponyms can be related to their superordinates in various ways, subsets of which tend to come together within a given semantic domain. In the semantic domain of verbs of communication, troponyms denotes the speaker's objective or drive for communicating. Even though troponymy culminates in hierarchical structure for verbs parallel to hyponymic structure for nouns, they vary significantly. Verbs tend to have superficially branched structure. In most cases the number of hierarchical levels does not exceed four. Moreover, within a semantic domain, not all verbs can be grouped into a single hierarchy, under a single unique beginner.

7.6.9 Opposition Relations and Entailment

Opposition relations are psychologically significant not only for adjectives, but also for verbs. It is found that after synonymy and troponymy, opposition relations are the most frequently coded semantic relations in building database for verbs. The semantics of opposition relations among verbs is complex. As far as Malayalam is concerned there is no morphologically derived opposite verbs. Some of the oppositions found among nouns are absent in verbs. A number of binary oppositions have been shown by the verbs that include converseness, directional, orthogonal, and antipodal oppositions. Active and passive forms of transitive verbs can be taken as showing converse opposition. *avan~ avaLe konnu* is in converse relation with the passive expression *avaL~avanaal~kollappeTTu*. Thus, active–passive pairs of transitive verbs in Malayalam show converse opposition. The relation between the verbs *vaangnguka* 'buy' and *vil~kkuka* 'sell' is rather more complex. The lexical items that are directionally opposite are in directional opposition. The relationship which hold between the pairs such as *etticceeruka* 'arrive' and *puRappeTuka* 'reach', *varuka* 'come': and *pookuka* 'go' is directional opposition. Under this category are the verb pairs such as *uyaruka* 'rise' and *taazhuka* 'go down', *kayaRuka* 'ascend' and *iRangnguka* 'descend'. There are other oppositions with reference to change of state, manner, speed, etc. as exemplified below:

nir~mmikkuka 'build': *poLikkuka* 'demolish'
keTTuka 'tie': *azhikkuka* 'untie'
sammatikkuka 'agree': *viyoojikkuka* 'disagree'
valikkuka 'inhale': *viTuka* 'exhale'
naTakkuka 'walk': *ooTuka* 'run'

Not only the opposing features, even the presence or absence of a feature can also keep two items in opposition relation. These contrasting or distinguishing features can be arrived at by componential analysis of verbs.

The componential analysis of verbs shows that many verb pairs in an opposition relation also share an entailed verb. For example, the pair *vijayikkuka* 'succeed' and *paraajayappeTuka* 'fail' entails *pariSramikkuka* 'try'. 'A verb V1 that is entailed by another verb V2 via backward presupposition cannot be said to be part of V2. Part–whole statements between verbs are possible only when a temporal inclusion relation holds between these verbs' (Fellbaum 1990). On the basis of temporal inclusion, the set of verbs related by entailment can be classified exhaustively into two mutually exclusive categories as shown in the following tree diagram adopted from Fellbaum (1990):

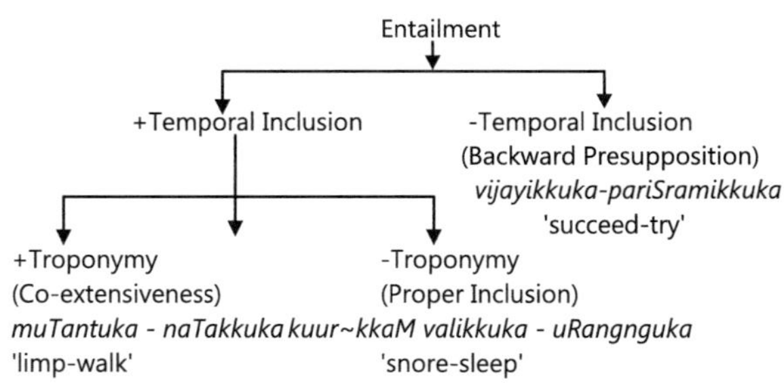

(Three kinds of entailment)

7.6.10 Causation and Entailment

The causative relation exists between two verbal concepts: one is causative (e.g. *koTukkuka* 'give') and the other is resultative (e.g. *kiTTuka* 'get'). Causation can be considered as a specific kind of entailment: if *V1* necessarily causes *V2*, then *V1* also entails *V2* (Fellbaum 1990).

puRattaakkuka 'expel' entails *viTTupookuka* 'leave'
uyar~ttuka 'raise' and *uyaruka* 'rise' (temporal inclusion)

We have distinguished four different kinds of lexical entailment that systematically interact with the semantic relations mapped in WordNet. These four kinds of entailment can be related as shown in the following tree (Fellbaum 1990):

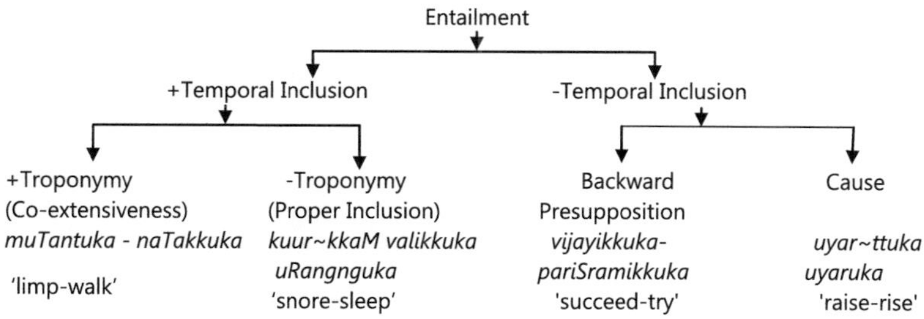

7.6.11 Syntactic Properties and Semantic Relations

In recent years, there is a trend incorporating syntactic properties in the lexicon itself. Viewing verbs in terms of semantic relations can also provide clues to an understanding of the syntactic behaviour of verbs. Incorporating the syntactic properties of verbs in the WordNet has to be explored for the better understanding of verb net.

7.6.12 Summing up of Verb Net

The following table sums up the lexical/semantic relations to be captured in the verb net.

Relations	Definition/sub types	Example
Synonymy	Replaceable events	*mayangnguka* 'sleep' · *uRangnguka* 'sleep'
Meronymy–hypernymy	From events to superordinate events	*paRakkuka* 'fly' · · *yaatraceyyuka* 'travel'
Troponymy	From events to their subtypes	*naTakkuka* 'walk' · *muTanthuka* 'limp'
Entailment	From events to the events they entail	*kuur~kkaM valikkuka* 'snore' *uRangnguka* 'sleep'
	From event to its cause	*uyar~ttuka* 'raise' · *uyaruka* 'rise'
	From event to its presupposed event	*jayikkuka* 'succeed' · · *pariSramikkuka* 'try'
	From even to implied event	*kolluka* 'murder' · *marikkuka* 'die'

(continued)

(continued)

Relations	Definition/sub types	Example
Antonymy	Opposites	*kuuTuka* 'increase' · *kuRayuka* 'decrease'
	Conversensess	*vil~kkuka* 'sell' · *vaangnguka* 'buy'
	Directional opposites	*puRappeTuka* 'start' · · *etticceeruka* 'reach'

7.7 Designing and Implementing WordNet

The WordNet automatically inherits all the powers of a thesaurus. It also resembles an online dictionary as it provides meanings for lexical items. Being superior to these two tools, WordNet provides much more information that has been loaded in an online thesaurus as well as in an online dictionary. The task of developing the online database can be conveniently divided into two interdependent tasks (Beckwith and Miller 1990). These tasks bear a vague similarity to the traditional tasks of writing and printing a dictionary:

- To write the source files that contain the basic lexical data—the contents of those files are the lexical substance of WordNet.
- To create a set of computer programs that would accept the source files and do all the work leading ultimately to the generation of a display for the user.

The WordNet system is divided into four parts based on the specific tasks assigned to them:

- Lexical resource system
- Compiler system
- Storage system
- Retrieval system

Lexical resource system contains source files. Lexicographers write WordNet's source files. They are the products of a detailed relational analysis of lexical semantics: a variety of lexical and semantic relations are used to represent the organization of lexical knowledge. The compiler system primarily compiles the lexical resource files into a database format and sends it to storage system to facilitate machine retrieval of the information in the WordNet. Storage system works as an intermediary between compiler system and retrieval system. The cooked database of the compiler system is stored in the storage system for retrieval.

The primary focus in WordNet construction is to ensure the degree of precision that is called for in a given information search and retrieval system and to eliminate any redundancy in the codification of the hierarchies. An interface is required in order to give a user access to information in the database. Interfaces enable end-users to retrieve the lexical data and display it via window-based tool or the command line. The interface provides a user with a variety of ways to retrieve and display lexical information. Different interfaces can be created to serve the purpose of different users, but all of them will draw on the same underlying database, and may use the same software functions that interface to the database files.

7.8 Malayalam WordNet Development Using Expansion Approach

Malayalam WordNet is being built using expansion approach (Vossen 1998). In this approach, synsets are created by referring to the existing WordNet of the chosen language. Hindi is used as a source language to create synsets of Malayalam. A synset linkage tool provided by Indian Institute of Technology, Bombay, is used to create synsets in Malayalam. This synset linking tool provides graphical user interface which shows Hindi synset on the left-hand side and provides interface to enter Malayalam synset on the right-hand side.

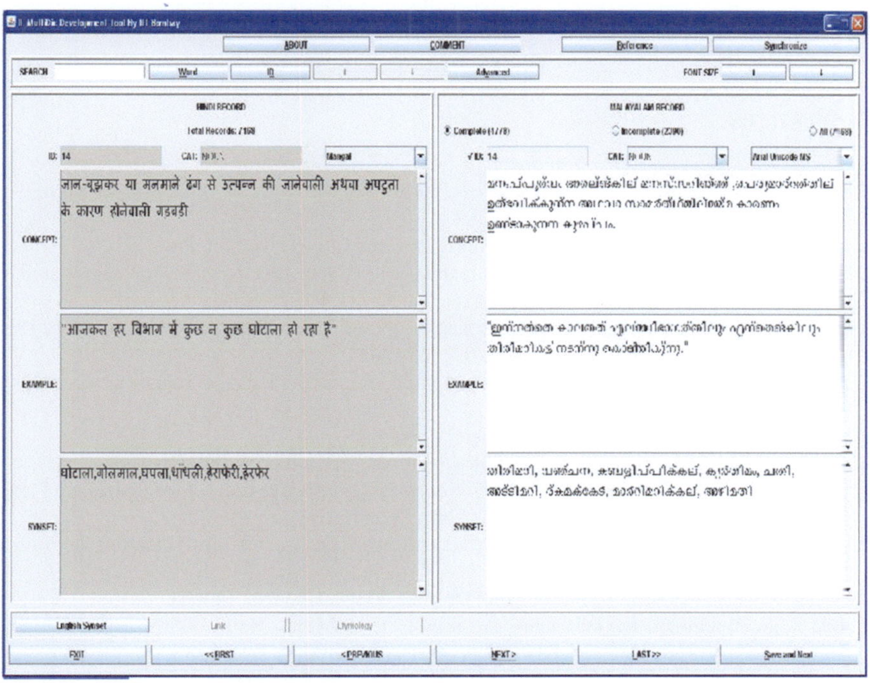

Lexicalization of concepts varies across languages, which leads to synsets that are present in one language but not in another language. In the present project, the lexical items are divided into six categories: (1) universal, (2) Pan-Indian, (3) in-family, (4) language specific, (5) rare and (6) synthesized. The lexical items covered consist of noun, verb, adjectives and adverbs. The main objective of the project is word sense disambiguation. For that sense, marking will be done at the next stage of the project. The sense making will be done on the corpus by using sense IDs as tags. This will enable word sense disambiguation in the text.

7.9 Conclusion

The theme of lexical semantics, computational lexicography, and computational semantics are expanding rapidly. The availability of machine-readable resources and newly developed tools for analysing and manipulating lexical entries makes it possible to build a massive WordNet for a language. In present state of affairs, it is quite feasible to build an efficient WordNet for Malayalam. Linkage of Hindi WordNet with Malayalam and other chosen Indian languages creates a multilingual resource for Indian languages which is useful for many NLP applications. However, variation in the lexicalization of the concepts across languages poses a major challenge in WordNet linking.

References

Beckwith, R., & Miller, G. A. (1990). Implementing a lexical network. *International Journal of Lexicography, 3*(4), 302–312.

Cruse, D. A. (1986). *Lexical semantics*. Cambridge: Cambridge University Press.

Fellbaum, C. (1990). English verbs as a semantic net. *International Journal of Lexicography, 3*(4), 278–301.

Fellbaum, C., & Miller, G. A. (1990). Folk psychology or semantic entailment? A reply to Rips and Conrad. The Psychological Review, 97, 565–570.

Gross, D., & Miller, K. J. (1990). Adjectives in WordNet. International Journal of Lexicography, 3(4), 265–277.

Leech, G. N. (1974). *Semantics*. Harmondsworth: Penguin.

Lehrer, A. (1974). *Semantic fields and lexical structures*. Amsterdam: North Holland.

Lyons, J. (1995). *Linguistic semantics: An introduction*. Cambridge: Cambridge University Press.

Lyons, J. (1977). *Semantics, 2 volumes*. New York: Cambridge University Press.

Miller, G. A. (1990). Nouns in WordNet: A lexical inheritance system. *International Journal of Lexicography, 3*(4), 245–264.

Miller, G. A. (1991). *Science of words*. New York: Scientific American Library.

Miller, G. A., Beckwith, R., Fellbaum, C., Gross, D., & Miller, K. J. (1990). Introduction to WordNet: An on-line lexical database. *International Journal of Lexicography, 3*(4), 235–244.

Nida, E. A. (1975a). *Compositional analysis of meaning: An introduction to semantic structure*. The Hague: Mouton.

Nida, E. A. (1975b). Exploring semantic structure. The Hague: Mouton.
Pustejovksy, J. (1995). *The generative lexicon*. Cambridge, Massachusetts: The MIT Press.
Pustejovksy, J. (2001). *Generativity and explanation in semantics. A reply to Fodor and Lepore*. Cambridge, Massachusetts: The MIT Press.
Vossen, P. (1998). *EuroWordNet: a multilingual database with lexical semantic networks*. London: Kluwer Academic Publishers.

Chapter 8
Creating Marathi WordNet

Lata Popale and Pushpak Bhattacharyya

8.1 Introduction

Marathi is the language spoken primarily by the native people of Maharashtra, a state of Indian subcontinent. There are about 90 million people who speak Marathi worldwide. It is the oldest of the Indo-Aryan regional languages. It is thought to be approximately 1300 years old, and it is considered that this language evolved from Sanskrit and Prakrit (a group of languages spoken in ancient India) (http://www.indianmirror.com/languages/marathi-language.html). It is written in Devnagari Script.

8.2 Expansion of Marathi WordNet from Hindi WordNet

8.2.1 Hindi WordNet (HWN)

Hindi WordNet, on which Marathi WordNet expanded model is based is inspired by Princeton WordNet. Currently, Hindi WordNet has 38985 synsets, of which 25857 are linked to English WordNet. Bilingual mappings are given by the lexicographers at IIT Bombay for the synsets which are not linked to English WordNet. HWN synsets are created by the following three principles of minimality, coverage, and replaceability. Each synset contains the synonymous words and the glossary which includes concept and example sentence/sentences. All the variant spellings are also included as synonymous words. HWN has only *noun,*

L. Popale (✉) · P. Bhattacharyya
Department of Computer Science and Engineering, IIT Bombay, Mumbai, India
e-mail: popale.lata@gmail.com

P. Bhattacharyya
e-mail: pb@cse.iitb.ac.in

N.S. Dash et al. (eds.), *The WordNet in Indian Languages*,
DOI 10.1007/978-981-10-1909-8_8

adjective, verb, and *adverb* categories of parts of speech. All examples are transliterated and expressed in italic, and English translations of them are written in normal text just below that.

English word:	leaf
Synonymous words:	patta, paat, parNa, patra, dal, chad, patrak, parat, bai
Concept:	peR-paudhe mein hone walaa bishes kar hare rang ka wah patlaa, halkaa abayab yo uski Tahaniyon se nikaltaa hai
Meaning:	The thin, light component of a plant, especially green in colour that originates from its branches
Example Sentence:	wah baag me gire sukhe patte ekatra kar raha hai "He is collecting fallen dry leaves in the garden".

8.2.2 Marathi WordNet (MWN)

Marathi WordNet is a system for bringing together different lexical and semantic relations between the Marathi words. It is being created from Hindi WordNet by using expansion approach. To create a synset in Marathi, the lexicographer first looks at each Hindi synset, grasps the meaning, and then creates the synset in Marathi by expressing the same concept. Hindi examples are translated in Marathi to create parallel corpora. But, if the translation looks unnatural, then, another example is given. The consistency about part of speech is retained, as is the custom of following variant spellings.
Example:

Noun:	*anghol*, *aanghol* and *ambaa*, *aambaa* (bath)
Adjective:	*andhaLaa, aandhaLaa* (blind)
Verb:	*karavane, karavine* (put to work)
Adverb:	*bharabharaa*, *bharMabharaaM* (quickly)

The orthographic rules are followed as set by the Marathi Mahamandal. The synsets are related to each other through semantic relations (hypernymy, hyponymy, antonymy, and meronymy) which are taken from Hindi WordNet.

Marathi WordNet creates senses based on Hindi WordNet sense ID's as pivot. The senses are created by following the sense ID for the synsets created in Hindi WordNet, and that enables us towards automatic hypernymy, hyponymy, etc., creation. The psycholinguistic principles that are followed for the relations mentioned above are thus followed for Marathi WordNet as well. It also enables us to follow the basic principles of WordNet sense creation, viz. coverage, minimality, and replaceability.

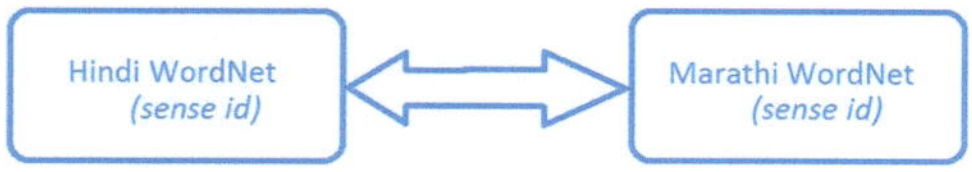

For example, paan, parNa, patrI, paat (leaf)

The thinner, lighter component of a plant, especially in green that originate from its branches

"He is collecting fallen dry leaves in the garden".

(R)(H)(E)(A)(Be)(Bo)(G)(K)(Ka)(Ko)(Ma)(Ml)(N)(O)(P)(S)(T)(Te)(U)

A. Ontology Nodes
B. Hypernymy (is a kind of ...)
C. Hyponymy (... is a kind of)
D. Meronymy—Component Object (part of ...)
E. Holonymy—Component Object (is a part of)
F. Holonymy—Member Collection (is a part of)
G. Holonymy—Portion Mass (is a part of).

8.3 Marathi WordNet Data Entry Tool

This is the MW data entry tool. There are seven tabs—*synsets, noun, adjective, verb, adverb, lookup, and ontology*. The entry is done in Unicode (Devanagari.) (Figs. 8.1 and 8.2).

A. *Synset tab*:

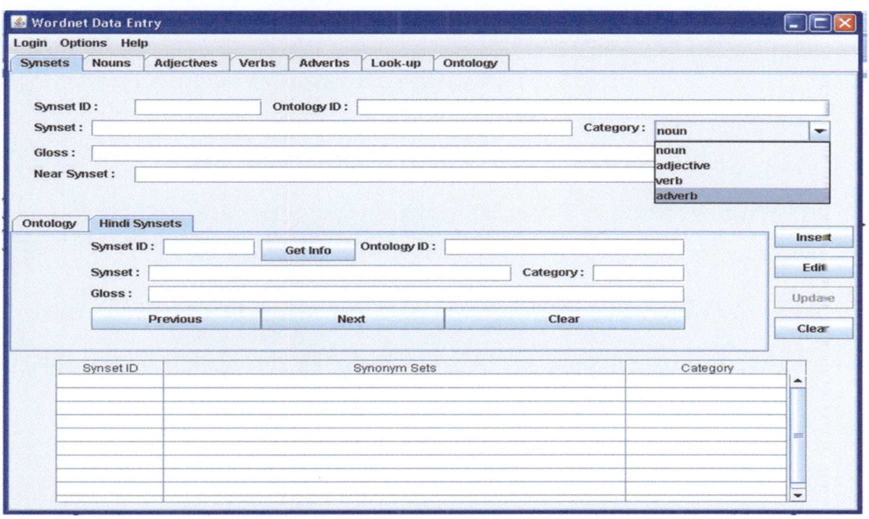

Fig. 8.1 WordNet data entry tool

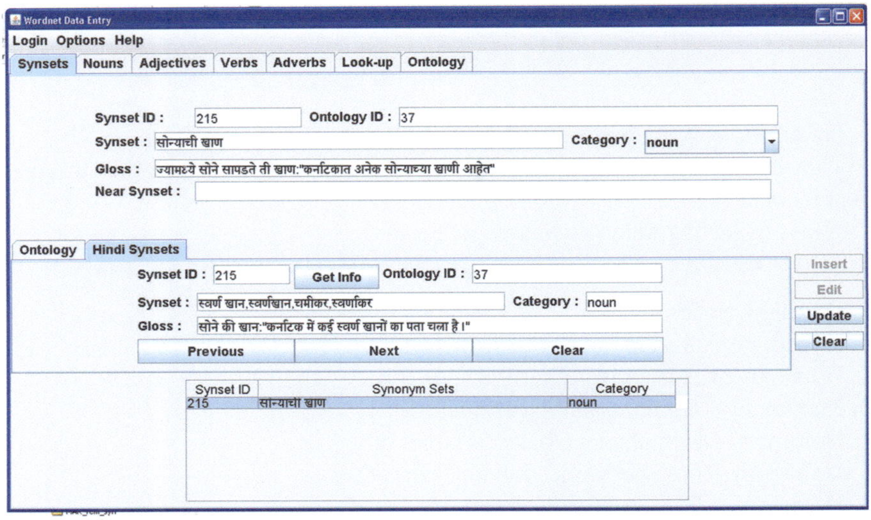

Fig. 8.2 Interface showing synset tab pan

This is the default tab pan and is used to insert, edit, update, or delete the entry.

1. **To enter a new synset**

    1. Enter the synset ID in *synset ID* field which should be the same as that of Hindi WordNet.
    2. Enter the synonym set in the *synset* field.
    3. Enter the gloss and example in the *gloss* field. The format is **gloss**: "**example**".
    4. Select the part-of-speech category.
    5. Write the ontology ID.

2. **To view/edit/update the synset**

    1. View the Synset

        i. Write synset ID in Synset ID field and press enter.

        OR

        ii. Write Word either in synset field or in near synset field and press enter.

    2. The synset(s) containing the searched word/searched synset ID is displayed at the bottom of the interface.
    3. Select the synset to be viewed.
    4. The synset contents are displayed in the respective boxes.
    5. To edit the synset, press *edit* button.
    6. Do the edition and press *update* button.

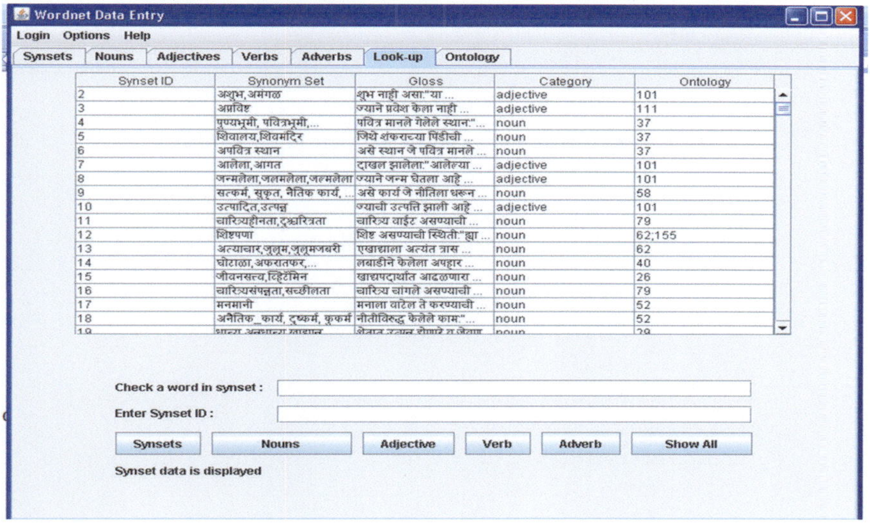

Fig. 8.3 Lookup tab

3. **To delete the synset**

    1. One cannot delete any entry but can make an entry NULL.
    2. Follow the steps (2.1–2.4).
    3. After the synset is displayed in respective boxes, delete all the contents and type "null" in the *synset* field.
    4. Press update button.
    5. The null synsets are not counted in the total synset numbers.
    6. One can later update the null synset.

Nouns, adjectives, verbs, and adverbs tab pans are currently not used for Marathi WordNet, but later on they will be used to provide other relations to Marathi synsets.

B. ***Lookup tab***:
This tab pan is used to view all the synsets arrange by IDs (Fig. 8.3).

C. ***Ontology Tab***:
This tab is used to view the ontology tree with node IDs, for the above-mentioned four parts of speech. Changes in the ontology nodes also can be made through this tab in the interface (Fig. 8.4).

8.4 Online MWN Interface

The link (http://www.cfilt.iitb.ac.in/wordnet/webmwn/wn.php) goes straight to the online Marathi WordNet interface. Here, the desired word can be searched for by typing it in the search box. The interface has Devanagari keyboard as well as phonetic transliteration facility as shown in the figure below (Fig. 8.5).

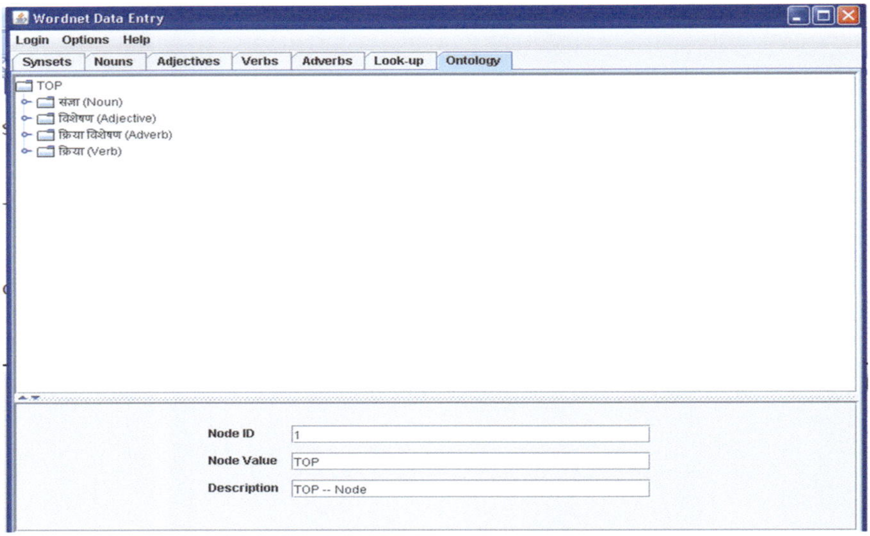

Fig. 8.4 Ontology tab

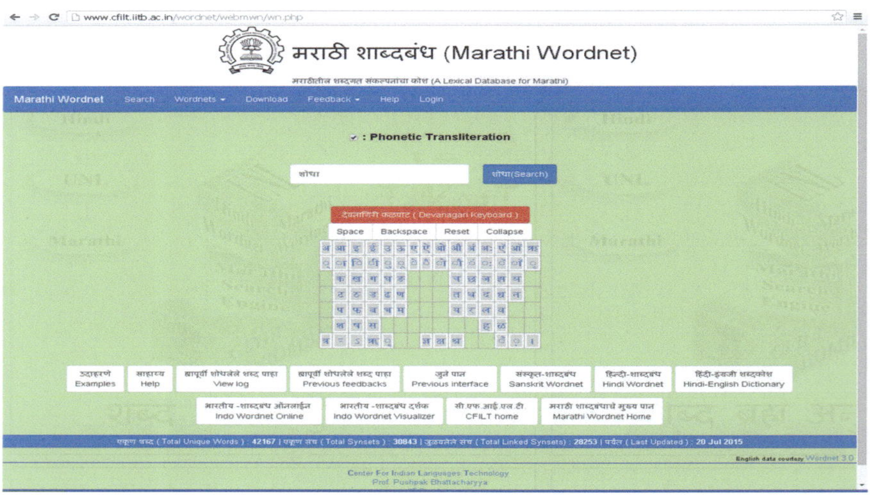

Fig. 8.5 Online Marathi WordNet interface

By clicking on the search button, all the senses of word which are present in WordNet. The status of the Marathi WordNet till date at the bottom of the interface; e.g., "*paan*" has 19 senses, but in the figure, only three are visible. One can scroll down to view all the synsets (Fig. 8.6).

Fig. 8.6 Interface showing the word "Paan"

8.5 Observations/Challenges

Marathi and Hindi languages are very similar to each other; therefore, they are called sister languages, but still the lexicographers face some problems. The prominent challenges are as follows.

8.5.1 Use of Phrasal or Compound, Coin Words or Borrowed Word for a Single Word

Sometimes, it is difficult to find a single word to express the concept of HWN; in such cases, we coin new words or use phrases or compound words. If this is also not possible, then we borrow the Hindi words. Here are a few examples where we have coined new words:

Hindi Synset	Marathi Synset
goroo-chora, goroo chora, maveshee chora (rustler, cattle thief)	*gurechora* (rustler, cattle thief)
baaloo chhalanii, baaloo chalanii (sand sieve)	*retachaalana* (sand sieve)
nikaaraguaaI, nikaaraguana (Nicaraguan)	*Nikaaraagviya* (Nicaraguan)

8.5.2 Phrasal or Compound Words

To link the synsets denoting objects which are differentiated by size, such as big or small, *chotaa* (small) or *lahaana* (small) for small size and *mothaa* (big) for big size is added before the word:

Hindi Synset	Marathi Synset
Borii, boriya, gonii—chotaa boraa "vaha dhaana se bhare bori ko kasa rahaa hai" small sack—small sack "he is tightening the sack filled with rice".	*lahaana pote* (small sack)
Sandukachi*—chotaa sanduk "sethaji ne sandukachi se paise nikaalkar mujhe diye"* small trunk—small trunk "Sethaji took out money from the small trunk and gave it to me".	*lahaana sanduka* (small trunk)
Tauni, tai, tavi*—chotaa tavaa "geeta tauni par roti seMka rahi haiM"* Small griddle—Small griddle "Gita is making chapati on the Small griddle".	*lahaan tavaa* (small griddle)
kulhaadii*—chotaa kulhaadaa "chikhuri kaakaa kulhaadi se lakadii phaada rahe haiM"* small axe—small axe "Chikhuri uncle is splitting a log with a small axe".	*lahaan kurhaada* (small axe)

8.5.3 Problems in Linking Colour Concepts

We do not get one single word to describe the following types of colours which describe the colour of an object:

Hindi Synset	Marathi Synset
mooMgiyaa*—mooMng ke se raMga kaa—"rahamaan ke gale maiM eka mooMgiyaa gamchaa lataka rahaa hai"* ***mooMgiyaa***—of the colour of green gram "There is a ***mooMgiyaa*** towel hanging around Rahman's neck".	*moogaachyaa rangaachaa* (of a colour of green gram)
amauaa*—kacche aama ke samaan rang "isa kiwaad ko amauaa se rang diijiye"* ***amauaa***—colour like that of a raw mango—"colour this door in amauaa".	*kachchyaa aambyachaa ranga* (colour like raw mango)
Pyaajii, pyaazii *—halake gulaabi rang kaa "shiilaa pyaaji saal odhi huii haiM"* **Pyaajii**—of a light pink shade—"sheela is wearing a pyaajii shawl".	*halakyaa gulaabi rangaachaa* (of a light pink shade)

(continued)

(continued)

Hindi Synset	Marathi Synset
Kapaasii*—kapaas ke phool ke rang kaa yaa bahut halke piile rang kaa "kapaasi saadzi maiM vah bahut acchii lag rahii thii"* **Kapaasii**—of a very light yellow colour: "She was looking very nice in a **Kapaasii** saari".	*halakyaa pivalyaa rangaachaa* (of a very light yellow colour)

8.5.4 Borrowed Words

Whenever there is a failure to coin a word or a phrase for a concept, it is simply borrowed the word from Hindi. Here are a few examples of borrowed words:

Hindi Synset	Marathi Synset
gul-ajaayaba, gulajaayaba*—eka phooladaara paudhaa* gulajayab—a kind of flowering plant	*gulajaayaba*
gulasharphii*—eka phooladaara paudhaa* **gulasharphii**—a kind of flowering plant	*gulasharphii*
chandalikaa*—eka prakaara kaa tambooraa* chandalika—a kind of stringed musical instrument	*chandalikaa*
sukeshii, sukeshaa-*jisake baal sundara, kaale, ghane evam lambe ho (mahilaa)* sukeshii- having beautiful, black, long and thick hair (lady)	*sukeshii*
Ashradheya- *jo shraddhaa ke yogya na ho* unrespectable—unworthy of respect	*ashradheya*

8.5.5 Difficult to Link the Hindi Synsets with Marathi Where Concepts Lack Specifications:

For example,

- *Raal—eka parkaar kaa kaMbal* (a type of blanket)
- *charak machalii—eka prakaar kii machalii* (a type of fish).

8.5.6 Two or More Concepts in One Synset

Sometimes we find that two or more concepts are merged in a single Hindi synset. In such a case we are unable to link to Hindi since there are different words for different concepts:

gatTaa, gatTara*—ghaas yaa lakadii kaa bozaa "lakadahaaraa sira par lakadii kaa gatTaa lekar jaa rahaa thaa";)*

Bundle—a package or load of wood or grass—The logger was carrying a bundle of wood on his head.

To represent the concept of the above synset, Marathi has two different words.

- *ghaas kaa bojhaa* (a package of or load of grass)—***bhaaraa*** → Marathi
- *lakadikaa kaa bojhaa* (a package of or load of wood)—***molii*** → Marathi

If we link it as ***bhaaraa***, then it will represent only the concept of ***ghaas kaa bojhaa***, and concept of ***yaa lakadii kaa bojhaa*** will be lost. Same kind of problem found in the following synsets also.

- ***phikaa****—jisameM shakkara, namaka yaa mircha aadi na dalaa yaa daalaa huaa ho "maiM phiikii chaaya pasanda karati huM")*

bland—in which there is no sugar, salt or pepper, chilli, etc—"I like bland tea".

- *jisameM shakkara na dalaa yaa daalaa huaa ho* (in which there is no sugar)—(***agoda, phikaa***) → Marathi;
- *jisameM namaka na dalaa yaa daalaa huaa ho* (in which there is no salt)—(***alanii, aalanii***) → Marathi;
- *jisameM mircha aadi na dalaa yaa daalaa huaa ho* (in which there is no chilli)—(***alanii, aalanii***) → Marathi.
- ***avaaMsanaa, avaasanaa****—kisi naye kapade, baratana aadii ko pahali baar prayog meM laanaa "meri dadi kisi khaas din hii chiijoM ko avaaMsatii thiiM")*

- **to use first time**—to use any new clothes, utensils, etc., for the first time: "My Grandmother used to use any thing for the first time on special days only".

- *kisi naye kapade ko pahali baar prayog meM laanaa* (to use any new clothes for the first time)—(***ghadii modaNe***) → Marathi;
- *kisi naye baratana ko pahali baar prayog meM laanaa* (to use any new utensils for the first time)—(***vaaparaalaa kaadhaNe***) → Marathi.

8.5.7 Some Adjectives Need Chaa or Lelaa Suffix

Though most of the adjectives are linked to Hindi, still sometimes we do not find proper word while creating adjectives. In such case, we take help of *chaa* or *lelaa* suffixes:

Hindi synset	Marathi Synset
dhalvaaM, dhaluvaaM (sloping)	*utaaraachaa, dhaaLaachaa* (sloping)
vivaahita (married)	*Lagnaachaa* (married)

(continued)

(continued)

Hindi synset	Marathi Synset
baDanakkaa (who has big nose)	*moTyaa naakaachaa* (who has big nose)
BaDakanaa (who has big ear)	*moTyaa kaanaachaa* (who has big ear)
indraka, indraka (of or related to god Indra)	*Indraachaa* (of or related to god Indra)

8.5.8 Others

Hindi Synset	Marathi Synset
anadhikaar, adhikaarhiinata (powerlessness)	*adhikaar nasataanaa* (powerlessness)
Beaaraam (without resting)	*aaraam na karataa* (without resting)
Gandhakii (sulphurous)	*halakyaa pivlyaa rangaachaa* (sulphurous)
mamiyauraa, mamiyaaur (mother's brother's house)	*maamache ghar* (mother's brother's house)
Mausihar (mother's sister's house)	*maavashiiche kiMvaa kaakaache ghar* (mother's sister's house)

8.6 Language-Specific Synsets (LSSs)

Along with creating Marathi synsets, we are creating language-specific synsets also. These synsets represent such concepts that are very specific to Marathi culture. To sure about of language-specific concepts, we use our knowledge, explore the Marathi cultural-specific websites and language-specific dictionaries, and discuss with Marathi native speakers before creating them. After creating LSS in Marathi, we create corresponding Hindi synsets. The LSSs fall in certain categories, such as food, ornaments, dance, games, clothing items, religion, which are described as follows:

- **Food**:
  paatavadii—*harabharyachyaa piTaata tikhata, miiTa, haLada ghaaloon, te shijavoona taataavara thaapatoona kelelii vadii: paatavadyaaNvara khobaryaachaa kiisa aanii kothiMbiira ghaalataat.*

Paatavadii—A type of steamed cake which is made from mixture of gram flour, salt, chilli powder, turmeric, etc.: "paatavadii is garnished with shredded coconut and coriander".
kadaboLe—*bhaajaniichyaa piTaapaasoona banavalelaa ardhavaatolyaa aakaraachaa telaata taLoon kelelaa padartha: "aalne divaaliichyaa pharaaL-aasaaTii kadaboLii banavalii".*

Kadbole—a semicircular fried dish which is made of roasted multigrain flour: "mother has made kadbole for diwali festival".

- **Ornaments**:
  kolhaapurii saaja—*maasaa, kamaLa, kaarale, chandra, baalpaana, shankha, naaga, kaasava, bhuNgaa ashii padake taarene samorasamora jodoona madhyabhaagii lolaka asalelaa haar: "tulaa kolhaapurii saaja khoopa shobhoon distoya".*

kolhaapurii saaja—A type of necklace: "kolhaapurii saaja looks nice".

pohehaara—*pohyaachyaa aakaaraachyaa sonyaachyaa lahanshyaa paataLa chakatyaa ekamekita guNtavoona tayaara kelelaa haar: "kamalaane divaaLiita pohehaara kelaa".*

Pohehaara—A type of necklace which is made by joining small thin golden chips shaped like beaten rice: "Kamala got made pohehaar in Diwali".

- **Dance**:
  laavanii—*mahaaraashtraache eka prasidha loknrutya: "laavaniiche aneka prakaar aaheta*
  Lavani—a famous folk dance of Maharashtra: "there are many types of Lavani".
  dhanagariinrutya, gajaanrutya—*mahaaraashtratiila ghatamathyaavarachyaa dhangaraaNche nrutya: "mii aaja pahilyaandaa dhanagariinrutya paahile".*
  Dhangari dance—a dance form of the Dhangar tribe who live in the hilly areas of Maharashtra: "I have seen Dhangari dance for the first time today".
- **Clothing items**:
  naUvaarii, navavaarii—*naU vaara laaMba asalelelii saadii: "tii naUvaarii nesate".*

Nauvaari—nine yard saari—"she wears **Nauvaari**"

- **Religion**:

bhootyaa—*bhavaaniichaa eka upaasaka, haa gaLyaata kavadyaaNchyaa maLaa ghaaloona, telakata vastre levuna aani haataata pota gheUna jogavaa mhanaje bhikshaa maagato "daaraata aalelyaa bhootyaalaa aaiine paise dile".*

Butya—a devotee of goddess Bhavani who wears oily clothes and garland of cowries holds rag in his hands and begs "Mother has given money to butya who came at the front of door".

kaanapiLanii—*navariichyaa bhaavaane laajaahomaachyaa velii navaryaa mulaachaa kaana piLanyachaa vidhii: "kaanapiLaniinantara saptapadiichaa vidhii zaalaa".*

kaanapiLanii—a kind of a marriage ceremony in which bride's borther twist the groom's ear: "saptapadii's ceremony is done just after the kaanapiLanii".

- **Game**:

zimmaa—*mulii ekamekiinkade tonde karoona ubhyaa raahoona paras-paraanchyaa panjyaavar panje maaroona khelataata to eka kheLa: "malaa zimmyaachii khoopa gaanii paatha aaheta".*

Zimma—a kind of game played by girls by facing each other and clapping each other's hands while singing. "I know many zimmaa songs".

aatyaapaatyaa—*ekaane dusryaalaa Taraaviik jaageta—paatiit—adakvaay-ache aani dusaryaane nisatoona jaanyaacha prayatna karaayachaa hyaa swaroopaachaa eka maharashtriya kheLa: "moole vyaayaamashaalepoodhe aatyaapaatyaa kheLata hotii".*

Aatyaapaatyaa—a kind of game: "Children are playing aatyaapaatyaa in front of gym".

8.7 Challenges in Making Hindi Synsets for Marathi LSS

Corresponding Hindi synsets have to be created for the existing Marathi language-specific synsets. While doing so, we came across some challenges. The biggest one is to translate the created Marathi LSS into Hindi. For this, the lexicographer should have good knowledge of Marathi as well as Hindi.

Marathi:

bagaada—*jaminiita pooralelyaa kiNvaa chaaltyaa gaadyaala pakkyaa basavalelyaa khaaNbaavariila aadavyaa laakadaata asalelaa aakadaa poTiita khupasoona tyaavar laNbakaLanyaachaa, navasa phedanyaachaa eka vidhii: "bagaadaachi prathaa aataa banda zaalii aahe".*

Hindi:

bagaada—*mannata poorii karane ke liye jamina maiN gaadii huI yaa chalatii gaadii maiN majabootii se bithaye staNbha para aadii lakadii para lagii huI aNkudii ko piiTa main ghoMpakara latakaane kii vidhi: "bagaada kii prathaa aba banda ho chukii hai".*

bagaada—hanging of a person on a hook in the pole which is horizontally fixed in another pole which is firmly vertically fixed in the ground or running vehicle to fulfil ones wish "custom of bagaada is almost dying".

After translation, Hindi lexicographer checks these translated concepts to finalize them, so that they can be uploaded to the database. Here, the Marathi lexicographer has to clear each doubt (regarding the concept, and sometimes regarding the words in the concept) of Hindi lexicographer while checking. Sometimes, for clearing the doubt, lexicographer has to show the images and video clip of the concept to support his/her claim him (e.g. showing video clip of ***baalyaanrutya***).

Some Marathi concepts need to be discussed with Hindi lexicographer to confirm whether the concept is language specific or not.

Marathi

saagargotaa—*dagada, gote Ityadii golaakaar vastooMnii kheLaavayaacha eka khela. jyaata 7/9/11 hyaa vishama saNkhyeta gote gheUna te jaminiivara taakoona tyaatiila eka gotaa haveta udavalaa jaato. udavalelaa gotaa khaalii yelparyaMta Itara raahilele gote ekaa haataanecha golaa karoona tyaacha haataane* *to vaara taakalelaa gotaa zelalaa jaato: "saagargotyaata vara phekalelaa gotaa khaalii padalaa kii kheLanaarii vyaktii baada hote".*

Saagargotaa—A kind of game.

kaatavata, kaathavata, kaathota—*bhaakariiche piiTa maLanyaachii kaana asalelii laakadii paraata: "siimaane kaatavatiita piiTa maLale".*

Kaatavata—a big wooden plate with handles to knead millet flour: "Seem kneaded the dough in kaatavata".

According to Marathi, above two synsets were LSSs. But after discussion with Hindi lexicographer, it was decided that the same concept exists in Hindi synsets ***goottaa*** and ***kaTautaa***, respectively.

Our future plan is to link as many of the Hindi words as possible and also increase Marathi WordNet data along with creating more language-specific synsets.

8.8 Applications of Marathi WordNet

8.8.1 Word Sense Disambiguation in Analysis (Sense Marking)

Main task of WordNet is to disambiguate diferent word senses. Most of the words have multiple meanings or senses. The task of marking each word in the sentence with the correct sense of the word is called Sense marking. Sense-marked corpus is a very important resource and is required by all supervised WSD algorithms and various other tasks of natural language processing.

To mark the senses in a corpus, a sense-marker tool is used. The Sense Marker tool is a graphical user interface-based tool developed using Java which facilitates the task of manual sense marking. The tool displays the different senses of the word available in the Marathi WordNet and allows the user to select the correct sense of the word amongst the given senses. The tool supports nine languages, viz. English, Hindi, Marathi, Tamil, Telugu, Kannada, Malayalam, Bengali, and Punjabi.

A news corpus in Marathi is being sense-marked at present. Articles from Marathi newspapers are selected, create files are created and saved them in a particular place. The Sense Marker tool (Fig. 8.7) is then opened. By clicking on "open" option to upload a saved file (Fig. 8.8). Next, the file is uploaded in the sense marking tool, and the language, font size, and edit word options are selected.

There are 2 panels in the tool (Fig. 8.9): first panel shows the texts of the uploaded file and other one shows the Marathi synset/synsets on selecting the word in the text file. Out of the given synsets, the synset which represents the word meaning in that particular context, is selected, keeping the part of speech in mind. The ID of the selected synset gets tagged to the word automatically (Fig. 8.10).

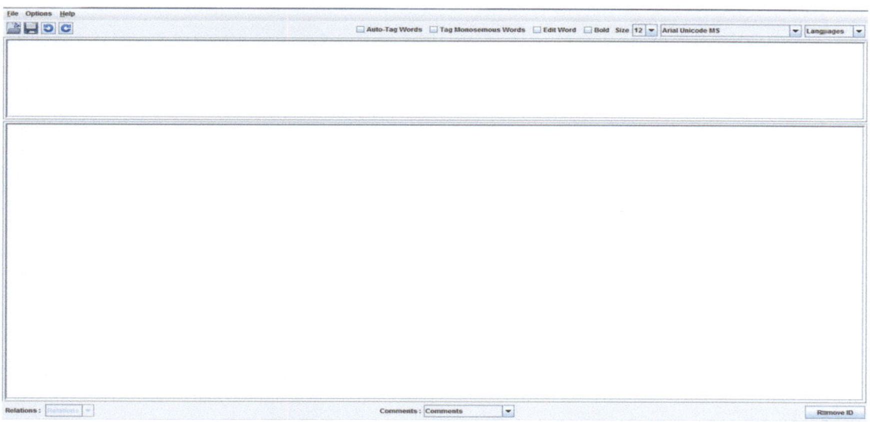

Fig. 8.7 Sense marker tool

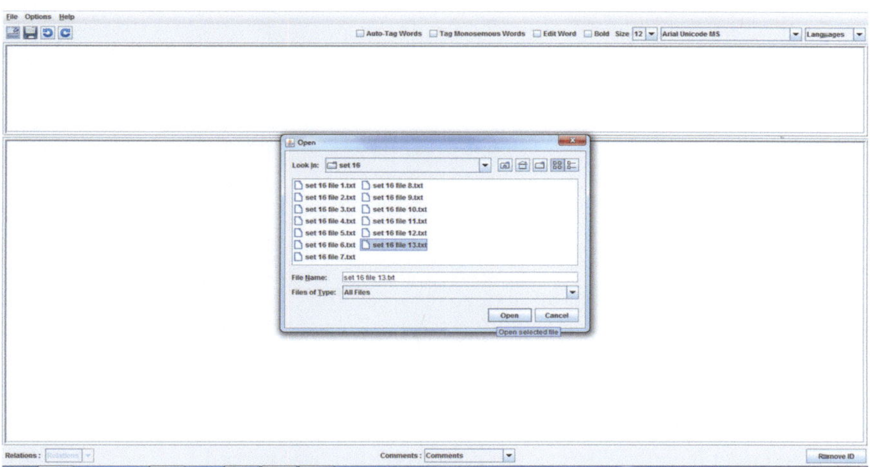

Fig. 8.8 Opening the file in the Sense marker tool

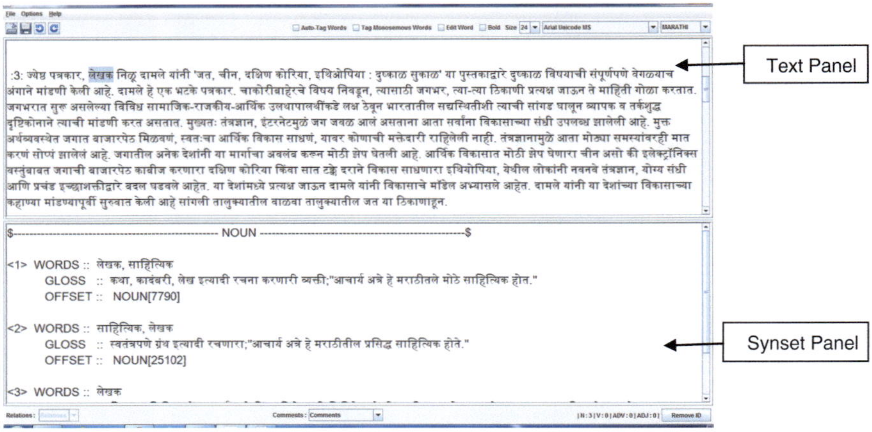

Fig. 8.9 Tool showing 2 panels

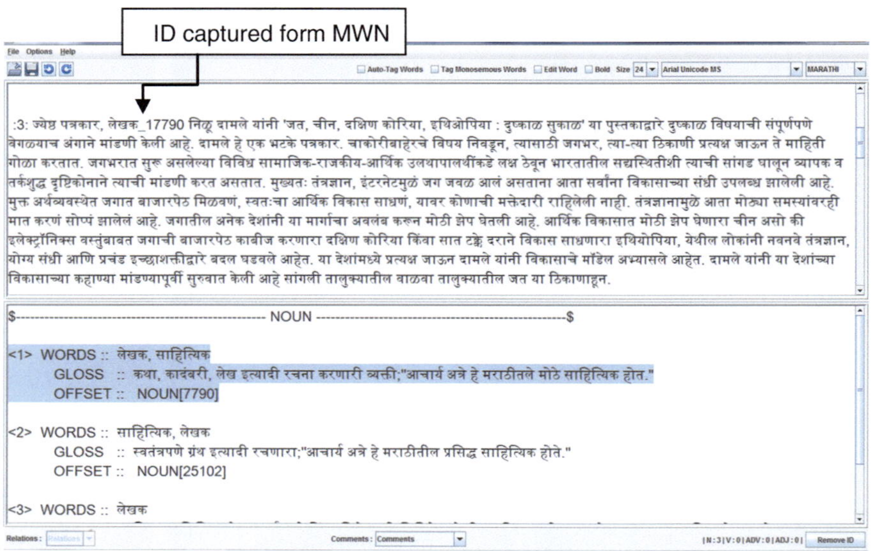

Fig. 8.10 Tool showing sense tagged word

Marathi WordNet is used as lexical resource for creating the sense-annotated corpus required for designing any WSD system for Marathi language. The WSD system thus created is very useful in machine translation systems for the correct translation of a word in Marathi language from other target languages and vice versa. Different senses of a word in Marathi language may have different translations into target language depending on the context of the word.

8.8.2 Machine Translation

Machine translation (MT) is automated translation. It is the process by which computer software is used to translate a text from one natural language (such as English) to another (such as Marathi).

To process any translation, human or automated, the meaning of a text in the original (source) language must be fully restored in the target language, i.e. in the translation. While on the surface this seems straightforward, it is far more complex. Translation is not a mere word-for-word substitution. A translator must interpret and analyse all of the elements in the text and know how each word may influence another. This requires extensive expertise in grammar, syntax (sentence structure), semantics (meanings), etc., in the source and target languages, as well as familiarity with each local region.

Human and machine translation each have their share of challenges. For example, no two individual translators can produce identical translations of the same text in the same language pair, and it may take several rounds of revisions to meet customer satisfaction. But the greater challenge lies in how machine translation can produce publishable quality translations.

Marathi WordNet is also useful for the rule-based machine translation (RBMT) system. These MT systems are based on the specification of rules of morphology, syntax, lexical selection, transfer, and generation. They use a bilingual or multilingual lexicon created from WordNets for creating different rules necessary for the correct translation.

Acknowledgments I would like to express my special thanks of gratitude to Mrs. Laxmi Kashyap, Mr. Gajanana Rane, Mr. Diptesh Kanojia, Ms. Sudha Bhingardive, Mrs. Madhuri Bhamble, and Mr. Nilesh Joshi and Shraddha Kalele who helped me in compiling the data, translations, etc., and special thanks to Mrs. Jaya Saraswati who helped me in editing.

References

Marashtra shabdakosh- 8 volumes.
Marathi paryayii shabdakosh—M. V. Bhatavadekar.
Bhartiya Sanskritiikosh—9 volumes.
Lekhankosh.
Grammar book by Damle.
WordNet 3.0.
Google Define:.
Thesaurus.com.
Marathi Vishwakosha—17 volumes.

Web Sources

http://www.cfilt.iitb.ac.in/~corpus/marathi/).

http://www.cfilt.iitb.ac.in/wordnet/webhwn/wn.php?nomorph=true&hwd=%E0%A4%AA%E0%A4%B9%E0%A5%81%E0%A4%81%E0%A4%9A.

http://www.indianmirror.com/languages/marathi-language.html.

http://www.systransoft.com/systran/corporate-profile/translation-technology/what-is-machine-translation/.

Chapter 9
Gujarati WordNet: A Profile of the IndoWordNet

Brijesh S. Bhatt, C.K. Bhensdadia, Pushpak Bhattacharyya, Dinesh Chauhan and Kirit Patel

Abstract Gujarati WordNet is built from the Hindi WordNet using the expansion approach. This paper presents experiences of building Gujarati WordNet. Various crucial issues relating to synset generation and linkage as well as the challenges relating to language-specific concepts are discussed. The paper also describes design of an online interface to access the WordNet.

Keywords Gujarati · WordNet · Synset · Concept · Hindi

9.1 Introduction

WordNet (Fellbaum 1998) is a machine-readable lexical database. Synsets are the basic building blocks of WordNet. Each synset represents a concept that is defined by a set of words in the language. Different synsets are linked using semantic and lexical relations such as hypernym–hyponym, holonym–meronym, antonym, and gradation. The WordNet for English language is developed at Princeton University. Following the *English WordNet*, WordNets for many other languages were developed across the globe. The first WordNet for Indian languages is *Hindi WordNet* (Chakrabarty et al. 2002), developed at the *Indian Institute of Technology*, Bombay. Recently, efforts are going on to develop WordNets for many other Indian languages. One such effort is to build Gujarati WordNet from Hindi WordNet using expansion approach.

B.S. Bhatt (✉) · C.K. Bhensdadia · D. Chauhan · K. Patel
Faculty of Technology, Department of Computer Engineering, Dharmsinh Desai University
Nadiad, Gujarat, India
e-mail: brij.s.bhatt@gmail.com; brij_bhatt@hotmail.com

P. Bhattacharyya
Department of Computer Science and Engineering, Center for Indian Language Technology, IIT-Bombay, Bombay, India

N.S. Dash et al. (eds.), *The WordNet in Indian Languages*,
DOI 10.1007/978-981-10-1909-8_9

The paper is organized as follows: Sect. 9.2 gives introduction to Gujarati language; Sect. 9.3 describes the Gujarati WordNet development approach; Sects. 9.4 and 9.5 describe the current status of the Gujarati WordNet and an online interface to access the Gujarati WordNet; and issues related to synset development are discussed in Sect. 9.6.

9.2 The Gujarati Language

Gujarati is a native language of Indian state of Gujarat and it is one of the 22 official languages of India. There are over 50 million speakers of Gujarati language. Gujarati belongs to Indo-Aryan family of the languages. As a descendent of Sanskrit, Gujarati language vocabulary contains four general categories of words: *tatsama, tadbhava, deshi*, and *videshi*.

Gujarati distinguishes between three genders: masculine, feminine, and neuter. Gujarati has two numbers, singular and plural. Adjectives agree with the gender and number of noun. Gujarati verb has [root + infinitive] structure and root verbs can be extended to make causative.

9.3 Gujarati WordNet Development Using Expansion Approach

Gujarati WordNet is being built using expansion approach (Vossen 1998). In this approach, synsets are created by referring to existing WordNet of related language. Hindi is used as a source language to create synsets of Gujarati language. Benefits of this approach are as follows:

- WordNet development process becomes faster as the gloss and synset of the source language is already available as reference.
- It provides linking between the synsets of different languages which can be used for machine translation applications.

A synset linkage tool, provided by *Indian Institute of Technology Bombay*, Bombay, is used to create synsets in Gujarati language. This synset linking tool provides graphical user interface which shows Hindi synset on the left-hand side and provides interface to enter Gujarati synset on the right-hand side.

Lexicalization of a concept varies across languages, which leads to synsets that are present in one language but not in another language. In order to handle this issue, synsets of the Hindi WordNet are divided into six different categories: (1) Universal, (2) Pan-Indian, (3) In-family, (4) language specific, (5) rare, and (6) synthesized. Universal, Pan-Indian, and In-family sets together represent synsets which are lexicalized in both Hindi and Gujarati. These synsets are developed in Gujarati WordNet by translating corresponding Hindi synsets.

The task of synset development for Gujarati language is further simplified by online availability of the lexical resources such as ***Bhagavad-Go-Mandal*** (Patel 1958) and ***Gujarati Lexicon*** (Chandaria 2006). *Bhagavad-Go-Mandal* was created in early twentieth century at princely state of Gondal in Kathiawad. It contains around 8.2 lacs words. It is accepted as a standard reference for Gujarati language by *Gujarat Sahitya Parishad* under the leadership of Mahatma Gandhi.

The *Gujarati Lexicon* is another more recent effort, by Ratilal Chandaria. The online interface of Gujarati lexicon provides easy access to meanings, synonyms, antonyms, idioms, proverbs, and phrases. These two resources together provide great help in building synsets.

9.4 Synset Linkage Status

Till date, 35599 synsets are built in the Gujarati WordNet. The category-wise count of synsets is as follows:

Part of speech-wise count of the synsets is as follows:

Noun	26503
Verb	2805
Adverb	445
Adjective	5828
Total	35599

9.5 Online Interface for Gujarati WordNet

A Web-based interface is developed to access Gujarati WordNet. The interface is accessible at http://www.cfilt.iitb.ac.in/gujarati. This Web site is developed using JSP and MySQL. The Web site provides facility to search a synset and its relations. Figure 9.1 shows a snapshot of the interface. Basic features of the Web site are as follows:

(a) **Virtual keyboard to enter text**: A virtual key board is provided on top right panel below the search box which allows user to enter text in preferred language.
(b) **Search synsets in 3 different languages**: Right-side panel allows user to see corresponding synsets in Hindi or English language. This gives a comparative view of synsets in different languages. This allows language learners and researchers to perform comparative study of languages.
(c) **Navigate through the different sense of the word**: Top left panel shows different senses for a word. Different senses can be browsed by pressing next synset/previous synset button.
(d) **Browse relations in different languages**: Left-side panel allows user to browse various lexical and semantic relations in any of the three languages.

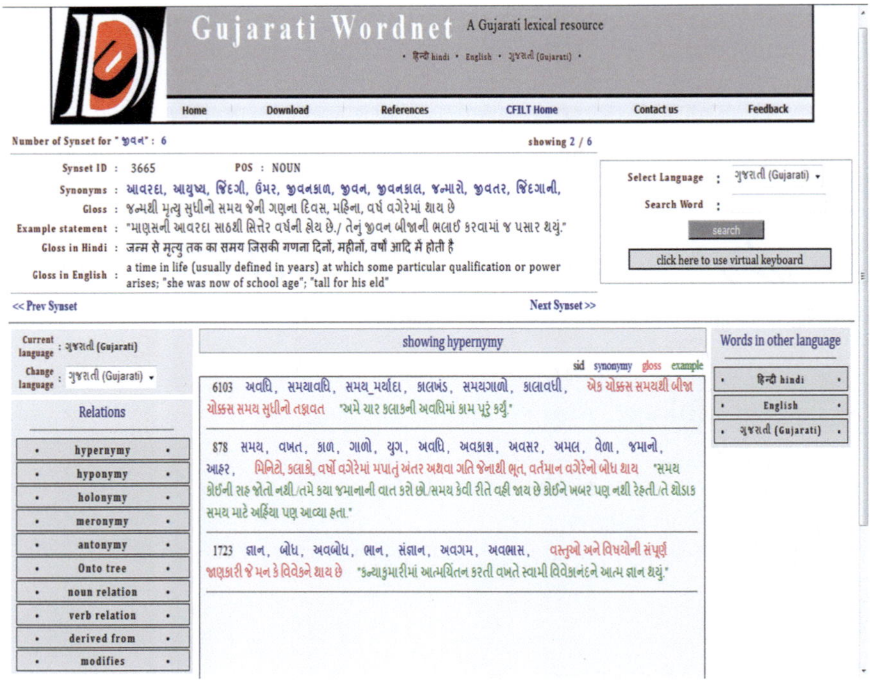

Fig. 9.1 Online interface to access the Gujarati WordNet

9.6 Issues Related to Synset Development

All universal, Pan-Indian, and in-family synsets of Hindi WordNet are translated into Gujarati WordNet. There are some synsets in Hindi language for which there is no lexeme in Gujarati, because of which it can not be created in Gujarati WordNet. Also there are some Gujarati language-specific concepts which can not be linked to Hindi WordNet. This section provides examples of such synsets.

9.6.1 Noun Synsets

(a) Difference in concept description

Concept	(turahI kI taraha kaa Eka bada baajaa) (turahI like one big musical instrument) (A big music instrument like turhi)
Example	(narasimhaa kI aawaaz door-door tak sunaI detI hain) (narasimhaa's sound to distance heard is) (narasimhaa's sound can be heard to far distance)
Synset	(narasimha, narasinga, gomukh)

No such concept is identified in Gujarati. However, there is a concept in Gujarati language for similar instrument which is used at war-front to announce beginning of a war.

(b) No indigenous lexeme in Gujarati

Concept (Itra kaa vyaapaar karanevala vyaktI)
(perfume's business person)
(A person who does business of perfume)
Example (aajakala Itra vyaparI nakalI Itra ka vyaapaara bhI karane lage hain)
(nowadays perfume seller duplicate perfume 's business also do)
(nowadays perfume sellers are doing business of duplicate perfume as well.)
Synset (Itra vyaaparI, Itra pharosh, attaara, gandhi)

There is no indigenous lexeme for this concept in Gujarati language.

(c) Difficulties in adoption

Concept (jo pravisHT na huAa ho)
(who entered not is)
(one who is not entered)
Example (apravisHTa mahemaano ko shighra hI bhItara pravesh karane de)
(apravishTa guest 's immediately inside enter let)
(immediately let the 'apravisht' guest enter inside)
Synset (apravisTa)

Though it can be translated into Gujarati, it is not a regular concept in the language.

(d) Non-availability of concept in Gujarati

Concept (jo akelaa charataa ya vicharaN karata ho)
(who alone grazing or moving)
(one who is grazing or moving alone)
Example (jungalI sUar Ek pruthakchara pashu hain.)
(wild boar one pruthakchara animal is)
(wild boar is an pruthakchara animal.)
Synset (pruthakachar)

There is no such concept in Gujarati language.

9.6.2 Verb and Adjective Synsets

Most of the verb and adjective synsets of Hindi WordNet were linked with Gujarati. However, there are some specific terms for which there are no words in Gujarat language. Some of the Hindi synsets which are difficult to create in Gujarati are as follows:

Concept (naye baratana ko pahalI baar kaam me laanaa)
(new vessel first time use)
(to use a new vessel for the first time)
Example (pooja ke samaya usane kaI baratana anavaanse)
(worship time he some utensil anavaanse)
Synset (anavaansanaa)

No such concept is identified in Gujarati language.

Concept (jisake pichhale pairo ko baandhakara charane ke liye chhoda gaya)
(whose hind legs tied up grazing left)
(one whose hind legs are tied up and left for grazing)
Synset (chhantaa)

There is no indigenous lexeme for this concept in Gujarati language.

Concept (jo atyaadhik maand khaata hai)
(who lots of 'maand' eats) (one who eats lots of 'maand')
Synset (madahaa)

There is no lexeme for this concept in Gujarati.

Concept (jo bhojana ke roop mein chavala aadi se adhik roTi hi khaata ho)
(who food in form of rice, etc. more 'roti' eats) (one who eats more roti then rice, etc.)
Synset (roTiha)

Though this word can be translated into Gujarati language, it is not a native concept used in Gujarati language.

Concept (jo pooja kiye jaane yougya ho (strI)
(who worship worth is (woman))
(One (woman) who is worth worship)
Synset (poojanIyaa)

This concept is specific to feminine gender. There exists a gender neutral lexeme in Gujarati. Above examples describe some of the synsets for which Gujarati synsets could not be created.

9.6.3 Language-Specific Concepts in Gujarati

While most of the day-to-day vocabulary of Gujarati language is similar to that of Hindi, there are some concepts which are very specific to Gujarati language. These concepts are mostly related to the unique features of Gujarati language and Gujarati culture.

Till date, 108 language-specific synsets are created for the Gujarati language. Few observations for the language-specific synsets are as follows:

- Language-specific synsets are created for culture-specific terms of Gujarati language.
- It covers words for the food items, places, local festivals, literature, etc.
- Most of the language-specific synsets are nouns.
- Most of the language-specific synsets are single-word synsets, i.e., there are not many synonyms.
- The language-specific synsets appear very lower down the WordNet hierarchy.
- For most of the language-specific synsets, there are no hyponymy concepts.
- The language-specific synsets are individuals or instances rather than concepts.

Some examples of the language-specific synsets are as follows:

Concept	(koi khaasa prasange kasumbo pIvaa maaTe bhegaa thavu.) (some special occasion 'kasumbo' drink get together) (to get together to drink 'kasumbo' on some special occasion.)
Synset	(Daayaro)
Concept	(Ek faL ke je lagna prasange var kanya na haathe bandhe chhe) (A fruit that marriage ceremony groom bride hand tie) (A fruit that the groom ties to the hand of the bride during marriage ceremony.)
Synset	(mIMdhaL)
Concept	(moksHa maaTe bhagavaan nu naama leta leta giranaara para thI padatu mukavu.) (moksHa for god's name uttering mount Girnar jump) (To jump from mount Girnar while uttering name of the God to achieve moksha)
Synset	(bheiravajapa)

9.7 Conclusion

Existence of Hindi WordNet and similarity between Hindi and Gujarati language helped development of Gujarati WordNet. Linkage of Hindi WordNet with Gujarati and other 16 Indian languages creates a multilingual resource for Indian languages which will be useful for many natural language processing applications. However, variation in the lexicalization of the concepts across languages poses a major challenge in WordNet linking.

Acknowledgments This work is done under project 'Indradhanush WordNet Development Project for Seven Indian Languages' financed by the Ministry of Communication and Information Technology, Govt. of India. We sincerely acknowledge the Dept. of Information Technology for providing support for the project.

References

Chakrabarty, D., Pande, P., Narayan, D., & Bhattacharyya, P. (2002). An experience in building the Indo WordNet—a WordNet for Hindi. In *International Conference on Global WordNet (GWC02)*, Mysore, India.

Chandaria, R. (2006). *Gujarati Lexicon*. http://www.gujaratilexicon.com.

Fellbaum, C. (1998). *WordNet: An electronic lexical database*. Mass.: MIT Press.

Patel, C. B. (1958) *Bhagvad-Go-Mandal*. http://www.bhagavadgomandalonline.com.

Vossen, P. (1998). *EuroWordNet: A multilingual database with lexical semantic networks*. London: Kluwer Academic Publishers.

Chapter 10
Issues in the Creation of Synsets in Odia WordNet

Panchanan Mohanty, Ramesh C. Malik and Bhimasena Bhol

Abstract Since languages differ from each other, it is difficult to find equivalents for the words and expressions of one language in another. So creating an inter-lingual WordNet in Odia vis-à-vis Hindi has been a challenging task. While dealing with the equivalence problems in Odia, creation of new expressions dominates the synsets involving various kinds of wage, derivation of nouns from nouns and adjectives, adjectives derived from nouns, and single-word Hindi synsets expressing complex ideas and kinship synsets. The other important procedure is borrowing that has been used widely in the domains of historical events, geographical locations, sociocultural practices, place names, personal names, flora and fauna, ecological entities, gods and goddesses, culture-specific items, etc. Apart from these, certain problematic issues of the Hindi WordNet, viz. wrong categorization of synsets, concepts with inadequate information and description, mismatch between concepts and synsets, and imprecise concepts have also been discussed with a view to sensitizing other Indian language WordNet developers regarding these deficiencies. At the same time, we expect the quality of the Hindi WordNet to improve if these problems are taken care of.

Keywords WordNet · Synset · Odia · New expressions · Borrowing · Kinship term · Compound verb · Conjunctive participle

10.1 Introduction

'WordNet is an on-line lexical reference system whose design is inspired by current psycholinguistic theories of human lexical memory', and also, 'it is a proposal for a more effective combination of traditional lexicographic information

P. Mohanty (✉) · R.C. Malik · B. Bhol
Centre for Applied Linguistics and Translation Studies, University of Hyderabad, Hyderabad, India
e-mail: panchananmohanty@gmail.com

N.S. Dash et al. (eds.), *The WordNet in Indian Languages*,
DOI 10.1007/978-981-10-1909-8_10

and modern high-speed computation' (Miller et al. 1990, p. 1). The main objective of WordNet was to describe the lexical and componential features of words and their use by the concerned linguistic community. WordNet contains linguistic data, such as syntactic, semantic, and pragmatic features of words which are important factors for designing a WordNet in a language. In order to create a WordNet for Odia on the basis of the Hindi WordNet, the major problems faced were of equivalence. While looking for Odia equivalents of Hindi words, the problems were of various kinds. We would like to highlight some of these issues in this paper.

All the synsets of Hindi WordNet have been divided into four lexical categories: noun, adjective, verb, and adverb. These cover different domains such as historical events, geographical locations, sociocultural practices, place names, personal names, flora and fauna, ecological entities, gods and goddesses, culture-specific items. In fact, creating equivalent synsets in Odia has been quite a challenging task. But one thing which we have religiously left untouched is the categories of synsets. In other words, the categories of the Hindi synsets have always been retained as such in Odia. So this discussion will focus on the problems of synset creation in Odia and their solutions.

10.2 Problems and Procedures in Odia Synsets Creation

Translation is the common method used for creating Odia synsets. While translating, the major problems were both linguistic and cultural. Since 'no two languages are ever sufficiently similar to be considered as representing the same social reality' (Sapir 1949, p. 69), translating from one language to another definitely poses problems as it is very hard to find one-to-one correspondence between two languages. Jakobson (1971, p. 235) states, 'Languages differ essentially in what they must convey and not in what they can convey. Each verb of a given language imperatively raises a set of specific yes/no questions, as for instance: Is the narrated event presented prior to the speech event or not? Naturally the attention of native speakers and listeners will be constantly focused on such items as they are compulsory in their verbal code'. That is why, translators often try to find out proper equivalents in the target language, and ultimately, this helps to solve many translation problems. According to Nida (1964, p. 91), 'Translation-problems, which are essentially problems of equivalence, may be conveniently treated under (1) ecology, (2) material culture, (3) social culture, (4) religious culture, and (5) linguistic culture'. In order to create synsets in Odia on the basis of the Hindi synsets, similar problems have been encountered, and efforts have been made to bridge the gap between the two languages. Let us now discuss these problems and the ways in which these have been solved.

10.3 New Expressions

Since languages and cultures differ from one another, it is difficult to find lexical equivalents of one language in another. So creation of new expressions becomes an important procedure to represent the source language (SL) concept in the target language (TL). Following this, new expressions have been created by combining the existing Odia words in order to express the meanings of the Hindi synsets which do not have equivalents in Odia.

10.3.1 Nouns Derived from Verbs

Hindi uses nouns derived from verbs, especially the ones which represent wages for various kinds, which is quite interesting. In Odia, on the other hand, such types of nouns are not commonly used as the general word for wage is used to represent any kind of wages. While providing equivalents for these single-word expressions, groups of words have been used in Odia. Therefore, this procedure has been very useful especially in creating synsets for different kinds of wages. For example:

Example 1

ID: 20708
CAT: NOUN
SL: Hindi
CONCEPT: chiRakne ki: mazdu:ri:[1]
sprinkling of wage[2]
EXAMPLE: usne prati ekaR daba: chiRka:i: paca:s rupae lie
he/she every acre medicine sprinkling wage fifty rupees took
SYNSET: chiRka:i:
sprinkling wage
TL: Odia
CONCEPT: *kichi chin'ciba:pa:iM dia:ja:uthiba: majuri*
something sprinkling for being given wage
EXAMPLE: *se ekaraprati ausadha chin'ciba: majuri paca:sa Tanka: nela:*
he/she acre per medicine sprinkling wage fifty rupees took
SYNSET: *chin'ciba: majuri, chin'ciba: mu:la, chin'ca: majuri, chin'ca: mu:la*
sprinkling wage

[1]Transliteration of the Hindi or Odia Text. This convention will be followed everywhere in this paper.
[2]Gloss of the Hindi or Odia Text. This convention will be followed everywhere in this paper.

In the above example,[3] the SL synset *chiRka:i:* is a noun derived from the verb *chiRakna:* 'to sprinkle', and the synset refers to 'the wage paid for sprinkling'. In Odia, there is no single word to express this concept. Therefore, it has been created as *chin'ciba: majuri*, *chin'ca: majuri*, *chin'ciba: mu:la*, and *chin'ca: mu:la* all of which mean 'sprinkling wage'. The words *majuri* and *mu:la* refer to 'wage', and *chin'ciba:* and *chin'ca:* mean 'sprinkling'. When these words are used together, they express the same meaning as *chiRka:i:* in Hindi. Here, we can examine another example:

Example 2

ID: 20919,
CAT: NOUN
SL: Hindi
CONCEPT: *jhoMkne ki: majdu:ri:*
Filling of wage
EXAMPLE:
jhoMkva: gulvar meM i:Mdhan ki: jhoMka:i: ma:Mg raha: hei
Filling person oven in fuel of wage for filling firewood in the oven asking is
SYNSET:
jhoMka:i:, jhoMkva:i:
the wage for filling firewood in the oven

TL: Odia
CONCEPT:
culire ja:La bhariba:paiM dia:ja:uthiba: majuri
oven in firewood filling for given wage
EXAMPLE:
lokaTi a:khusa:La culire ja:La bhariba: majuri ma:guchi
the man sugarcane mill oven in firewood filling wage is asking
SYNSET:
culire ja:La bhariba: majuri, culire ja:La bhara: majuri, culire ja:La bhariba: mu:la, culire ja:La bhara: mu:la, and *bha:Tire ja:La bhariba: majuri, bha:Tire ja:La bhara: majuri, bha:Tire ja:La bhariba: mu:la, bha:Tire ja:La bhara: mu:la*
the wage for filling firewood in the oven

In this example, the Hindi words *jhoMka:i:* and *jhoMkva:i:* are nouns derived from the verb *jhoMkna:* which means 'to cast fuel into an oven', and the synset refers to *jhoMkne ki: majdu:ri:* 'the wage for filling firewood in the oven'. There is no single-word verb in Odia to express this concept. Therefore, the equivalents in Odia have been created using phrases such as *culire ja:La bhariba: majuri*, *culire*

[3]In this paper, [T, Th, D, Dh, R, Rh, L] have been used for the voiceless unaspirated retroflex stop, voiceless aspirated retroflex stop, voiced unaspirated, retroflex stop, voiced aspirated retroflex stop, voiced unaspirated retroflex flap, voiced aspirated retroflex flap, and retroflex lateral respectively.

ja:La bhara: majuri, *culire ja:La bhariba: mu:la*, *culire ja:La bhara: mu:la*; and *bha:Tire ja:La bhariba: majuri*, *bha:Tire ja:La bhara: majuri*, *bha:Tire ja:La bhariba: mu:la*, *bha:Tire ja:La bhara: mu:la* where the words *culire* and *bha:Tire* mean 'in the oven'; *ja:La* means 'firewood'; *bhariba:* and *bhara:* mean 'filling'; and *majuri* and *mu:la* mean 'wage'. All these words have been put together to give the meaning of the Hindi words *jhoMka:i:* and *jhoMkva:i:*.

There are a few more examples which show the use of specific words for paying wages in Hindi where Odia has no equivalents for them. For example, the Hindi word *kata:i:* (ID: 21093) refers to 'the wage for spinning'. But there is no single word in Odia for representing this concept. So the Odia equivalents have been made *su:ta:kaTa: majuri* and *su:ta:ka:Tiba: majuri* which is a combination of the following words *su:ta:kaTa:* or *su:ta:ka:Tiba:* for 'spinning' and *majuri* for 'wage'. These phrases express the equivalent meaning of the Hindi word *kata:i:*.

Similarly, the Hindi word *boa:i:* (ID. No: 6926) refers to 'the wage for sowing seeds'. It can be created as *buNiba: majuri* and *buNa: majuri*. But the verb root *buN-* is ambiguous in Odia in the sense that it refers to both 'sowing (seeds)' and 'weaving (cloth or net)'. In order to make it unambiguous and specific, Odia equivalents have been created by adding appropriate words to the verb, i.e. *bihana buNiba: majuri*, *bihana buNa: majuri, manji buNiba: majuri*, and *manji buNa: majuri* where *bihana* and *manji* mean 'seed', *buNiba:* and *buNa:* mean 'sowing', and *majuri* means 'wage', and the synset means 'the wage for sowing seeds'.

There are differences in cultural and occupational activities between the Hindi and Odia speech communities for which it is difficult to find equivalents for such Hindi words in Odia. The above terms used in Hindi for paying wages for different types of occupations are not found in Odia and that is why this difficulty occurs.

10.3.2 Derivation of Nouns from Nouns and Adjectives

We find a number of Hindi nouns that have been derived by adding prefixes or suffixes. But the same is not possible in Odia even though both these languages belong to the Indo-Aryan family. When we follow the Hindi way, the outcomes do not give appropriate meanings. So to create such equivalents in Odia, the Odia morphological practices have been followed. For example:

Example 1

ID: 22283, CAT: NOUN
SL: Hindi
CONCEPT:

upshaman	*na*	*hone*	*ya:*	*na*	*daba:ne*	*ki:*	*kriya:*
abatement	not	happening	or	not	pressing	of	action

EXAMPLE:

indriyon	*ki:*	*da:sata:*	*apratikriya:*	*ke*	*hi:*	*pariNa:m*	*hai*
senses	of	enslavement	absence of reaction	of	too	consequence	is

SYNSET:
apratikriya:
absence of reaction

TL: Odia
CONCEPT:

sa:nta naheba:	*ba:*	*prasamita naheba*	*prakriya:*
not pacifying	or	not abating	action

EXAMPLE:

indriyaguRikara	*da:satvahela:*	*pratikriya:hi:nata:ra*	*pariNa:m*
the senses of	enslavemen became	unresponsiveness of	consequence

SYNSET:
pratikriya:hi:nata:
the state of absence of reaction

In this example, the SL word *apratikriya:* as a noun refers to *upshaman na hone ya: na daba:ne ki: kriya:* which means 'the state of remaining unabated'. It is a noun, which has been formed by adding the negative prefix *a-* to the noun *pratikriya:* 'reaction', which is also found in Odia, but there is no word such as *apratikriya:* in Odia. In order to create an equivalent in Odia, the negative suffix *-hi:nata:* 'absence of something' has been added to *pratikriya:*. The product *pratikriya:hi:nata:* is an equivalent to Hindi *apratikriya:*.

This above example shows how some nouns in Hindi are created by adding prefixes to other nouns. There is another Hindi example (ID: 23272) *abha:vna:* that refers to 'absence of thought'. It is also formed by adding the negative prefix *a-* to the noun *bha:vna:* 'thought' because the word *abha:bana:* is not used in Odia. So the negative suffix *-hi:nata:* has been added to *bha:bana:* leading to creation of *bha:bana:hi:nata:* 'absence of thought' or 'thoughtlessness'.

There are some other Hindi nouns which have been made with prefixes or suffixes added to the root word, but it is difficult to provide direct equivalents for these nouns in Odia. Let us consider the following example:

Example 2

ID: 16413, CAT: NOUN
SL: Hindi
CONCEPT:

atyadhik	*gahri:*	*hone ki:*	*avastha:*
too much	deep	becoming	situation

EXAMPLE:

samudr ki:	*anavaga:hita:*	*se*	*sabhi:*	*paricit heiM*
sea of	condition of unsuitability for bathing	from	all	familiar are

SYNSET:
anavaga:hita:
condition of unsuitability for bathing due to excess depth of water

TL: Odia
CONCEPT:

atyadhika	*gabhira*	*heba:ra*	*abastha:*
excess	deep	being of	situation

EXAMPLE:

samudrara	*ataLa*	*gabhi:rata:*	*bisayare*	*samaste*	*ja:Nanti*
sea of	bottomless	depth	regarding	all	familiar are

SYNSET:
ataLa gabhi:rata:, ati gabhi:rata:, sugabhi:rata:
bottomless depth

In this example, the Hindi synset *anavaga:hita:* refers to the concept *atyadhik gahri: hone ki: avastha:* which means 'the state of being too deep'. The word *anavaga:hita:* is a noun which has been created by adding the negative prefix *na-* and the nominal suffix *-ta:* to the root *avaga:h-* 'to bathe'. Thus, the word *anavaga:hita:* literally means 'the condition of unsuitability for bathing due to excess depth of water'. This Hindi word does not have a direct equivalent in Odia. Therefore, expressions such as *ataLa gabhi:rata:*, *sugabhi:rata:*, and *ati gabhi:rata:* have been used for rendering the same meaning where the word *ataLa* means 'bottomless', the prefix *su-* means 'good', the word *ati* means 'very', and the word *gabhi:rata:* means 'depth'.

It is found in both the examples that the above SL synsets are not used in Odia the way they are used in Hindi. Though the above Hindi nouns have been created by adding prefix and suffix, the Odia nouns have been created by adding suffix to the already existing nouns.

10.3.3 Verbs Derived from Adjective or Nouns

Some verbs are used in different ways in Hindi compared to their equivalents in Odia. Creating synsets for such Hindi verbs in Odia was difficult, and in this situation, new expressions have been created in Odia. For example:

Example 1

ID: 13195, CAT: VERB
SL: Hindi
CONCEPT:

achi:	*tarah*	*banna: ya:*	*hona:*	
good	type	to be made	or	to become

EXAMPLE:

bi:ma:ri: ke	*ba:d*	*ab*	*uska:*	*shari:r*	*gaTh raha: hei*
illness of	after	now	his	body	is being built

SYNSET:
gaThna:
to be built

TL: Odia
CONCEPT:

bhala	*bha:bare*	*gaRiheba:*
good	in a way	to be made

EXAMPLE:

rogaru	*uThiba:pare*	*ebe*	*ta:*	*deha*	*sustha heuchi*	
illness from	rising after	now	his	body	healthy	is becoming

SYNSET:
sustha heba:
to become healthy

In this example, the SL synset *gaThna:* which is a verb refers to 'to be built well' in connection with regaining health. But in Odia, there is no single-word verb to express this meaning. So it has been created as *sustha heba:*. This verb is a conjunct verb in Odia where the adjective *sustha* means 'healthy' and the verb *heba:* means 'to become', and all of these together express the meaning for the Hindi verb *gaThna:*. In this context, we can analyse the following example:

Example 2

ID: 14326, CAT: VERB
SL: Hindi
CONCEPT:
bartanoM ko upyog meM la:ne se pu:rv usmeM pa:ni: bharkar rckhna:
utensils to use in bringing before it in water filling to be kept
EXAMPLE:
ma:M ghaRe ko kam se kam cObi:s ghaMTe aMba:sti: hei
mother pitcher to less from less twenty four hours keeps water before use
SYNSET:
aMba:sna:
to keep a new utensil filled with water for some time before use

TL: Odia
CONCEPT:
ba:sanaguRika byabaha:ra kariba: pu:rbaru sethire pa:Ni bhartikari rakhiba:
utensils use doing before it in water filling to be kept
EXAMPLE:
ma:a: nu:a: ba:sanare ati kamre cabis ghaNTa: pa:Ni bhari rakhanti
mother new utensil in very little twenty four hour water filling keep
SYNSET:
nu:a: ba:sanare pa:Ni bhari rakhiba:, nu:a: ba:sanare pa:Ni pura:i rakhiba:, nu:a: ba:sanare pa:Ni bhartikari rakhiba:
to keep a new utensil filled with water for some time before use

In this example, the Hindi verb *aMba:sna:* refers 'to keep a new utensil filled with water for some time before use'. This process of treating a new earthen or metal pot before use is common, but there is no specific verb in Odia to convey this idea. So it has been rendered as *nu:a: ba:sanare pa:Ni bhari rakhiba:*, *nu:a: ba:sanare pa:Ni pu:ra:i rakhiba:* and *nu:a: ba:sanare pa:Ni bharti kari rakhiba:*. The Odia expressions *nu:a: ba:sanare* 'in a new utensil', *pa:Ni bhari*, *pa:Ni pu:ra:i, pa:Ni bharti kari* 'having filled water', and *rakhiba:* 'keeping' together convey the meaning of the Hindi verb *aMba:sna:*.

There are some other Hindi verbs which have created problems for creating equivalents in Odia. The Hindi verb (ID No: 15494) *magha:rna:* refers to *a:ga:mi: varSha:ritu meM dha:n bone ke lie ma:gh ma:s meM hal cala:na:* which means 'to cultivate land in the month of Magha (January–February) to make it ready for sowing paddy in the rainy season'. Though this phenomenon is found in Odisha, there is no specific verb in Odia to express it. Therefore, *ma:ghua:Ni ca:sapa:iM haLa kariba:* has been created in order to provide the equivalent meaning to the Hindi verb. Here, *ma:ghua:Ni* 'related to the month of Magha', *ca:sapa:iM* 'for cultivation' and *haLa kariba:* 'to plough' together express the meaning of magha:rna:.

10.3.4 Adjectives Derived from Nouns

There are some adjectives in Hindi that have been created by adding certain suffixes to nouns. Since such suffixes are not usually used in Odia, the Hindi equivalents in Odia have been created by adding other suffixes to the nouns. For example:

Example 1

ID: 17292, CAT: ADJECTIVE
SL: Hindi
CONCEPT:
vidya:lay ka: ya: vidya:lay se sambandhit
school of or school with related
EXAMPLE:
vidya:layi: va:ta:varaN ko gurukul ke va:ta:varaN ke samakakR bana:ne ka:
school of environment to gurukul of environment of equal making of
prayatn kiya: ja:na: ca:hie
attempt done going wants
SYNSET:
vidya:layi:, vidya:layi:n, vidya:layi:y, sku:li:, pa:Thsha:ley
related to school

TL: Odia
CONCEPT:
bidya:Laya ba: bidya:Layasaha sambandhita
school or school with related
EXAMPLE:
bidya:Layara ba:ta:baraNaku gurukuLara ba:ta:baraNasaha sama:na kariba:la:gi
school of environment to gurukula of environment with equal doing for
a:me cesTa:kariba: ucita
we try should
SYNSET:
bidya:Layara, skulra, bidya:Laya sambandhi:ya, skul sambandhi:ya
school about

In the above example, the SL synset contains the adjectives *vidya:layi:*, *vidya:layi:n*, *vidya:layi:y*, *sku:li:*, and *pa:Thsha:ley* mean 'of a school or related to a school'. These adjectives have been created by adding the suffixes *-i:*, *-i:n*, *-i:y*, to the noun *vidya:lay;* the suffix *-i:* to the noun *sku:l*, and *-ey* to the noun *pa:Thsha:la:* 'school'. As these adjectives are not used in Odia, the possessive case suffix *-ra* 'of' and the adjective particle *sambandhi:ya* 'related' have been added to *bidya:Laya*, and *skul* leading to creation of the adjectives *bidya:Layara*, *skulra*, *bidya:Laya sambandhi:ya*, and *skul sambandhi:ya* which are equivalents of Hindi synset. Another example can be discussed here:

Example 2

ID: 26877, CAT: ADJECTIVE
SL: Hindi
CONCEPT:
ka:rya:lay ka: *ya:* *ka:rya:lay se* *saMbaMdhit*
office of or office with related
EXAMPLE:
a:j *ka:rya:layi:* *ka:moM ko* *nipTa:ne meM* *hi:* *ra:t* *ho gai:*
today official works to accomplishing in only night happened
SYNSET:
ka:rya:layi:
official

TL: Odia
CONCEPT:
ka:rya:Layara *ba:* *ka:rya:Layasaha sambandhita*
office of or office with related
EXAMPLE:
a:ji *a:phisika* *ka:ma sabu* *sa:riba:beLaku* *ra:ti* *hoigala:*
today official works all accomplishing time to night happened
SYNSET:
a:phisika
official

Here, the SL synset is an adjective *ka:rya:layi.* This refers to *ka:rya:lay ka: ya: ka:rya:lay se sambandhit* which means 'of an office or related to an office'. This adjective has been created by adding the suffix *-i:* to the noun *ka:rya:lay* 'office', and this is acceptable in Hindi. But in Odia, such an adjective cannot be derived from the noun *ka:rya:Laya.* Again in the written variety, the adjective *a:phisika* is in currency though it has been derived from the English word 'office', which is more frequently used in Odia than the word *ka:rya:Laya.*

It is clear from the above example that the formation of adjectives from nouns by adding suffixes in Hindi and Odia is not the same though both of them belong to the Indo-Aryan language family. Hindi adjectives are usually formed by adding prefixes or suffixes to nouns, whereas in Odia, if a noun does not have an adjective, it can also be used as an adjective without changing its morphological form. The SL synset (ID No. 7323) *cama:ri:* refers to *cama:r ka: ya: cama:r se sambandhit* is in adjective category. As there is no adjective of *cama:r* in Odia, the same noun *cama:ra* has been used as an adjective.

10.3.5 Single-Word Synsets Expressing Complex Ideas

There are certain Hindi synsets which consist of single words, but express relatively complex ideas. Such synsets in different categories such as noun and verb cannot be expressed in single words in Odia. For this purpose, more words have to be used together to create Odia equivalents to express appropriate meaning. For example:

Example 1

ID: 9562, CAT: NOUN
SL: Hindi
CONCEPT:

saphed	*shari:r*	*aur*	*ka:li:*	*cOMc*	*va:la:*	*kabu:tar*
white	body	and	black	beak	having	pigeon

EXAMPLE:

chat par	*kalTore*	*ka:*	*ek*	*joRa:*	*baiTha: hua:*
terrace on	pigeon with black beak and white body	of	one	pair	sitting

SYNSET:
kalTora:
pigeon with black beak and white body

TL: Odia
CONCEPT :

dhaLa:	*shari:ra*	*o*	*kaLa:*	*thaNTathiba:*	*pa:ra:*
white	body	and	black	beak having	pigeon

EXAMPLE :

cha:taupare	*joRe*	*kaLa:*	*thaNTathiba:*	*dhaLa:*	*pa:ra:*	*basichanti*
terrace on	two	black	beak having	white	pigeon	sitting are

SYNSET :
kaLa: thaNTathiba: dhaLa:pa:ra:, kaLa: cancuthiba: dhaLa:pa:ra:, kaLa: than Tia: dhaLa: pa:ra:
pigeon with black beak and white body

In the above example, the SL concept *kalTora:* is in noun category, and this refers to 'a pigeon which body is white and beak is black'. This is an example which shows how a single word in Hindi expresses a complex concept. There is no single word in Odia which can convey the same meaning. So while creating the expression in Odia, it has been made as *kaLa: thaNTathiba: dhaLa: pa:ra:*, *kaLa: cancuthiba: dhaLa: pa:ra:*, and *kaLa: thaNTia: dhaLa: pa:ra:* where *kaLa:* means 'black', *thaNTathiba:*, *cancuthiba:* or *thaNTia:* mean 'having a beak', *dhaLa:* means 'white', and *pa:ra:* means 'pigeon'. We can examine another example with a verb which expresses such type of complex concept below:

Example 2

ID: 18850, CAT: VERB
SL: Hindi
CONCEPT:
khet meM paRi hui: suPkhi: pattiya:M, gha:seM a:di jala:kar ra:kh sameta khet ko jotana:
field in fallen dry leaves, grasses etc. having burnt ash with field to plough
EXAMPLE:
kisa:n khet ko ra:vana: raha: hei
farmer field to is ploughing after burning the dry leaves, grass, etc. lying there and scattering the ashes
SYNSET:
ra:vana:a:
to plough the field after burning the dry leaves, grass, etc. lying there and then scattering the ashes

TL: Odia
CONCEPT:
khetare paRithiba: sukhila: patra gha:sa a:di jaLa:i sehi pauMsaku kheLa:i haLakariba:
field in fallen dry leaves, grasses etc. having burnt that ash to having spread plough
EXAMPLE:
krusakaTi khetare paRithiba: sukhila: patra gha:sa a:di jaLa:i sehi pauMsaku kheLa:i haLakaruchi.
the farmer field in fallen dry leaves, grasses etc. having burnt that ash to having spread is ploughing
SYNSET:
sukhila: patra gha:sa a:di jaLa:i sehi pauMsaku kheLa:i haLakariba:
to plough the field after burning the dry leaves, grass, etc. lying there and then scattering the ashes

There are some synsets that do not have equivalents in the cultural milieu of Odisha. The Hindi verb *ra:vna:na:* refers to *khet meM paRi: hui: su:khi: pattiya:M, gha:seM a:di jala:kar ra:kh samet khet ko jotna:* which means 'to plough a land after burning the dry leaves, grass, etc. lying there and scattering the ashes'. The situation does not generally occur in the way it is conveyed through the SL synset as the farmers in Odisha mainly weed out the grass in an uncultivated land and let it dry there. It is less frequently seen that the farmers burn the grasses and scatter the ashes in the field. However, there is no single word in Odia to express this concept. So the Odia synset has been created as *shukhila: patra gha:sa a:di jaLa:i sehi pauMsaku kheLa:i haLakariba:*. Here, the word *shukhila:* means 'dry', *patra gha:sa a:di* means 'leaves, grass, etc.', *jaLa:i* means 'having burnt', *sehi pa:uMsaku* means 'those ashes', *kheLa:i* means 'having scattered', *haLa kariba:* means 'to plough'. All these words combined together give the meaning 'to plough the field after burning the dry leaves, grass, etc. lying there and scattering the ashes', which is an equivalent to the Hindi synset *ra:vana:na:*.

10.4 Kinship Relations

Kinship terms denote some definite relations, and these terms are culture specific. So when it comes to translation, these are very difficult to translate from one language to another. Similar problem has been faced while dealing with the translation of the adjectival forms of some kinship terms which have been discussed below. Since such single-word adjectives are not used in Odia, new expressions were created by combining the existing Odia words for equivalence. Let us discuss the following examples:

Example 1

ID: 6992, CAT: ADJECTIVE
SL: Hindi
CONCEPT:

phu: pha:	*ya:*	*phu:a: se*	*utpann*
father's sister's husband	or	father's sister from	born

EXAMPLE:

uska:	*phuphera: bha:i:*	*ek*	*na:mi:*	*cikitsak*	*hei*
his	father's sister's son regarded as cousin	one	famous	doctor	is

SYNSET:
phuphera:
related through or pertaining to father's sister's husband

TL: Odia
CONCEPT:

piusa:	*ba:*	*piusi:nkaTha:ru*	*janmita*
father's sister's husband	or	father's sister from	born

EXAMPLE:

Ta:ha:ra	*piusi:pua bha:i*	*jaNe*	*na:mi:*	*cikitsaka*
his	father's sister's son regarded as cousin	one	famous	doctor

SYNSET:
piusi:pua, piisi:pua
father's sister's son

In the above example, the SL synset is *phuphera:*. This kinship adjective refers to 'born to father's sister's husband', but while referring to dictionary, it was found to be 'related through or pertaining to father's sister's husband'. In Odia, when we refer to any person from father's sister's family, we relate him/her with father's sister since she is close to father. *phua:* in Hindi refers to *piusi:* 'father's sister' in Odia. So, in order to give the closest meaning to the adjective *phuphera:* 'born to father's sister' or 'related through or pertaining to father's sister's husband', it has been created as *pius:i pua* and *piisi: pua,* where *pius:i* or *piisi:* is 'father's sister', and *pua* is 'son'. Though the synset appears to be in noun form, it has been categorized as adjective where it gives the adjectival meaning 'pertaining to father's sister's husband'. This is because some nouns are also used as adjectives in Odia when they do not have other adjectival forms. However, the TL synset *pius:i pua bha:i* and *pi:si pua bhai* 'father's siter's son' provide closest equivalent to the SL term *phuphera: bha:i:,* 'father's sister's son regarded as cousin'. We can see another similar example here:

Example 2

ID: 7011, CAT: ADJECTIVE
SL: Hindi
CONCEPT:
ma:ma: se *utpann*
mother's brother from born
EXAMPLE:
mohan mera: mamera: bha:i: hei
mohan my mother's brother's son regarded as cousin is
SYNSET:
mamera:

TL: Odia
CONCEPT:
ma:muTha:ru *ja:ta*
mother's brother from born
EXAMPLE:
mohan mora mauaLa: pua bha:i
mohan my mother's brother's son regarded as cousin
SYNSET:
mauLa: pua, mamu pua

In this example, the SL synset *mamera:* is 'born to mother's brother'. Since there is no single-word equivalent of this SL kinship adjective in Odia, the words *mauLa: pua* or *ma:muM pua* have been taken as equivalent. These words are generally nouns which mean 'mother's brother's son', and here, these have been used as adjectives which gives the same meaning as *mamera:*. However, the SL term *mamera: bha:i:* 'mother's brother's son regarded as cousin' has been created as *ma:mu pua bha:i* or *mauLa: pua bha:i* in Odia for close equivalent where the word *bha:i* is used for a 'male cousin' in both Hindi and Odia. In ID No. 9876, the SL synset *mausera* is another kinship adjective which means 'related to mother's sister's husband', and the TL word has been made as *mausa:* which is a noun but used as an adjective in Odia. So the SL term *mausere sasur* has been made as *mausa: sasura* 'wife/husband's mother's sister's husband' as this is widely used in Odia.

10.5 Borrowing of Synsets

A number of concepts found in Hindi WordNet are language specific, e.g. names of persons, places, geographical locations, food items, historical places and events, culture-specific items, occupational instruments, different kinds of dress and dress materials, domestic articles, gods and goddesses, rituals, festivals, and names of religion-related items which do not have equivalents in Odia. So they have been borrowed into Odia, sometimes directly and sometimes with phonological adjustments. In fact, whenever we could not find an equivalent in Odia for a Hindi item in spite of all our efforts, we resorted to borrowing. Consider the following example:

Example 1

ID: 20073, CAT: NOUN
SL: Hindi
CONCEPT:
ek peR se pra:pt gahare la:l raMg ka: gol phal
one tree from obtained deep red colour of round fruit
EXAMPLE:
shi:la: a:lu:bukha:ra: kha: rahi:hai
Sheela alubukhara eating is
SYNSET:
a:lu:bukha:ra:
alubukhara

SL: Odia
CONCEPT:
goTie gacharupra:pta ga:Rh na:li rangara gol phaLa
one tree from obtained deep red colour of round fruit
EXAMPLE:
shi:la: a:Lubakhara: kha:uchi
Sheela alubukhara is eating
SYNSET:
a:Lubakhara:, a:Lubukha:ra:, a:Lubokha:ra:
alubakhara alubukhara alubokhara

In this example, the SL synset *a:lu:bukha:ra:* does not have an equivalent in Odia. Actually, *a:Lubakhara:* is 'a kind of plum that has acid taste'. It is not grown within the geographical location of Odisha, and so there is no equivalent for it in Odia. In this situation, the Hindi word has been borrowed and naturalized as *a:Lubakhara:, a:Lubukha:ra:,* and *a:Lubokha:ra:* in Odia.

A number of synsets in Hindi refer to a variety of animals, birds, trees, and some mythological characters from the *pura:Nas*. When such words do not have equivalents in Odia, they have been borrowed with certain adjustments. Let us take an example:

Example 2

ID: 26503, CAT: NOUN
SL: Hindi
CONCEPT:

iMDoneshiya:	*meM*	*pa:i:*	*ja:neva:li:*	*ek*	*praka:r ki:*	*bhEMs*	
Indonesia	in	being	found	one	type	of	buffalo

EXAMPLE:

su:ba:	*acha:*	*du:dh*	*deti: hai*
suba	good	milk	gives

SYNSET:

सूबा,	सूबा	भैंस
su:ba:,	*su:ba:*	*bhEMs*
suba,	suba-buffalo	

TL: Odia
CONCEPT:

iNDonesia:re	*miLuthiba:*	*eka*	*praka:ramaiMsi*	
Indonesia in	being found	one	type	buffalo

EXAMPLE:

suba:maiMsi	*bhala*	*khi:ra*	*die*
suba buffalo	good	milk	gives

SYNSET:
suba:maiMsi
suba buffalo

In this example, the SL synset *su:ba:* refers to *iMDoneshiya: meM pa:i: ja:neva:li: ek praka:r ki: bhEMs* which means ‘a particular type of buffalo found in Indonesia’. This type of buffalo is not found in India, and it is highly unlikely that it will be understood in the same context by the Odia speakers. It is the fact that, in Odia, the word *su:ba:* also means ‘a former province’. In order to overcome this problem, the synset *suba:* has been borrowed with the word *maiMsi* for ‘buffalo’ added to it, and the TL synset is *suba:maiMsi* so that the users can decode the synset easily.

10.6 Wrong Categorization of Synsets

All the synsets in Hindi WordNet have been created according to their lexical categories, but some of them are found to be in wrong grammatical category. However, while dealing with this problem, the categories of these incorrectly categorized synsets have not been changed. Attempts have been made to provide TL synsets on the basis of the SL concepts while keeping the categories intact. Let us discuss the following example:

Example 1

ID: 1105,CAT: ADJECTIVE
SL: Hindi
CONCEPT:

jo	*karneva:la:*	*ho*
whoever	doer	is

EXAMPLE:

bhagva:n	*hi:*	*sab*	*ka:moM*	*ke*	*karta:*	*haiM,*	*ham*	*to*	*nimitt*	*ma:tr*	*haiM*
God	only	all	works	of	doer	are	we	only	medium	mere	are

SYNSET:
kartta:, karta:, karta:r, karanha:r, karaNha:r
doer

TL: Odia
CONCEPT:
kariba:ba:la:
doing person
EXAMPLE:

bhagaba:n	*hiM*	*sabu*	*ka:marakartta:,*	*a:me*	*ta*	*nimitta*	*ma:tra*
God	only	all	works of doer,	we	only	medium	mere

SYNSET:
kartta:, prabhu, ma:lika
doer

In this example, the Hindi synset *kartta:* has been categorized as an adjective. But synset refers to *jo karneva:la: ho* which means 'a person who does something' or in other words 'a doer', and thus, it is a 'noun'. When we see the usage of the synset, the example sentence also shows that the word has been used as a noun because the phrase *sab ka:moM ke kartta:* means 'doer of all works' is in genitive case and its object must be a noun, and the same can occur in Hindi. This confirms that the synset belongs to noun category. However, the Odia synset retains the word *kartta:* and new synonyms such as *prabhu* and *ma:lika* have been added to it, and all these words mean 'doer', the same as the SL synset. We can observe another example here:

Example 2

ID: 10870, CAT: ADVERB
SL: Hindi
CONCEPT:
a:ge ya: sa:mne
ahead or in front
EXAMPLE:
unhoMne kha:ne ki: kuch ci:jeM pesh ki:M
they eating of some things presentationdid
SYNSET:
pesh, ha:zir, ja:jir
presentation

TL: Odia
CONCEPT:
a:gare ba: sammukhare
ahead or in front
EXAMPLE:
sema:ne a:ma sa:mna:re kichi kha:dyadrabya paribeShaNa kale
they our in front some eatables served did
SYNSET:
sa:mna:re
in front

In the above example, we find that the SL synset *pesh*, *ha:zir*, and *ha:jir* are in the category of adverb. This words refer to the concept *a:ge ya: sa:mne* ‘ahead or in front’. Here, there is no problem with the SL concept as the meaning of the words and the category match each other, but from the usage in the example sentence, it is clear that the synset *pesh* is not an adverb. The Hindi words like *pesh* and *ha:zir/ha:jir* have been categorised as indeclinables and adjectives respectively; and never as adverbs. Since we have not changed the category of the synsets, and we have created the synsets according to the concepts, the TL synset has been made as *sa:mna:re* ‘in front’ which is in the adverb category, and thus, the TL synset matches the concept unlike the SL synset.

There are also some other Hindi words which have been categorized wrongly. The word (ID No: 1648) *riNprada:ta:* has been categorized as an adjective. In fact, it means ‘a person who lends money’ or ‘a money lender’, and it is quite natural that it falls in the category of ‘noun’. Sometimes nouns may be used as adjectives according to their usage. But here, the usage shows that the word is a noun which is a common name for a person who lends money. Despite this, the Odia synset retains the same word *ruNada:ta:* as an adjective. The reason behind this is that the team’s decision was not to change the category in any case and also that the nouns in Odia can be used as adjectives without any morphological changes.

10.7 Concepts with Inadequate Description

Generally, the synsets are created following the information given in the concepts. So the concepts are expected to give a detailed description of the synsets. But some Hindi synsets do not provide sufficient information in the concepts, and for this reason, it has been very difficult while dealing with such synsets during the creation of equivalents in Odia. Let us take an example:

Example 1

ID: 23390, CAT: NOUN
SL: Hindi
CONCEPT:
ek praka:r ka: phul
one type of flower
EXAMPLE:
guldaste me:M raMg-biraMgi: liliya:M saji: hai
the bouquet in colourful lilies decorated are being
SYNSET:
lili
lily

TL: Odia
CONCEPT:
eka praka:raphula
one type flower
EXAMPLE:
phulatoRa:Ti ran'gaberan'ga lilire sajjita hoichi
bouquet the colourful lily in decorated being is
SYNSET:
lili
lily

In the above example, the SL concept *ek praka:r ka: phu:l* refers to 'a kind of flower'. There are innumerable kinds of flowers found in the world, and it is not clear which particular flower the concept talks about and the concept is not a proper description of the flower named *lili*. It would have been much better, if the concept had described the colour, shape, size of this flower as well as the kind of plant that bears it. However, the concept in Odia has been retained as *eka praka:ra phula* like the SL concept because the aim of the team was not to change the concept but to create synsets on the basis of the SL concepts. We can see another example below:

Example 2

ID: 20919, CAT: NOUN
SL: Hindi
CONCEPT:
ek *dvi:p*
one island
EXAMPLE:
sha:lmali: ka: varNan pura:No meM milta: hei
Shalmali of mention puranas in found is
SYNSET:
sha:lmali:
Shalmali

TL: Odia
CONCEPT:
Eka dvi:pa
one island
EXAMPLE:
sha:lmali:ra barNana: pura:Nre miLe
Shalmali of mention puranas in is found
SYNSET:
sha:lmali:
Shalmali

In this example, the SL concept *ek dvi:p* 'an island' talks about any island found on earth, and it does not give any particular information about the island *sha:lmli:*. So the concept here does not specify the synset. A more appropriate concept would have given the information about the island including its geographical location and other identifying features which would have helped the reader to find a connection between the synset and the concept. Here also, the Odia concept retains it as *eka dvi:pa* the same as it is found in the Hindi concept.

There are a number of such examples, where the concepts have been rendered in Odia as they are in Hindi. In some cases, words have been added to the synsets for a better comprehension. For example, in ID No: 27401, the TL synset 'Snow' has been made 'Charles Percy Snow' in Odia because the word 'Snow' may create confusion as it also refers to 'frozen water vapour falling from sky'.

10.8 Mismatch Between Concepts and Synsets

There are some synsets in Hindi where the relation among the concept, example, and synset is found mismatching, and sometimes they also convey ambiguous meanings. This creates difficulty while making synsets. Let us discuss an example in this regard:

Example 1

ID: 7198, CAT: NOUN
SL: Hindi
CONCEPT:
patr a:di likhne ke lie visheSh ru:p se kaTe hue ya: bane hue ka:Gaz
letter etc. writing for special type from being cut or being made paper
EXAMPLE:
yaha:M har praka:r ki: lekhan-sa:magri: uplabdh heiM
here every type of writing materials available are
SYNSET:
lekhan-sa:magri:, lekhan sa:magri:, lipisajja:, sTeshnari:
writing materials, stationery

TL: Odia
CONCEPT:
ciThipatra a:di lekhiba:pa:iM bisheShabha:bare prastuta hoithiba: ka:gaja
letters etc. writing for in a special way being prepared paper
EXAMPLE:
eTha:re sabu praka:ra lekhana sa:magri: miLe
here all type writing materials are available
SYNSET:
lekhana sa:magri:, ShTesna:ri:
writing materials, stationery

In this example, we find that there is no relation between the SL concept and the SL synset because the concept is *patr a:di likhne ke liye visheSh ru:p se kaTe hue ya: bane hue ka:Gaz*, i.e. 'a kind of paper cut or made in a special way for writing letters, etc.', which means a 'letter card'. On the other hand, the SL synset *lekhan-sa:magri:* means 'writing and other office materials', which generally includes a number of common stationery items such as pen, pencil, paper, envelopes. Thus, there is a clear mismatch between the concept and the synset. We can see another example here:

Example 2

ID: 34533, CAT: NOUN
SL: Hindi
CONCEPT:
lekar *ja:na:*
having taken going
EXAMPLE:
itna: *sa:ma:n uTha:kar* *le* *ja:na:* *mujhe* *bha:ri:* *paR raha: ha/*
this much goods having lifted take going me heavy falling is/
a:p *inheM* *bhi:* *apne* *sa:th* *le ja:eM*
you them too own with take
SYNSET:
le *ja:na:*
take going

TL: Odia
CONCEPT:
kichi *nelapare* *jiba:*
something taken after going
EXAMPLE:
eteguRie *jinisa* *neikari* *jiba:* *mopa:iM* *kasTakara*
this much goods having taken going me for difficult
SYNSET:
neikari jiba:, *neiki* *jiba:*
having taken going

In the above example, the SL synset *le ja:na:* refers to the concept *lekar ja:na:*. In fact, the meaning of both the synset and the concept is different. The synset *le ja:na:* is primarily a compound verb, and the concept *lekar ja:na:* is a conjunctive participle, but both can be used as a 'verbal noun', and here, we find that the synset has been categorized as noun. The compound verb *le ja:na:* consists of two verbs, where the first verb *le* means 'to take', and the second verb *ja:na:* means 'to go', and the compound verb conveys the meaning of only the first verb *le,* and the second verb *ja:na:* remains silent. So the synset gives the meaning 'to take away'. On the other hand, the concept *lekar ja:na:* being a conjunctive participle, the meaning is expressed from both the verbs *lekar* 'taking' and *ja:na:* 'going', and thus, the verb means 'to go away after taking something'. If, for better comprehension, we examine the verb *le ja:na:* 'to take away' along with other compound verbs such as *a: ja:na:* 'to come', *kha: ja:na:* 'to eat', we find that these do not give similar meaning as the verbs *lekar ja:na:* 'to go away after taking something', *a:kar ja:na:*, 'to go away after coming' and *kha:kar ja:na:* 'to go away after eating'. So the abovementioned concept and the synset do not match with each other. Considering these, the TL concept has been made as *kichi nelapare jiba:* 'to go away after taking something', and the SL synset has been made as *neikari jiba:* and *neiki jiba:* both conjunctive participles which keep the meaning close to the concept. The other important point to be mentioned here is that the SL synset has been used in the example as a verb, i.e. *le ja:eM* which is the present tense of the compound verb *le ja:na:*. Since the category of the synset is stated to be a noun, the second example sentence in Hindi has been dropped in Odia.

10.9 Imprecise Concepts

There are certain concepts which do not convey a clear and precise meaning. It was difficult to understand such concepts, as a result of which creating equivalents in Odia was difficult. Here, we can discuss the following example:

Example 1

ID: 195, CAT: ADJECTIVE
SL: Hindi
CONCEPT:
sa:mneva:le ka:
front person of
EXAMPLE:
tumha:ra: ghar bhi: bahut pya:ra: hai
your house also much loving is
SYNSET:
tumha:ra:, tera:
your

TL: Odia
CONCEPT:
sa:mana: lokara
of front person
EXAMPLE:
tuma ghara bahuta sundara
your house much beautiful
SYNSET:
tuma, tama, tumara, tamara, to, tora, a:paNanka, a:paNankara
your

In the above example, the SL concept is *sa:mneva:le ka:* 'of the person present in the front', and the SL synset consists of *tumha:ra:* and *tera:* both second person pronouns used here in adjective category. Generally, the pronoun *tumha:ra:* 'your' is used for both semi-honorific singular number and non-honorific plural number, and the pronoun *tera:* 'your' is used in non-honorific singular number in Hindi. In this example, the concept does not limit the meaning of the synset because it may also refer to a person or persons present in front, for whom third-person possessive pronominal form can be used, such as *is ka:, us ka:, is ki:,* and *us ki:* in non-honorific singular number and *in ka:, un ka:, in ki:,* and *un ki:* in both honorific singular number and non-honorific plural number. Again, the pronouns *a:p ka:* and *a:p ki:* 'your', for masculine and feminine gender, respectively, are used for honorific singular and non-honorific plural number, and they have the same possessive function. Considering all these, we can say that it would have been more precise if the concept had been made as *sa:mne upasthit aur sambodhit honeva:le vyakti ka:* 'of the person present in the front and being addressed to', and this concept will express the intended meaning more faithfully than the existing one. However, the concept remains unchanged in Odia, and in order to provide equivalents, the Odia synset has been made as *tuma, tama, tumara, tamara, to, tora, a:paNanka, a:paNankara where tuma, tama, tumara, tamara* are used for both semi-honorific singular number and non-honorific plural number; *to* and *tora* for non-honorific singular number; and *a:paNanka* and *a:paNankara* for honorific singular number and non-honorific plural number pronouns.

Example 2

ID: 2658, CAT: ADJECTIVE
SL: Hindi
CONCEPT:
jiska: shari:r choTa: ho
Whose body small becomes
EXAMPLE:
mujhe nanhe-munne bacce ache lagte heiM
to me small sized children fond of are
SYNSET:
nanha-munna, nanha munna, nanha, nanhaM, laghuka:y
small sized

TL: Odia
CONCEPT:
Ja:ha:ra shari:ra choTa
whose body small
EXAMPLE:
mote kuni pila:ma:ne bhala la:ganti
to me small children fond of
SYNSET:
kuni, sa:na, choTa, Tiki, kaTi
small

The SL concept *jiska: shari:r choTa: ho* means 'anyone whose body is small', whereas the SL synset is *nanha-munna* 'of small size' which is used especially for a human child. The synset does not match with the concept in this example because the concept indicates a broader meaning, and it can be applicable to any living or non-living being. On the other hand, the term *nanha:-munna:* is only used to indicate any human child, not any other living or non-living being. However, in Odia, the synset has been made as *kuni, sa:na, choTa, Tiki, kaTi* all of which indicate both living and non-living being, and thus, they match the concept.

10.10 Conclusion

The present paper has dealt with the problems encountered while creating synsets in Odia based on the Hindi WordNet. In order to create Odia synsets, the procedures of new expressions and borrowing have been used widely. The procedure of new expression has been used mostly to resolve the problems of synsets dealing with different kinds of wage and kinship relations. The other important issues discussed in this paper are wrong categorization of synsets, concepts with inadequate description, mismatch between concepts and synsets, imprecise concepts in Hindi with suggestions as to how to improve these in future.

Acknowledgments The authors are thankful to Dr. Smita Mohanty, Dr. H.K. Patra, Ms. Gouri Sahoo, and Dr. R.R. Mohapatra for their help during the preparation of various drafts of this paper.

References

Jakobson, R. (1971). On linguistic aspects of translation. *Selected writings* (Vol. 2, pp. 232–239). The Hague: Mouton.
Miller, G. A., Beckwith, R., Fellbaum, C., Gross, D., & Miller, K. (1990). Introduction to WordNet: An on-line lexical database. *International Journal of Lexicography, 3*(4), 235–244.
Nida, E. A. (1964). Linguistics and ethnology in translation problems. In: D. Hymes (Ed.), *Language in culture and society* (pp. 90–100). Bombay: Allied Publishers Private Ltd. (Indian reprint).
Sapir, E. (1949). *Culture, language and personality: Selected essays*. In: D. G. Mandelbaum (Ed.) Berkeley: University of California Press.

Chapter 11
Building Telugu WordNet Using Expansion Approach

S. Arulmozi and M.C. Kesava Murty

Abstract WordNet building activities in Dravidian languages started with the work of Tamil WordNet (Project partially funded by Tamil Virtual University.) at AU-KBC Research Centre utilizing Rajendran's (2001) ontological classification of Tamil vocabulary. The first phase of the work on Dravidian WordNet (comprising WordNets in four major Dravidian languages, viz., Kannada, Malayalam, Tamil, and Telugu) was initiated with funding from Ministry of HRD, Government of India, and the work was carried out for Kannada at University of Hyderabad, Malayalam at Amrita Vishwa Vidyapeetham, Tamil at Tamil University, and Telugu at Dravidian University. Currently, the second phase of the Dravidian WordNet (with funding from DeitY, Government of India) is being carried out at Dravidian University (Telugu), Amrita Vishwa Vidyapeetham (Malayalam), Tamil University (Tamil), and University of Mysore (Kannada). In this paper, we describe the construction of synsets for Telugu language. Based on the Hindi WordNet synsets, we developed synsets (synonym sets) in Telugu using the expansion approach. This chapter is organized as follows: Sect. 11.2 gives a brief account on the morphological features of Telugu language. This section also provides the language technology activities pertaining to Telugu language. Section 11.3 details the Telugu synset building activity, challenges/problems faced during the construction of synsets in general, and construction of synsets pertaining to kinship and address terms in particular. The last section summarizes the work.

S. Arulmozi (✉)
Centre for Applied Linguistics and Translation Studies,
University of Hyderabad, Hyderabad 500046, Telangana, India
e-mail: arulmozi@uohyd.ac.in

M.C. Kesava Murty
Dravidian University, Kuppam, India
e-mail: kesavamurty.mc@gmail.com

N.S. Dash et al. (eds.), *The WordNet in Indian Languages*,
DOI 10.1007/978-981-10-1909-8_11

Keywords Ontological classification · Dravidian WordNet · Synsets · Expansion approach · Kinship terms · Address terms · Statistical account · Web interface

11.1 The Telugu Language

Telugu belongs to the South Central Dravidian subgroup of the Dravidian family of languages (Krishnamurti 2003). It has recorded history from sixth century A.D. and literary history dating back to eleventh century A.D. Telugu language was awarded the Classical Status in 2008 by the Indian government. It is the second most spoken language after Hindi in India. Telugu has been the language of choice for lyrical compositions for its vowel ending words, rightly called the 'Italian of the East.'

The vocabulary of Telugu is highly Sanskritized in addition to the Persian-Arabic borrowings /kaburu/'news,' 'information,' /javābu/'answer'; Urdu / tarāju/'balance.' It does have cognates in other Dravidian languages such as / puli/'tiger,' /ūru/'village'; /tala/'head' (these cognates are available in Tamil and Malayalam).

Words in Dravidian languages, especially in Telugu, are long and complex; i.e., because of its suffixation, words are build up from many affixes that combine with one another. Telugu, like other Dravidian languages, is highly rich in morphology and hence agglutinative in nature; it also allows polyagglutination.

Telugu has the state-of-the-art Morphological Analyzer[1] and Telugu–Hindi, Hindi–Telugu, Telugu–Tamil, and Tamil–Telugu MT systems.[2] In addition to this, the Resource Centre for Indian Language Technology Solutions-Telugu (RCILTS) established by the Ministry of Communications and IT, Govt. of India, during 2000–2003 has developed several products, services, and knowledge bases pertaining to Telugu language. They include Drishti, the first comprehensive OCR system in Telugu, Tel-Spell, Spell checker for Telugu, Telugu Corpus (9.2 m words),[3] etc. This effort on building a WordNet for Telugu is the first of its kind along the lines of Hindi WordNet.

[1]Developed by G. Uma Maheswar Rao at the Centre for ALTS, University of Hyderabad.

[2]Consortia on Indian-Language-Indian Language MT systems established by MCIT, GoI.

[3]Achievements of RCILTS-Telugu, TDIL.

11.2 Construction of Telugu WordNet

For the construction of WordNet, there are two basic approaches, viz., merger approach and expansion approach (Vossen 1998). With regard to the Indian languages, the expansion approach is the most followed method. Similarly, in the construction of Telugu WordNet, we also follow the expansion approach; i.e., Hindi WordNet synsets are taken as a starting point of departure. The concepts provided along with the Hindi synsets are first conceived and appropriate concepts in Telugu are manually provided by language experts. The Telugu synsets are then built based on the concepts created keeping in view the three principles, viz., Minimality, Coverage, and Replaceability (Bhattacharya 2010).

11.2.1 Categorization of Synsets

(A) Initially, synsets in Hindi were categorized into two broad categories: (i) core synsets and (ii) common synsets. Subsequently, WordNets (particularly synset creation) in Indian languages were developed based on this categorization. Core synsets comprised of vocabulary from day-to-day communication, whereas common synsets consisted of vocabulary which is common across major Indian languages. These synsets were created using an offline tool (standalone interface) in most of the Modern Indian languages including Telugu.

(B) Since the core and common synset categorization had some discrepancies and based on the inputs from all synset developers in Indian languages, a six-way categorization of synsets was created in 2010. The six-way categorization is given below:

  (i) *Universal synset:* synsets which have an indigenous lexeme in all the languages of the world (e.g., sun and earth)
  (ii) *Pan-Indian synset:* synsets which have indigenous lexeme in all the Indian languages but no English correspondence (e.g., paapad).
  (iii) *In-family synset:* synsets which have indigenous lexeme in the particular language family (e.g., bava/bavamariti distinction in Dravidian family of languages).
  (iv) *Language-specific synset:* synsets which are unique to a language (e.g., bihu in Assamese, puutareekulu in Telugu).
  (v) *Rare synset:* synsets which express technical terms (e.g., ngram).
  (vi) *Synthesized synset:* synsets created in the language due to influence of another language (e.g., pizza).

(C) Even though the six-way categorization had solved most of the discrepancies, still it had problems in linking synsets across Indian languages, and hence, it was decided to come up with a two-way categorization by the end of 2010 as follows:

 (i) *Universal synsets:* synsets which have an indigenous lexeme in all the major Indian languages as well as English.
 (ii) *Indian synsets:* synsets which have an indigenous lexeme in all the major Indian languages but do not have a correspondence in English.

 So, the creation of synsets in Telugu had taken a long stride (be it core or common categorization, or six-way categorization, or Universal and Indian synsets). As briefed above, for the building of Telugu synsets, we used the Offline Tool provided along with Hindi WordNet synsets. This standalone interface allows users to view the Hindi synsets, concepts, example sentence on the one side and simultaneously keying the target language (Telugu in our case) synsets, concepts, and example sentence. The tool also has the Princeton WordNet English synsets interlinked. This helps the language experts to cross-check with English WordNet synsets. Below we present the challenges/problems faced in the construction of synsets from Hindi into Telugu.

11.2.2 Expansion from Hindi into Telugu

During the construction of Telugu synsets, we have encountered certain issues, while rendering corresponding synsets and concepts in Telugu. The problems are of different sorts, viz., in connection with rendering equivalents, especially translational equivalents from Hindi into Telugu; change of parts-of-speech category while creating synsets; lexical gaps; cross-linkages in synset relations; and language-specific synsets.

11.2.2.1 Lexicographical Concerns

As mentioned earlier, Hindi concepts are first conceived and appropriate concepts are provided along with synsets in target languages. But during this process, problems occurred when we are faced with concepts that have no appropriate equivalents. For example,

1. HWN ID: 7531
Concept: /cAIlsa sera kI eka taula/which means 'a measure of 40 kg'.

For this concept, there is no corresponding equivalent in Telugu. This is because there are different usages in different dialects of Andhra Pradesh and Telangana.

For example, in Rayalaseema dialect which is spoken Kuppam, the measure is equal to 10 kg, whereas in Kadapa (which also is a part of Rayalaseema dialect) it is 14 kg. So there are no standard usages even within same dialect. But if one has to populate the synsets (to justify coverage principle), then one has to keep all dialectal variations as synonyms of a particular lexical item. In this case, in Telugu WordNet, we have provided equivalent as */manu/* keeping aside what it means as a measure in Telugu.

2. HWN ID 24:
Concept: /mAdA Sera/ which means 'a female tiger'

For the above concept, there is no problem in assigning equivalent concepts and synsets, but when it comes to providing equivalent sentences (which we mostly translate for developing parallel corpora), we come across difficulty. In most cases, we do not use gender while providing translations. This is not the case with this concept alone, but in all the concepts involving gender. For example, there are concepts such as female rat (HWN ID 335) and female parrot (HWN ID 1278). These are problematic synsets because there is no such distinction straightaway available in Telugu rather one has to forcefully use equivalent denoting female.

11.2.2.2 Kinship in Telugu WordNet

When we come to WordNet building activities in Indian languages, Hindi WordNet which is the pioneer is taken as the source language for building WordNets. As discussed earlier, Hindi WordNet's concepts are taken as a starting point and WordNets are getting built using the expansion approach. In the outset, this approach looks trivial and economical considering the interlinking of synsets of different languages. But when it comes to kinship relations, however, Hindi concepts create problems while assigning synsets in Dravidian languages, especially in Telugu. Let us examine a few in the following pages.

In all, there are 54 concepts in Hindi WordNet which involve kinship relations. For the purpose of this discussion, only the problematic concepts are taken into consideration which needs special attention.

1. HWN ID 7379:
Concept: /bhai ka ladka/ which means 'brother's son'

When it comes to Telugu, providing concept is a problem. Straightforward, one can assign /sōdaruni koḍuku/. But when assigning synsets, one comes across ambiguity in the concept, i.e., whose (male/female) brother's (younger/elder) son.

2. HWN ID 1804.
Concept: /bhai ki ladkhi/ which means 'brother's daughter'

This is similar to the one given in 1 above; whether one has to provide /anna kūturu/ or /tammudu kūturu/or both.

3. HWN ID 683:
Concept: /māmā ki laDaki/ which means 'uncle's daughter'

The concept in Telugu can be given as /māma kūturu /. But, when it comes to providing synsets, one faces the problem in elder–younger distinction. In the case of Telugu, if it is elder daughter then it is /vodhina/ and younger is /maradalu/.

4. HWN ID 2861:
Concept: /māmā ka laDakā/ which means 'uncle's son'

The concept in Telugu can be given as /māmā kodukku/. But, when it comes to providing synsets, one faces the problem in elder–younger distinction. In the case of Telugu, if it is elder son then it is /bāva/ and younger is /bāvamaridi/.

5. HWN ID 6992:
Concept: /phuphēra/ which means 'father's sister's husband'.

The equivalent in Telugu is: /māma/
Whereas in /phūphī/ in Hindi refers to
Telugu: /mēnatta/'father's sister' in Telugu.

Male referent point of view

Hindi /phupherā bhāi/can be translated into Telugu as /mēnatta koḍuku/'father's sister's son' but this can be used only as address term.

/bāva/If he is elder—as address and reference terms
/bāvamaridi/If he is younger—as address and reference term
/bāmmardi/If he is younger—as address and reference term

Female referent point of view

/mēnatta kūturu/'fathers's sister's daughter'
/vadina/'father's sister's elder daughter'—This is address and reference term
/maradalu/'father's sister's younger daughter'—This is only a reference term.

Kinship terms denote some definite relations and are culture specific. So these are very difficult to translate from one language to another. Kinship relations in Hindi like /bhatija/'brother's son' could not be linked directly in Dravidian languages and particularly in Telugu since there are many terms available which can be attributed to denote this concept, depending on gender of the speaker and whether the referent or speaker is elder or younger to him.

6. HWN ID 7011:

Hindi: /mamērā/is 'related to mother's brother.'
/mamērā bhāi/, i.e., 'mother's brother's son'
Telugu: /mēnamāma koḍuku/
/bāvamaridi/- If he is younger—as address and reference term (or)
/bāmmardi/- If he is younger—as address and reference term

7. HWN ID: 7028

Kinship relations in Hindi such as /bhatīja/'brother's son' could not be linked directly in Telugu since they are multiple terms available which denote this concept, depending on gender of the speaker and whether the referent or speaker is elder or younger to him.

For this Hindi concept, there is no straightforward equivalent in Telugu, but there exists different terms for this concept, a couple of which are mentioned below:

Male point of view

/tammuḍi koḍuku/'younger brother's son'
/chōṭe bhāi kā bēṭā/

/anna koḍuku/'elder brother's son'
/badē bhāi kā bēṭā/
Both cases can be equal to the Telugu equivalent usage /koḍuku/only as reference term. It is not used as an address term.

Female point of view

/tammuḍi koḍuku/'younger brother's son'
/chōṭe bhāi kā bēṭā/

/anna koḍuku/'elder brother's son'
/badē bhāi kā bēṭā/

Both cases can be equal to the Telugu equivalent usage /alluḍu/as address and reference term.

In the above examples, only few of the problems faced while constructing synsets in Telugu using Hindi concepts are presented. The reason for this is twofold; viz., first, Hindi concepts are built based on most commonly used words, so one can see how shallow the synsets are and secondly, it is a problem of two different language families in the expansion approach. In Trauttman (1995) words, one needs a hierarchy of constructs, the genetic constructs—Dravidian and Indo-Aryan—and the synthesizing construct of Indian kinship to distinguish the Dravidian data from the non-Dravidian.

11.3 Conslusion

While WordNets are being developed for almost all the major Indian languages, one should give special attention while constructing synsets which is the core of WordNet. As seen from the examples above, it exemplifies that constructing WordNet based on Indo-Aryan languages into Telugu (as well as in Dravidian languages) is not a trivial task. It is also clear that kinship relation in Hindi WordNet is shallow, and hence, one has to take into account different culture-specific constructs into consideration. This brings us to some interesting challenges in the construction of WordNets: How to integrate language-independent constructs in IndoWordNet? How to handle problems such as male–female distinction in IndoWordNet and vice versa? Elder–younger, distinction which is prominent is Telugu? How to represent kinship hierarchy in WordNet? The only solution at this point of time is to look into Domain Ontology within the framework of WordNet Domains.

Acknowledgments The work on Telugu WordNet activity is a part of the larger effort on building a Dravidian WordNet and the work has been sponsored by the Ministry of Human Resource Development, Government of India (during the I Phase) and DeitY, Ministry of Communications and Information Technology, Government of India (II Phase).

References

Bhattacharya, P. (2010). 'IndoWordNet', In *Proceedings of Lexical Resources Engineering Conference (LREC 2010),* Malta.

Brown, C. P. (1857). *A grammar of the Telugu language*. Madras: Christian Knowledge Society's Press.

Burrow, T., & Emeneau, M. B. (1984). *Dravidian etymological dictionary*. New Delhi: Munshiram Manoharlal Publishers.

Cruse, D. A. (1986). *Lexical semantics*. Cambridge: Cambridge University Press.

Fellbaum, C. (Ed.). (1998). *WordNet: An electronic lexical database*. Cambridge, MA: MIT Press.

Krishnamurti, Bh. (1961). *Telugu verbal bases*. Berkeley: University of Chicago Press.

Krishnamurti, Bh. (2003). *The Dravidian languages*. Cambridge: Cambridge University Press.

Krishnamurti, Bh, & Gwynn, J. P. L. (1985). *A Grammar of Modern Telugu*. New Delhi: Oxford University Press.

Miller, G. A. (1995). WordNet: A lexical database for english. *Communications of the ACM, 38*(11).

Narayan, D., Chakrabarty D., Pandey P., & Bhattacharyya, P. (2002). An experience in building the Indo WordNet—a WordNet for Hindi. In *International Conference on Global WordNet*, Mysore.

Rajendran, S. (2001). *taRkaalat tamizhc coRkaLanjciyam [Modern Tamil Thesaurus]*. Thanjavur: Tamil University Publication.

Trauttmann, T. R. (1995). *Dravidian kinship*. New Delhi: Vistaar Publication.

Vossen, P. (1998). *EuroWordNet: A multilingual database with lexical semantic networks*. Dordrecht: Kluwer Academic Publishers.

Chapter 12
Challenges, Problems, and Issues Faced in Language-Specific Synset Creation and Linkage in the Kashmiri WordNet

Aadil Amin Kak, Farooq Ahmad, Nazima Mehdi, Mansoor Farooq and Muneera Hakim

Abstract The first half of the present paper highlights some of the issues that are faced while creating language-specific synsets in Kashmiri. It also discusses the necessity of the standards and guidelines for group work. It thoroughly describes some of the issues of untranslatability and transliteration. It focuses on the need of field work while creating language-specific synsets in the language. The second half of the paper discusses the problems faced while linking synsets with the Hindi WordNet. It gives some description regarding the areas where problems are faced which include domains such as concept creation, example translation, maintenance of category, and English–Hindi linking.

Keywords WordNet · Kashmiri · Synsets untranslatability · Transliteration concepts translation · Linking

12.1 Introduction

A standard is an agreed, repeatable way of doing something or considered by an authority or by general consents a basis of comparison: an approved model or a universally or widely accepted, agreed upon, or established means of determining what something should be. It contains a technical specification or other precise criteria designed to be used consistently as a rule, guideline, or definition. To increase the reliability and the effectiveness of group work, a set of common standards is needed. Standards are created by bringing together the experiences and expertise of all interested parties such as the regulators and the different language groups in our case.

A.A. Kak (✉) · F. Ahmad · N. Mehdi · M. Farooq · M. Hakim
Department of Linguistics, University of Kashmir, Srinagar, India
e-mail: aadil.kak@gmail.com; aadilaminkak@yahoo.com

N.S. Dash et al. (eds.), *The WordNet in Indian Languages*,
DOI 10.1007/978-981-10-1909-8_12

During the ongoing work of creation of language-specific synsets, a need is felt for common standards/guidelines. Different language groups are working on different languages which represent or contain within them different cultural backgrounds, different tastes, different likings, etc, and it is obvious that these factors will bring along different outlook and different priorities during the process of synset creation. One language group will give priority to one aspect and another language group to other aspect. Thus, in order to create a uniform system of working, there is a need to build common and explicit set of collectively created standards/guidelines. Overall, a need has been felt for building explicit standards/guidelines in the following aspects for synset creation.

12.2 Definition of Language-Specific Synset (LSS)

Regarding the question of language-specific synsets (LSSs), the basic concept of Language specificity is vague. The questions which arise are

(a) Does language specific mean that the particular concept is unique to the language or culture in question, and absolutely unavailable in the other languages and cultures of the entire world?
(b) Does language specific mean that the particular concept is unique in a particular group of languages (Indian languages in our case)?

In the case of (a) above, it is physically impossible to claim the uniqueness of a particular concept in such a multilingual and multicultural entity as the whole world. In truth, it will never be possible to verify any language-specific synset from that perspective. However, if (b) above is taken into consideration, especially in the case of a group of languages, then language specificity can be considered and the validity of language-specific synsets can be assured. This can go a long way when we take the present group of languages and compare it with other groups, and we might in a way be able to talk about a broader dimension of language specificity. This appears to be the only viable solution to this issue.

Another related issue which will be considered in this realm is which concepts should be and which concepts should not be included? Consider prominent personalities of a culture or language, and unknown to other cultures and languages. Can they be included? Consider important shrines, temples, mosques, etc., of a culture which are unknown to other culture. Can they be included? This does not stop at the level of personalities and important places but goes on to include a number of other concepts. However, their inclusion is fraught with a number of problems. One of the main problems is that if all such cultural items are included, then the list will start including somewhat less prominent items, lesser known items, and selectively known items, and finally, it will start including almost everything. This will make the whole exercise childish and unprofessional. If these and similar items are to be included, then the best way would be to issue a set of standards which will enable one to understand what to include and what not to include.

12.2.1 Types, Subtypes, and Derivations

One more problem which we are facing is that of types and subtypes, part–whole relation terms, etc. The basic issue here is that some concepts, though subtypes of other concepts, have an innate 'strength' in themselves which makes one to put these 'subtypes of concepts' as an individual concept. This can be understood by looking at the concept of 'animal' and the concepts of *dog, horse, ape,* etc. And when we move further down, we have the concept of 'ape' and its subtypes *orangutan, gorilla, chimpanzee, and bonobo*. Should these be included as subtypes or as types?

Another related aspect is regarding the handling of other similar issues. Consider the example given below (Table 12.1). The word *kəli:nnakhshɨ* is a term which literally means 'design of a carpet'. The other terms are the types of carpet designs, which in themselves are important terms as well. This can be somewhat compared to the concept of 'painting' and the concepts of *impressionism, cubism, gestural abstraction, expressionism, pop art*, and so on. And, from the perspective of LSS, what should be done? One important thing which should be considered here is that though these terms may look like parts of the larger term but from a local perspective, these 'types' terms may have a standing of their own.

From the perspective of a local, these types have an identity of their own, so should they be considered as individual entities or subtypes of a larger entity.

12.2.2 Part–Whole Relation

In a similar fashion, we have examples of part–whole relation as shown below (Table 12.2). The problem is whether to regard all the 'parts' as separate synsets or not.

12.2.3 Problem of Derivatives

One more problem is that of derivatives. Consider some more examples from Kashmiri (Table 12.3). It is not clear for us whether both the terms shown in the above example are two separate language-specific synsets or not. That is, there is not any strict criteria on which we can decide this.

Table 12.1 Difference between a cover term and its subtypes

Cover term	Types
kəli:nnakhʃɨ (Carpet design)	khaswunnakhʃɨ, aḍawa:rda:rnakhʃɨ, ḍajiḍa:rnakhʃɨ, tsalwunnakhʃɨ
tsũ:ʈ (apple)	ambur, delshus, dɔd ambur, mahrə:dʒʲ, chamu:ra, and tre l

Table 12.2 The interface of part–whole relation of components

Whole	Parts
kã:gɨr (Kashmiri fire-pot)	kə:n (willow twig of which the whole kangir is made of) kɔnɖul (inner earthenware bowl) tsa:lan (wooden or metallic instrument/spatula to turn the fire, ash or coal within the kangir) ko:p (upper part of the kã:gɨr made of wicker) tsok (bottom part of the kã:gɨr made of wicker) wolut (a strip of willow wrapped spirally around the handles of the kangri) lənɖ (handle of the kangir) nas (bridge between the two handles of the kangir) kan (hoop into which the tsa:lan is tied) khopur (wicker basket woven around the earthenware bowl)

Table 12.3 Problem of derivatives in Kashmiri

Kashmiri	Meaning	Hindi
tʃha:v	The process of cooking rice by putting it on low heat and covering it in the final stage of cooking	Not known
atʃho:v	That rice which has not been prepared following the proper procedure of atʃha:v	Not known
o:m	Raw, not cooked or boiled	Not known
adɨ o:m	Half cooked	Not known

12.2.4 Problem of Cultural Untranslatability

Sometimes, it becomes virtually impossible to convey the meaning of words as they require to be conveyed, where the 'sense' of a particular sentence or document cannot be expressed in the target language. Catford (1965) distinguishes two types of untranslatability: linguistic and cultural. The linguistic untranslatability occurs when there is no equal lexical or syntactic substitute in the target language (TL) for a source language (SL) item.

Catford's category of linguistic untranslatability is rather straightforward. His second category, that is cultural untranslatability, is more problematic. Linguistic untranslatability is caused due to differences in the SL and the TL, whereas cultural untranslatability is caused due to the absence of the particular cultural significance of a linguistic term in the TL for a relevant situational feature. Consider the example from Kashmiri given below:

Kashmiri /tsəndɨr va:ri doh tʃʰu mɔrdɨ sɨdi e:sa:li sava:bɨ khə:trɨ pi:r peva:n la:gɨnʲ/
Hindi /tsəndrivar ke din murda vʲekti ki ʃanti ke lije pɪr bulaje dʒate he/

The problem here is that the reader will have a concept of the term based on his or her cultural context and will apply that particular view accordingly. Insofar

Table 12.4 Lack of adequate linguistic expression in translation

Kashmiri	Hindi
CONCEPT: mɔrdɨ sɨndi marnɨ patɨ gɔɖnitʃ tsəndɨrva:r EXAMPLE: tsəndɨr va:ri doh tʃʰɨ mɔrdɨ sɨndi e:sa:li sava:bɨ khə:trɨ pi:r peva:n la:gɨnʲ SYNSET-KASHMIRI: tsəndɨrva:r	CONCEPT: murde ke mərne ke bad pehlı somvar EXAMPLE: tsəndrɨvar ke din murda vjektı ki ʃantı ke lije pır bulaje dʒate he/ SYNSET-HINDI: tsəndɨrva:r
CONCEPT: khandrʊk akh rasɨm jatʰ mãz mahrenʲ khandrɨ brõnh kẽh doh sran karnay che rozan EXAMPLE: malas behnɨ patɨ cha mahrenʲ prənʲ nera:n SYNSET-KASHMIRI: malas bihʊn	CONCEPT: ʃadi ki wo ek rasam dʒis me dulhan ʃadi ke kuch din pehle nahaye bage:r rehti he EXAMPLE: malas bihʊn ke bad dulhan ka raŋ nikhar a:ta he SYNSET-KASHMIRI: malas bihʊn
CONCEPT: khã:druk akh rasɨm jemi doh sə:ri ə:ʃna:v tɨ hamsa:i rəlith səmith tomul tʃhi tʃhaʈa:n EXAMPLE: kẽh luk tʃhi tomul tʃhaʈnɨkʲ doh w:azɨ ti laga:n SYNSET-KASHMIRI: tomul tshaʈun	CONCEPT: ʃadı kı ek rasam dʒisme səbhi riʃtedar aur paɽosi mil kar ʃadi ke tʃavəl saf kərte he EXAMPLE: kutʃh log tomul tʃhaʈun par wazwan bhi ləgate he SYNSET-HINDI: tomul tshaʈun

as language is the primary modelling system within a culture, cultural untranslatability must be de facto implied in any process of translation. Once again it was Popovič (1970) who has attempted to define untranslatability without making a separation between the linguistic untranslatability and the cultural untranslatability. Popovic, however, distinguishes two types:

(a) A situation in which linguistic elements of the original language cannot be replaced adequately in structural, linear, functional, or semantic terms in consequence of lack of denotation or connotation.
(b) A situation where the relation of expressing the meaning, i.e., the relation between the creative subject and its linguistic expression in the original does not find an adequate linguistic expression in the translation.

In the present work, we face such problems in translating the concept and example from source language Kashmiri to the target language Hindi. Let us consider some of the examples presented below (Table 12.4).

Another issue which raises its head is how Hindi should handle this. In the above examples, the Kashmiri synsets are transliterated into Hindi. However, we look at the examples *tsəndɨrva:r* which literally means 'Monday', and *tomultsʰaʈun* literally means 'to clean rice'. It is, therefore, opined that these culture-specific terms should be transliterated.

12.2.5 Problem of Focus

There are usually two aspects of cultural elements, the structural aspect (which focuses on the structure or the physical aspect) and the functional aspect (which

Table 12.5 Problem of focus for language-specific item

Language-specific item	Function	Structure
samava:r	Used to make tea and *kehwa* Used to keep tea and *kehwa* warm and tasty	Made of copper Bulging at centre with special base and cap Contains a cylindrical fire pot in the centre
kā:gɨr	Used to keep the body warm during winter by taking it inside the *pheran*	It has an earthen pot around which a cage of canes is weaved Has a base and conical top

focuses on the function or use). Ideally, during the process of concept creation, both those aspects need to be given due importance. However, since the length of the concepts needs to be limited, therefore, both the aspects cannot be taken in the concept. In the process of concept creation, one of the aspects gets priority. The question which arises here is should the lexicographer focus on the structural or the functional aspect of a language-specific item. To explain the phenomenon let us illustrate by some examples (Table 12.5).

12.2.6 Problem of Transliteration

There is a basic difference in the sound systems of different languages. Let us consider that Hindi and Kashmiri have similarities as well as differences between the sounds and sound sequences used in these languages. Now, the problem which arises is what should be done in such a situation where Kashmiri synset contains non-Hindi sound/sounds. Some examples are given below (Table 12.6). In this case, the best option is perhaps nativization by naturalization of the sounds.

There is a general lack of resources for LSS especially in the case of Kashmiri. It is not possible for a lexicographer to know each and every LSS, and experience with dictionaries also did not seem very helpful. Therefore, field survey was conducted with good results. So, it might be tentatively proposed that for LSS, targeted field method can be a fruitful option. We have different fields of activities specific to a culture and thereby to the language or language terms associated with that culture. For example, in Kashmir, there is a lot of technical jargon associated with different occupations, e.g. handicrafts. Now assuming a lexicographer to be

Table 12.6 Nativization of sounds naturalization

Kashmiri word with phonetic form	Sound lacking in Hindi
dɔd (milk)	'ɔ'
Shur^{j} (children)	'j'
tsa:s (cough)	'ts'
ə:s	'ə:'

aware of all these terms or a dictionary contain them is absurd. There appears no other option but to do some fieldwork in this direction.

12.3 The Linkage Network

WordNet is a lexical database which groups words into sets of synonyms called 'synsets', provides short general definitions, and records the various semantic relations between these synonym sets. The purpose is twofold: to produce a combination of dictionary and thesaurus that is more intuitively usable and to support automatic text analysis and artificial intelligence applications.

The Indradhanush WordNet, a part of the IndoWordNet, has the basic purpose of developing a concept-based multilingual dictionary for Indian languages. It involves the following three steps:

(a) Concept development,
(b) Providing example/examples of the given concept, and
(c) Inputting a set of synonyms representing that particular concept.

In the given snapshot (Fig. 12.1), all the end products of the three above-mentioned processes are observed. Going into the history of WordNet development in the Indian context, Hindi WordNet was the first and most comprehensive WordNet in Indian languages, and when other languages started getting involved, a general consensus was to take Hindi as the pivot language. However, after working on different languages, it does appear that linking Hindi with other languages from a WordNet perspective does have its share of issues. Some of these are discussed below.

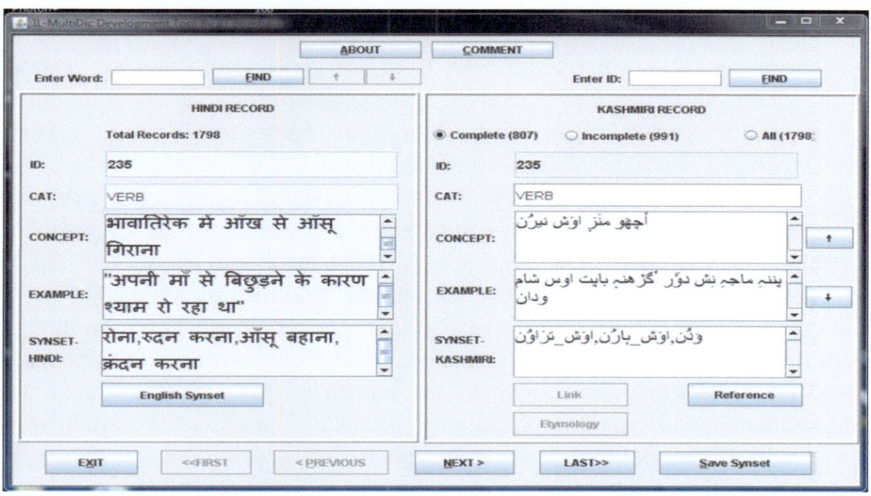

Fig. 12.1 Snapshot showing synset creation

12.4 Problems Faced While Linking

12.4.1 Conceptual Inadequacies

The first and foremost thing which needs to be taken into consideration is the issue of conceptual inadequacy. By conceptual inadequacy, it is meant here that the concepts should not be inadequate, and this is more so true of the pivot language which is Hindi. The expression like *ek prakar ka* 'of one type' seems to be very vague and unprofessional. With concepts of such nature, it becomes difficult to identify what the concept is all about. Instead of giving such a vague description as *ek prakaar ka peeD* 'a type of tree', a linguist can put the whole information into a single word as [+tree] and can add other features if required. Consider the following examples.

Example 1:

Synset	Hindi	Kashmiri
ID: 19052		ID: 19052
Concept	/ek prəkar ka ped/	Son-specificity
Example	/dʒatli plaʃ ke prəkar ka hota he/	Not conceived
Synset	/dʒatli/	Not clear
ID: 568		ID: 568
Concept	ek prəkar ka poda dʒiske bɪdʒ dal ke rʊp, me khaje dʒate he	/su kul jeth krɔthɨ da:l tʃ^{h}e ne:ra:n/
Example	blʊjɪ miʈʈɪ ərhər ke lije upjukit hotɪ he/ ərhər ek dəlhənɪ poda he	/asi tʃu gari ba:gas manz krɔthɨ da:li kul/ krɔthɨ kul tʃu da:li da:r kul/
Synset	ərhər, tuar, tʊr, tusrɪ, ərrə, tor, adik, adikɪ, vanar	/krɔthɨ da:li kul, krɔthɨ kul/

In the above given example, it is very clear that the concept is not well defined for the given synset member. The given concept means any plant-bearing pulses (i.e. *dal*) and not particularly *arharkape:*ɖ or *po:da*. Thus, there is not any particular feature in the concept which restricts it to this particular kind of tree.

In order to handle such problems, it is proposed that a component which comprises of componential analysis or something similar or feature-based should be introduced and associated with the concepts. This method will convey the concept more clearly and in a more professional manner. The idea of whether or not to incorporate a strict form of feature system is a proposal which has to be thought about in detail. But it appears that (a) if a formal feature-based system frame is agreed upon and (b) if lexicographers are trained in it, the task will definitely become much easier. The formalization of the feature-based system should work as a very important tool for removing ambiguity. Furthermore, this can lead to the concept being more formal (a set of yes-es and no-s) which probably can be more WordNet builder and machine friendly.

12.4.2 *Language Differences*

Language differences more so in the case of how languages handle certain concepts and issues can also be problematic at times. Consider the example no: 2 given above. Here, the Hindi synset uses the word ‘ərhər’ as well as for the plant is same. In case of Kashmiri, there are two different words. It has the word *krɔthɨkul* for the plant *ərhər* and a separate word *krɔthɨda:l* for its pulses.

12.4.3 *Lack of Single-Word Equivalents*

Another problem arises in linking synsets when the source language has a single-word synset, and there is no parallel single-word synset in the target language. The solutions proposed to this problem are as follows:

(a) Short description
(b) Coin a new word (neologism)
(c) Transliteration

The last two seem very unnatural from the native speaker’s perspective. This leads to the selection of a) as far as possible. However, in doing so, it becomes difficult at times to use that description in the example in the same sense which the synset member conveys. Sometimes, the category maintenance of such synsets becomes difficult as well. Consider the examples to understand this problem.

Example 2:

ID: 547	Hindi	Kashmiri
Concept	dʒo tjagne ja tʃhoɖne jogi ho	jus trə:vith hekav
Example	tʃori, dhurtə adı tjadʒjekərəm he	tsu:r, dupandalə:zi: be:tri tʃi tra:vnas la:jak ka:r
Synset	tjadʒje, tjadʒnijə, paritjadʒi, tadʒnıj, hei, vadʒri, apri, avdri	tra:vnas la:jak, məʃra:vnas lajak

Example 3:

ID:398	Hindi	Kashmiri
Concept	veh vadrji dʒiske dono bhago ko ek dʊsre par aghat karke badʒaja dʒata he	tim sa:z jim akh əkis sə:tʲ ʈa:s dith vainɨ tʃi jiva:n/
Example	mandʒıra ek tal vadrji he	mandʒi:rɨ tʃu akh əkis sə:tʲ va:jan vo:l sa:z
Synset	ghanvadrji, ghanvadrji, talvaədrji, talvadrji	ʈhasɨ və:lʲ sa:z, ʈa:sɨ da:r sa:z

In the above examples, the description is given in Kashmiri instead of a single-word equivalent. When such descriptions are used in the given examples of the synset usage, they do not fit in; rather, they are made to fit in forcefully. In Kashmiri, the sentence '*tsu:r, dupandalə:zi: be:tri tʃi tra:vnas la:jak ka:r*' does not seem quite natural.

12.4.4 Problem of Translating Examples

Sometimes, it becomes virtually impossible to convey the meaning as one important factor which should be considered is that languages are not associated with a uniform culture. Instead, each language has a different culture associated with it. However, there are certain languages, for example, Hindi and Urdu which share a somewhat common culture to some extent. In these languages, the meaning equivalence could be achieved to a certain extent. There would be lesser problems of untranslatability in general and cultural untranslatability in particular. The point which needs to be focused here is the role of culture in determining the meaning of linguistic terms. According to linguistic relativism, meaning of the linguistic terms is relative to culture, and according to cultural relativism, the meaning of cultural elements whether concrete or abstract is relative to the particular culture in which they are present. In the present work, the 'example translation' in a given synset becomes complex when the example is too cultural or the linguistic terms used in the example have cultural significance. Consider the following examples

Example 4:

ID:11359	Hindi	Kashmiri
Concept	ʃiv ka upassək ja baght	ʃiv sund baghat ja: ma:nan vo:l
Example	ʃiv mandir mẽ ek ʃev ne dhunɪr mari he	ʃiv mãdras mãz tʃʰi ʃiv baghat mast gəmətʲ
Synset	ʃev, paʃʊpit, ʃivbaght/	ʃiv baghat

12.4.5 Generalization of Concepts

The factors of language and cultural differences play a very important role in determining equivalents to the linguistic concepts (lexemes) of one language from another. The native language draws the lines to divide the conceptual continuum of the members of a culture in a unique way. Thus, the conceptual units may not be equal in different languages. That is why it is said that 100 % equivalence of a linguistic term in other language is impossible. This problem becomes grave when this difference is acute like the one mentioned here in the examples below.

Example 5:

ID:4332	Hindi	Kashmiri
Concept	dãt adi gaɽa kər khəɖ, kʃitjadhav karna	dãd be:tri tsənith dʒismas zakhəm ja: vɔzdʒa:r gatshun/
Example	rat ko sote səme mətʃhər ne bəhut kaʈa	ra:t kʲut dits me mahev varjah ʈɔpɨ /təmʲ hʲot me athas tsop/
Synset	ka:ʈna	tsop hʲon, ʈɔph dinʲ

The problem in the example is that of generalization of concepts in Hindi which encompass more than one concept in Kashmiri. In the example above, *kaʈna* in Hindi refers to a general 'bite', be it by human, mammal, bird, insect, reptile. However, in Kashmiri, the bite by a human or mammal is usually *tsop*, by an insect or snake is *ʈɔph*, and by a bird is *dig*, etc. A similar case is observed in the example below.

Example 6:

ID:1123	Hindi	Kashmiri
Concept	kisɪ vəstu adi ke nɪtʃe ka bhag	kuni tʃi:zuk təlim hisɨ
Example	is bərtən ke təle mẽ tʃed he/ mõtʃɪ dʒʊte ka təla bədəl rəha he	tath ba:nas tʃu tsəkis god/ va:tul tʃu bu:ʈuk talɨ pot badla:va:n/
Synset	təla, təlla	tsok, talɨ pot/

The Hindi synset 'təla' can have more than one Kashmiri equivalent such as*talɨpot and tsok* which are two different concepts in Kashmiri.

12.4.6 Problem of Category Maintenance

In certain instances, it was very difficult to maintain the same part-of-speech or grammatical category of the synset equivalents in Kashmiri as that of Hindi. This is because the use of a lexical item differs from language to language. Language use is a very complex phenomenon which develops differently in different languages due to the effect of various factors which operate differently in different societies and cultures. Some of the factors which determine the patterns of use of a language are cultural (norms, beliefs, practices, etc), language and social contact, borrowing (words, structures, sounds, etc.), etc. If a synset is used, say as an adjective in Hindi, it is not necessary that it will be used as an adjective in Kashmiri as well. Consider the following examples.

Example 7:

ID:27111	Hindi noun	Kashmiri adjective
Concept	veh dʒo nidra mẽ ho ja soja huva ho	jemis ninder a:si ja jus ʃẽgith a:si
Example	soje ko mat dʒagav	ʃõgmut ʃakhɨs ma karun huʃa:r
Synset	soja, sota, sota huva, supt	ʃõgmut /ʃaŋith

In the above given example, the equivalent synset in Kashmiri *ʃõgmut* is not used as noun but is usually used as an adjective.

Example 8:

ID:896	Hindi adverb	Kashmiri reflexive pronoun
Concept	swadhın rʊp se	bej sındi dakhlı varəːi
Example	veh pretek karji swadhıne kərna tʃahta he	su tʃʰu preth kãhn kəːm pəːnʲ panai jetshaːn karɨnʲ
Synset	swadhınt, swatr rʊːp se	pəːnʲ panai, dakhlɨ varəːi

In the above given example, the sense of the Hindi synset (having adverb as category) used in the given example does not have that sense equivalent as adverb in Kashmiri. Instead, we convey such sense by using reflexive.

12.5 Conclusion

To conclude the paper, we can say that there must be proper guidelines to which each language group should remain bound. A set of proper procedures, standards, and rules will go a long way in building a useful WordNet schema, more so pertaining to the Indian language scenario. Building a WordNet with multiple languages does have its share of issues. The present paper discusses the problems faced during linking Kashmiri with Hindi synsets. Moreover, it also discusses some major issues relating language-specific synsets. The paper briefly also proposes some ad hoc solutions to some of the issues.

References

Catford, J. C. (1965). *A linguistic theory of translation: An essay on applied linguistics*. Oxford: Oxford University Press.

Popovič, A. (1970). The concept of 'shift of expression' in translation analysis. In J.S. Holmes, F. deHaan & A. Popovič (Eds.), *The Nature of Translation: Essays on the theory and practice of literary translation* (pp. 78–90). The Hague: Mouton.

Chapter 13
Language-specific Synsets and Challenges in Synset Linkage in Urdu WordNet

Rizwanur Rahman, Mazhar Mehdi Hussain and Niladri Sekhar Dash

Abstract The Urdu WordNet is being developed following the process used to develop the Hindi WordNet by using the Expansion Approach. This paper, in the first part, presents some of our experiences that we gathered in the process of building the Urdu WordNet as a part of the IndoWordNet. Many crucial issues and questions relating to Language-specific Synset generation are discussed at length in the first part of the paper with some examples taken from the Urdu and other Indian languages. In the second part, it attempts to reflect on some of the linguistic and technical difficulties that we have encountered in the act of linking the Hindi synsets to the similar terms of the Urdu WordNet. We have linked the Urdu synsets to the Hindi synsets in a very rational manner taking into consideration the similarities noted in senses and concepts denoted by the terms. This work tries to give wider coverage of the lexicon and concepts available in the Urdu language and used by its speakers.

Keywords Urdu · Hindi WordNet · Synset linking · Concepts · Senses · Language-specific synset

R. Rahman · M.M. Hussain (✉)
Centre of Indian Languages, Jawaharlal Nehru University, New Delhi, India
e-mail: ilci.jnu@gmail.com

R. Rahman
e-mail: rrahmanjnu@gmail.com

N.S. Dash
Indian Statistical Institute, Kolkata, India
e-mail: ns_dash@yahoo.com

N.S. Dash et al. (eds.), *The WordNet in Indian Languages*,
DOI 10.1007/978-981-10-1909-8_13

13.1 Introduction

As a part of the IndoWordNet (Saraswati et al. 2010), we, the members of the Urdu WordNet development team, have worked for the identification and linkage of the Language-specific Synsets (LSS) for the Urdu WordNet. We have faced a great deal of difficulties in selecting the specific concepts, explaining these concepts, and generating equivalent synsets for the other Indian languages as modeled in the EuroWordNet (Vossen 1998). We have also made an attempt to record the difficulties that we have faced in the process due to lack of specific guidelines for creating LSS in the IndoWordNet (Bhattacharyya 2010). Moreover, we have understood that there was a need for training to the people involved in this highly complex linguistic task to teach and guide them in the act of selection of LSS, defining their uniqueness and explicating the concepts embedded in these synsets so that the common users as well as other language users could rightly comprehend these forms to have a better insight about the language.

In this present paper, we have made two attempts. First, we have tried to record the experience we have accumulated at the time of providing translational or conceptual equivalents of the synsets that are presented in the Hindi WordNet. In this part, many theoretical issues and practical challenges have come up and we had to address all these in the context of generation of equivalents. Next, in the second part, we have noted that finding our unique synsets for Urdu is a highly challenging task, as most of the terms that are available in Urdu are also found in Hindi. In a rare case, we come across some Urdu terms or concepts that are novel to Hindi or other Indian languages. If this has been a real challenge for us to link such Urdu terms to Hindi counterparts in a sensible manner, we can take into consideration the similarities of concepts denoted by the terms. The present paper is a short narration of the journey through the meanders of Urdu WordNet that desires to stand as a good replica of the Hindi WordNet with regard to the numbers and types of terms considered to constitute the form and content of the IndoWordNet.

13.2 Approaches Used for Identifying LSS in Urdu

Finding concepts specific to a particular language is quite a difficult task. And since it is not easy to find unique terms in Urdu with relation to Hindi, we had to adopt a kind of unique approach which has been quite useful to identify the concepts specific to Urdu. Most of these concepts are cited in this section with some examples. We have applied the following steps to finalize a the language-specific concepts in Urdu:

(a) Collection of Unique words from various linguistic sources,
(b) Collection of unique concepts from social practices,
(c) Verification of the words and concepts, and
(d) Categorization of the concepts based on their senses.

In the task of collection of words from texts and concepts from various cultural contexts, we had to mimic the task of a lexicographer in which we are given responsibilities for identifying the terms and words from various available printed and digital sources and cultural practices, in which these terms and words denote unique concepts. After thorough cross-lingual reference and verification, we picked up those words the concepts of which are not found in other languages. In this task, we have used the following resources to collect and to verify language-specific concept-based terms.

(a) Standard Urdu dictionaries
(b) Urdu literary and non-literary texts
(c) Urdu cultural texts, and
(d) Urdu journals and magazines

Since finding out the LSS for Urdu is a highly challenging process, after much effort, we have been able to compile a list of nearly 250 words, which, to our assumption, may be termed as unique synsets as they have no conceptual equivalence in other languages—neither in Hindi nor in other Indian or neighboring languages.

This leads us to the second stage where we have made attempts to explore the language-specific nature of the concepts that are put to verification. Once a concept identified to be unique for Urdu is placed for verification with Hindi terms to confirm it is unique at all for Urdu. The entire process of manual selection and verification is done in the following manner:

Step 1: Identify a concept to be specific or unique to Urdu,
Step 2: Check whether the concept is absent in Hindi and other languages,
Step 3: If identified as specific to Urdu, send it to experts for confirmation, and
Step 4: After confirmation, mark its unique status in Urdu.

The next stage involves systematic categorization of the language-specific concepts available in Urdu. The concepts that are shortlisted to be unique in Urdu are classified into two broad types, as follows:

(a) Unique concept—a concept unique to Urdu and
(b) Unique word—an Urdu word that needs paraphrasing in other languages.

A major chunk of the time devoted to the project is consumed for the purpose of creating LSS for Urdu following the processes mentioned above. Initially, more than 700 concepts/words are identified as unique; after rigorous cross-verification with information availed in various authentic sources, finally, a list of 250 words is selected and marked as unique concepts in Urdu; and because of their unique identity, these are treated as LSS for the language. The list so far includes nearly 225 named entities and 25 adjectives; it has no verb or pronominal form. It may be an interesting area of exploration to know why only the named entities and adjectives are found to be unique in a language, while words of other part-of-speech are normally missing in the list.

13.3 Domains of Use of LSS in Urdu

The concepts or words which are identified as LSS for Urdu language belong mainly to culture and literature domains. This simply establishes our long-preserved assumption that a language community normally differs from its neighboring communities due to its own cultural elements and practices which may not be available in neighboring language communities. For elucidation, some examples are presented below.

ID : 116002
Category : Adjective
Concept : wo jo qaseeda padhta ho
Example : aslam ke walid sahab aek achhe qaseeda khaan hain
Synset : qaseeda khaan

ID : 116003
Category : Noun
Concept : qaseeda takhleeq karne kaa amal yaa fun
Example : 1857 se qabl urdu mein qaseeda nigari ka fun urooj par tha
Synset : qaseeda nigaari

Id : 116011
Category : Noun
Concept : ilme arooz mein radeef se pehle aane waalaa lafz
Example : urdu ghazal ke har sher ke doosre misre ke akheer mein radeef se pehle qaafiya laanaa laazmi hota hae
Synset : qaafiya

Id : 116057
Category : Noun
Concept : sunnat naamaaz ki woh bees rakatein jo ramzaan mein ishaa ke baad aur witr se pehle padhi jaati haen
Example : aslam ramzaan ke mahine mein paabandi se taraaweeh ki namaaz padhta ha
Synset : taraaweeh

There are many such examples the analysis of which makes it clear that these terms normally refer to some named entities and qualities that are prevailing in Urdu but missing in all other languages, including Hindi. A sensible and attentive collection of more terms of this kind from the language, may perhaps, lead this language to showcase its linguistic concepts that are unique to this language as well as can help to enrich the conceptual world of the other language communities.

13.4 The Linking Issues

Urdu is technically classified as an Indo-European language belonging to the Western Hindi branch of the language tree. Since it shares root with Hindi, linguists like to put Hindi and Urdu in one language group with four distinct dialect variations, namely *Hindi, Urdu, Dakhni* (spoken in Deccan province), and *Rekhta* (used in Urdu poetry). The dialects differ from each other in the same way the languages do. The two distinct ways of speaking of Hindi and Urdu diverge them into two different languages due to the degree of difference than the type of difference. Scholars have described these differences in terms of the differences noted between the American and the British English.

The present Urdu WordNet is developed with a lexical database obtained from the Hindi WordNet (Chakrabarty 2002). It is noted that the Hindi WordNet includes words from almost all North Indian dialects and languages. It is also noted that many words of the Hindi WordNet are actually taken from various dialects and this affirms the richness of Hindi language (Saraswati et al. 2010). Interestingly, from our assessment, we have noted that one-third of the Hindi lexical database includes words, which can easily be called as lexical items of Urdu. Such close lexical commonality can simply be attributed to the common heritage of the two Indian languages (i.e., Hindi and Urdu), which differ mostly on the level of orthography (i.e., script) and, to a certain extent, on the level of pronunciation. Although there are some subtle differences in use of syntactical structures and the pattern of lexical usage, these are not so prominent that they can arrest the attention of common language users and can be used as salient marks of identification of the two language varieties. Strikingly, in spite so much of closeness at phonetic, lexical, syntactic, and semantic levels, we have encountered a number of problems in linking the Urdu terms with the Hindi synsets. Some of these issues are addressed in the following sections.

13.5 Methods for Creation of Urdu Synset

The methods that we have applied for creating Urdu synsets include the followings:

(a) Translation,
(b) Transliteration,
(c) Derivation, and
(d) Explanation.

In order to create Urdu synsets, in many occasions, we have adopted the process of translation of the Hindi synsets into Urdu. While translating Hindi texts into Urdu, we have come across several translation problems and to overcome these, we have followed appropriate strategies. The problems that we have faced, mainly evolved from translating culture-specific items, deciphering actual contextual meanings of ambiguous concepts, and finding out most appropriate conceptual equivalent words and terms from the Urdu language. These problems mostly cropped up while we are trying to find Urdu terms for universal synsets, pan-Indian synsets, and adjectives. The challenge was far less pressing in the case of adverbs and verb forms.

The most daunting problem that we faced in linking synsets is finding out a word-to-word perfect lexical match from Urdu. In most cases, both Hindi and Urdu have the same lexical item to refer to a named concept (e.g., *assmaan* 'sky'). In this case, the use of the same term in Urdu, similar to that of Hindi, is the most sensible solution. On the other hand, in the case of derived words of Hindi, especially for adjectives and adverbs, we have faced serious challenges as absolute equivalence is missing. To come up with an amicable solution, we have rigorously referred to the existing dictionaries (e.g., Urdu–Hindi, Hindi–Urdu, English–Hindi, and Hindi–English). Finally, in the case of non-availability of suitable Urdu words, we have adopted the process of neologism where, we have, keeping the source concept in mind, created new words in Urdu by using the standard method of derivation. In most of the cases, Urdu multiword units (made with two/three words) are used to express the concept of a single Hindi word unit. Paraphrasing is mandatory in such a situation where the concept is new and the term referring to the concept is foreign to the target language community.

13.6 Methods of Affixation

Let us consider some Hindi words made up with affixes and their Urdu equivalents (Table 13.1). If we looks carefully at the examples given in the table, we can find that two or three Urdu words are used to express the sense expressed in single Hindi word (two words for ID Nos. 1, 2, 41, and 102) and three words for ID Nos. 3, 7, and 140). The reason behind this problem lies in Hindi affixation system where prefixes and suffixes are normally tagged with the words as an integral part of the word. And at the time synset generation in Urdu, we need to adopt paraphrasing method to address the issue of affixation in Hindi.

In the same fashion, the following list (Table 13.2) indicates how such prefixes and suffix can be handled during linking the synsets in the Urdu WordNet.

Table 13.1 Hindi words and their Urdu equivalents

ID	Hindi synset	Urdu synset equivalents
1	ajanmaa, ajaat, anutpann	na-zaaidah, na-paed, ghair-paeda shudah
2	amaangalik	bud-bakht, bud-qusmat, bud-naseeb
3	apravisht	ghair-daakhil shudah
7	aagat, samaagat	aayaa huaa, tashreef farmaa, tashreef laaya huaa
41	sa sahaae, sahayak yukt	baa sahaara
102	abhukt bhogi	ghair saarif
140	anukirt, amaulik, anusarit	naqal shudah, kaapi ki hui, naqal ki hui

Table 13.2 Negative affixes during synset linking in Urdu WordNet

ID	Hindi synset	Urdu synset
1	ajanmaa, ajaat, anutpann	na-zaaidah, na-paed, ghair-paeda shudah
2	amaangalik,	bud-bakht, bud-qusmat, bud-naseeb
3	apravisht	ghair-daakhil shudah
329	anaechchhik	ghair-aikhteyaari, be-iraadah
691	a-ashthiheen	baghair-haddi waalaa
836	asamirdhiprad	ghai- khush haal kun

Table 13.3 Hindi synsets with different prefixes in Urdu

ID	Hindi synset	Urdu synset
16	sacharitrataa	nek kirdaari, raast kirdaari, raast baazi
41	sa sahaae, sahayak yukt	baa sahaara

In this list the Hindi words have used the prefix *a-* as a negative prefix for all the words. This has been expressed by several prefixes (e.g., *bud-*, *be-*, *na-* and *ghair-*) of Arabic and Persian origin, to generate the same sense in Urdu. Although these are common Urdu words, most of them do not find mention in standard Urdu dictionaries.

Let us see the following list (Table 13.3) of Hindi synsets with another kind of prefix. The Hindi prefix *sa-* has been rendered into Urdu as *baa-*, *nek-*, and *raast-* although they cannot be used interchangeably across all words, as there is some morphological conventions in use of these affixes with Urdu words, although, at the same time, there is no such rule, which may dictate or govern their usages. The list also shows that the Urdu synset (ID No. 41) does not find its entry into dictionary while all the words of Urdu synset under ID No. 16 are found in almost all the standard dictionaries in Urdu.

Finally, let us consider another category of Hindi words, which are difficult to render into Urdu, because despite the existence of the concept in the language, no single word has been entered into the Urdu dictionary (Table 13.4). In the examples given below, there are Urdu equivalents words for each Hindi word but they do not find their entry in the dictionary as these have been newly formed to meet the present requirement of the language. In most case, Urdu words such as *shudah, pazir, naaqabil, kaa paaband*, and *kaa* have been used as suffixes for creating these new words.

Table 13.4 Non-availability of Urdu equivalents for Hindi synsets

ID	Hindi synset	Urdu synset
8	ajanmaa, ajaat, anutpann	zuhuu pazir, paedeaa shudah, paidaish shudah
670	niyamit	ausulo zawaabit kaa paaband
1512	amanchniye	na qaabile pesh kash
1832	gavya	gaye kaa

13.7 Problems in Lexical Equivalence

The most crucial problem which we have faced while linking the synsets is related to word-for-word equivalent between Hindi and Urdu. The most difficult part was the process of coining words for Hindi words containing more than one affixes from noun, adjective, and adverbs. Some of the examples are presented below (Table 13.5) as illustrations.

To solve this problem, in most of the cases, we had to adopt two different strategies: either the Hindi synset has been explained and paraphrased in Urdu, or a new set of words have been created in Urdu to address the problem of neologism, as is the case in ID No. 9905 and ID No. 11692.

13.8 Difficulties in Concept Transfer

A peculiar problem which we have faced while linking the synsets was the difficulty in transferring the concept of Hindi into Urdu. It was not possible to coin new words in Urdu for many terms or synsets used in Hindi. The only solution was to transliterate the Hindi term into Urdu, as appropriate Urdu words were not available or exiting Urdu terms were unable to match the semantic range expressed by the Hindi terms. Some examples are cited below (Table 13.6) to explain the problem.

This problem has evolved mostly from Hindu religious terminologies, ceremonies, prayers, names of gods and goddesses, etc., as these terms fall under a different category. Although efforts have been made to find or coin new terms in Urdu for such words, they do not exactly express the meaning or the sense expressed in Hindi terms.

Table 13.5 Problems of Lexical Equivalence between Hindi and Urdu

ID	Hindi synsets	Urdu equivalents
119	aabhaamandal	minaaraye noor
9905	ratnaar	surkhi mail
1117	airshyaaheentah	baghair hasad ke
1447	vidhiheentah	be saliqah andaaz mein
1455	uddeshheentah	bi ghair maqsad ke
1812	adhikaarpurvak	baa ikhteyar tariqe se
2066	aadyopaant	ibtadaa taa aintaha
4250	dridhtaapurvak	mustahkam andaaz mein
6364	darshnaarth	ziyaarat ke liye, baraye ziyaarat
10738	aajaanubahu, mahaabaahu	lambe baazu waalaa, tawil baazu waalaa
11692	nabhchar	falak parwaaz
12279	aghoshit	ghair aelaan shudah
29135	akshamasheel	na qaabile maafi

Table 13.6 Transliteration of Hindi synsets into Urdu at lexical level

ID	Hindi	Urdu synset
11169	antarjaanu	aukdun, antarjanu
18850	raavanaanaa	raawnaanaa
23188	abhyaa	abhyaa
3811	bauraa	baura
1176	dantulaa	dantulaa
1359	shaakt	shaakt

13.9 Conclusion

In the first part of the chapter (Sects. 13.2 and 13.3), we have tried to present some ideas for augmenting the *IndoWordNet* with language-specific concepts of Urdu. The approach we have used is almost same with that of the methods commonly followed all other language groups. The most notable deficiency of this approach is that there is no filter to check the overlap of concepts across the languages as there is a high possibility that some concepts or words thought to be specific to a particular language or variety may also appear in other languages.

In the second part of the chapter (Sects. 13.4, 13.5, 13.6, 13.7, and 13.8), we have made some attempts to reflect on some of the difficulties which we have faced during the process of linking Hindi synsets into the Urdu WordNet. In addition to the linguistic issues mentioned here, there are some technical problems as well. One of the major issues was related to alignment of texts between the two languages. The other important issue was related to use of non-linguistic characters in text, as it was assumed that it may pose difficulty at the time of entering text into the tool.

Keeping all these issues in view, we have tried to generate Urdu equivalents for the Hindi synsets as far as these have been equivalent in sense denotation, concept transfer, and general cognition. It is expected that this present study will provide necessary insights required for developing a general WorldNet for Urdu with wider coverage of lexicon and concepts available in the language and used by its speakers.

References

Bhattacharyya, P. (2010). IndoWordNet. *Lexical Resources Engineering Conference 2010 (LREC 2010),* Malta, May, 2010.

Chakrabarty, D., Pande, P., Narayan, D., Bhattacharyya, P. (2002). An experience in building the Indo WordNet—a WordNet for Hindi. *International Conference on Global WordNet (GWC02),* Mysore, India.

Saraswati, J., Shukla, R., Goyal, R. P., Bhattacharyya, P. (2010). Hindi to English wordnet linkage: Challenges and solutions. *Proceedings of 3rd IndoWordnet Workshop,* ICON 2010.

Vossen, P. (1998). *EuroWordNet: A multilingual database with lexical semantic networks.* London: Kluwer Academic Publishers.

Chapter 14
Sanskrit WordNet at Indian Institute of Technology (IITB) Mumbai

Malhar Kulkarni

Abstract The present article reports about the development of Sanskrit WordNet at IIT Bombay, India. After highlighting the importance of Sanskrit in the gamut of Indian Languages, this paper in brief presents how Sanskrit WordNet came into being. It also describes the expansion approach with which it was built. It also notes down the features of the online interface of Sanskrit WordNet and the features of the database of Sanskrit WordNet. It also points out the contribution made by Sanskrit WordNet to the development of WordNets in India. Finally, it states future challenges faced by Sanskrit WordNet, notable amongst them is to bring it on par with the English WordNet developed at Princeton University, USA.

Keywords Sanskrit · WordNet · Expansion approach · Database · Tatsama · Tadbhava · Indian constitution

---

I would like to thank the Ministry of Human Resource Development (MHRD), Government of India which funded the creation of Sanskrit WordNet through the Central Institute of Indian Languages (CIIL). I also thank the authorities of the Indian Institute of Technology Bombay (IITB) which hosted Sanskrit WordNet through the Center for Indian Language Technology (CFILT), Department of Computer Science and Engineering (CSE) as well as Department of Humanities and Social Sciences (HSS). I also thank a number of research scholars mentioned hereafter who worked as Lexicographers: Dr. Chaitali Dangarikar, Dr. Irawati Kulkarni, Dr. Tanuja Ajotikar, Tejasvini Kinjavadekar and Dr. Nilesh Joshi and those who worked as system administrators: Abhishek Nanda, Salil Joshi, Ganesh Bhosle, Sudha Bhingardive, Hanumant Redkar and Diptesh Kanojia. Thanks are also due to the members of International Sanskrit Computational Linguistics Consortium who gave various inputs which helped improve the versions of the resource. I also thank the publishers of various papers related to Sanskrit WordNet published in their volumes. Thanks are also due to the authorities of the Global WordNet Association as well as the Global WordNet Grid which included Sanskrit WordNet in the list of WordNets all over the world.

M. Kulkarni (✉)
Department of Humanities and Social Sciences, Indian Institute of Technology Bombay, Powai, Mumbai, India
e-mail: malhar@iitb.ac.in

N.S. Dash et al. (eds.), *The WordNet in Indian Languages*,
DOI 10.1007/978-981-10-1909-8_14

14.1 Introduction

This is a brief sketch of the development of Sanskrit WordNet, an online resource built under the leadership of Professor Pushpak Bhattacharyya, Department of Computer Science and Engineering, Indian institute of Technology Bombay, Mumbai, India.

Sanskrit WordNet is a part of a larger project called IndoWordNet undertaken by a consortium of Indian universities and institutions where WordNets of different Indian languages are built and linked with each other.

Sanskrit is an important language amongst the whole list of languages that are spoken in India as it is historically linked with most of the Indian languages in one way or another. Currently, it is considered to be one of the 23 official languages of the Government of India and is the second official language in the Indian state of Uttarakhand, India. Below is a statistics of people recorded to be the speakers of Sanskrit in the census conducted by the Government of India (Table 14.1).

Table 14.1 Census of India 2001

Scheduled languages in descending order of speaker's strength			
S. No.	Language	Persons who returned the language as their mother tongue	Percentage to total population
1	Hindi	422,048,642	41.03
2	Bengali	83,369,769	8.11
3	Telugu	74,002,856	7.19
4	Marathi	71,936,894	6.99
5	Tamil	60,793,814	5.91
6	Urdu	51,536,111	5.01
7	Gujarati	46,091,617	4.48
8	Kannada	37,924,011	3.69
9	Malayalam	33,066,392	3.21
10	Oriya	33,017,446	3.21
11	Punjabi	29,102,477	2.83
12	Assamese	13,168,484	1.28
13	Maithili	12,179,122	1.18
14	Santali	6,469,600	0.63
15	Kashmiri	5,527,698	0.54
16	Nepali	2,871,749	0.28
17	Sindhi	2,535,485	0.25
18	Konkani	2,489,015	0.24
19	Dogri	2,282,589	0.22
20	Manipuri	1,466,705	0.14
21	Bodo	1,350,478	0.13
22	Sanskrit	14,135	N

In fact, the Constitution of India, through article 351, acknowledges the importance of Sanskrit amongst Indian languages when it says that modern Indian languages like Hindi should use Sanskrit as a backbone in developing scientific and technical terminology in various branches of learning.

14.2 Article 351: Constitution of India

It shall be the duty of the union to promote the spread of the Hindi language, to develop it so that it may serve as a medium of expression for all the elements of the composite culture of India and to secure its enrichment by assimilating without interfering with its genius, the forms, style and expressions used in Hindustani and in the other languages of India specified in the Eighth Schedule, and by drawing wherever necessary or desirable, for its vocabulary, primarily on Sanskrit and secondarily on other languages. (Directive for development of the Hindi language. 1 Ins. by the Constitution (Seventh Amendment) Act, 1956, s. 21. THE CONSTITUTION OF INDIA (Part XVII.—Official Language.—Arts. 349—351.) p. 216).

This article in the constitution of India also highlights the salient feature of the grammar of Sanskrit composed by Panini around 500 BCE in sutra style, namely the high degree of word productive capacity.

Sanskrit is also an oldest language in the Indo-Aryan language family in India. In public opinion, it is considered to be the mother of the mother tongues (i.e. modern Indian languages).

As a result of being the oldest language in the Indo-Aryan family, the relationship between Sanskrit and modern Indo-Aryan languages is deep and worth several studies. The words borrowed from Sanskrit in their original form part considerable chunk of the vocabulary in modern Indian languages. Such words are called Tatsama. The other type of words are called Tadbhava. These are words which are borrowed from Sanskrit but their phonological form is changed according to the behaviour pattern of that modern Indian language. The other two types are called deshi and videshi, meaning, local and foreign, respectively. The primary criterion adopted for this kind of classification of vocabulary in Indian languages seems to be 'relation to Sanskrit'.

All these facts stated above make it a compelling case for the existence of an online resource of Sanskrit that is linked with the similar resources of modern Indian Languages, namely Sanskrit WordNet.

Therefore, it was no surprise to find amongst researchers a feeling to create such a resource. And some researchers came forward and started thinking about developing such a resource. Mohanty and Adhikari Das (2012) present their thoughts about a prospective Sanskrit WordNet that they proposed to build. However, they did not publish further on the availability of their resource. A researcher in Germany thought of automatically creating Sanskrit WordNet but did not continue. It was with some effort that Professor Pushpak Bhattacharyya submitted a proposal to build Sanskrit WordNet to Central Institute of Indian

Languages (CIIL), Ministry of Human Resource Development, Government of India and got it approved. He was supported by the team of researchers available at IIT Bombay at that time. This happened in 2008. Since then researchers are engaged in the development of Sanskrit WordNet. This development was done manually. The first public report of building of Sanskrit WordNet came out in the Global WordNet Conference (GWC) 2010 hosted by IIT Bombay. Since then further reports regarding development of Sanskrit WordNet have been regularly appearing in the subsequent instalments of GWC, in Matsue, Japan in 2012; in Tartu, Estonia in 2014 and in Bucharest, Romania in 2016 and elsewhere. These reports are available in the proceedings of all these conferences.

14.3 Expansion Approach

The Sanskrit WordNet was built using expansion approach where a resource is built on the basis of an already existing similar resource. The base resource for Sanskrit WordNet was Hindi WordNet (HWN) that was already in the process of development at IITB. By doing this, we ensured that when these two resources get linked to each other there is some standardization in place. We adopted certain policies and principles towards achieving this end. They are as follows:

(1) The synset ID that the HWN has created would be the same in the Sanskrit WordNet.
(2) As far as possible, the gloss in the Sanskrit WordNet would remain close to the gloss in the HWN.
(3) As far as possible, the example in the Sanskrit WordNet would remain close to the example in the HWN.
(4) As far as possible, the part of speech mentioned in the HWN would be adhered to in Sanskrit WordNet.

In order to implement these policies, we created an interface in which HWN entries would be readily available together with the synset ID number, and the lexicographers will have to enter the Sanskrit WordNet entry in the other part of the interface (Figs. 14.1 and 14.2).

By adopting to these general policies and principles, we have created so far 34904 synsets. They are divided across part of speech categories, statistics of which is shown below (Fig. 14.3):

14.4 Features of the Online Interface of Sanskrit WordNet

Sanskrit WordNet is hosted at www.cfilt.iitb.ac.in. It's motto is: *saṁ giraṁ cinuyāma* (Let us cull (words of a) language). This was specifically composed to suit the task at hand at Sanskrit WordNet by Malhar Kulkarni in the Vedic style

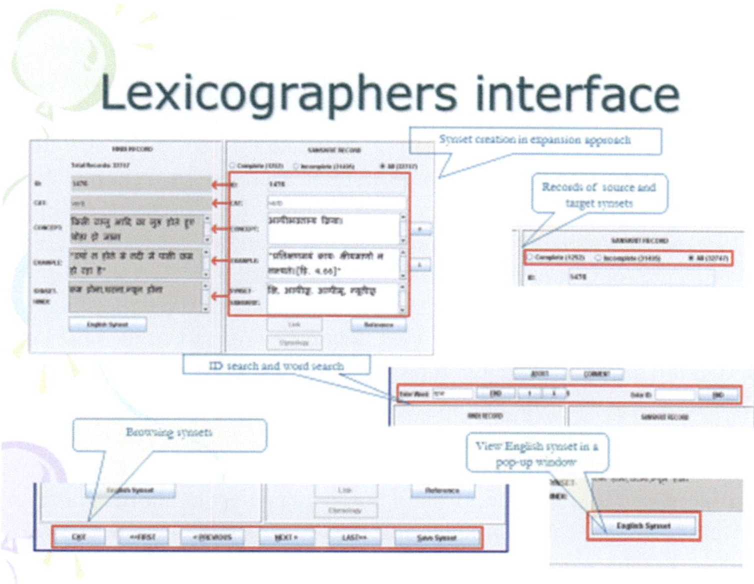

Fig. 14.1 Lexicographer's interface: Sanskrit WordNet 2008

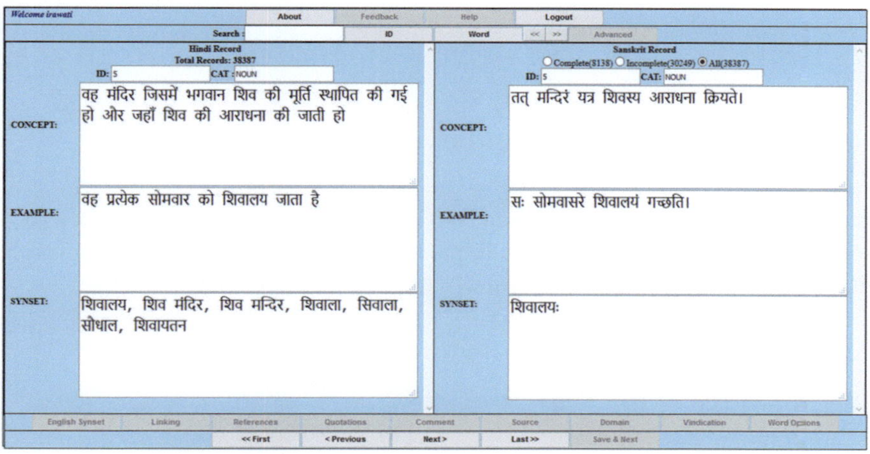

Fig. 14.2 Lexicographer's interface: Sanskrit WordNet 2015

	Noun	Verb	Adjective	Adverb	Total
Sanskrit	29356	1247	4032	264	**34904**

Fig. 14.3 Current statistics: Sanskrit WordNet

which is reflected by separating the preverb from the verb. Once we click on the Sanskrit WordNet button, we go to the interface of Sanskrit WordNet. On this interface, we have a virtual key board typing into which one can search the entry in the Sanskrit WordNet. Since the morphological behaviour of an adjective in Sanskrit is same as the noun it qualifies, we decided to store the adjective in the root form. We decided to store the nouns in their declined form (nominative singular). Therefore, when one searches for a noun, he/she has to type in the noun in the declined format in this keyboard. And when one searches for an adjective, he/she has to type in the root word using the virtual key board.

After one enters the word using virtual key board in the space provided and one clicks on the search button, one gets the entries related to the word searched, displayed in the next interface. On top of this web page the part of speech category is mentioned along with the number of meanings of the searched word available in Sanskrit WordNet. Below this, each and every meaning is placed in a separate box which contains (i) words expressing that meaning- in black (bold) with the searched word in blue, (ii) the gloss or the explanation of the meaning in green and (iii) an example which contains the first member of the set of words mentioned above in faint black.

Below these are the buttons for relations and languages. R is the button for relations and initials of each language would be the button for that respective language (A-Asamese, Be-Bengali, etc.). The button for relations show the lexical relations hypernymy–hyponymy of the meaning expressed by the set of words as well as ontological nodes.

14.5 Features and Contributions of Sanskrit WordNet

Regularly working to catch-up with HWN, the Sanskrit WordNet is now in a position to be on par with the HWN in terms of number of synsets. Following can be cited as contributions of Sanskrit WordNet:

14.5.1 Source of the Synsets

During the initial stages of the development of the Sanskrit WordNet, we discussed on the selection of concepts that should be a part of each and every resource. The team of Sanskrit WordNet proposed to use the concepts available in Bharatiya Vyavahara Kosha, a print lexicon consisting of 14 language data linked with each other. This issue was discussed in the subsequent workshops of the consortium, and a call was taken about the availability of such concepts in different languages. On the basis of this exercise, the synsets were classified into following classes: universal, pan-Indian, language family specific and language specific.

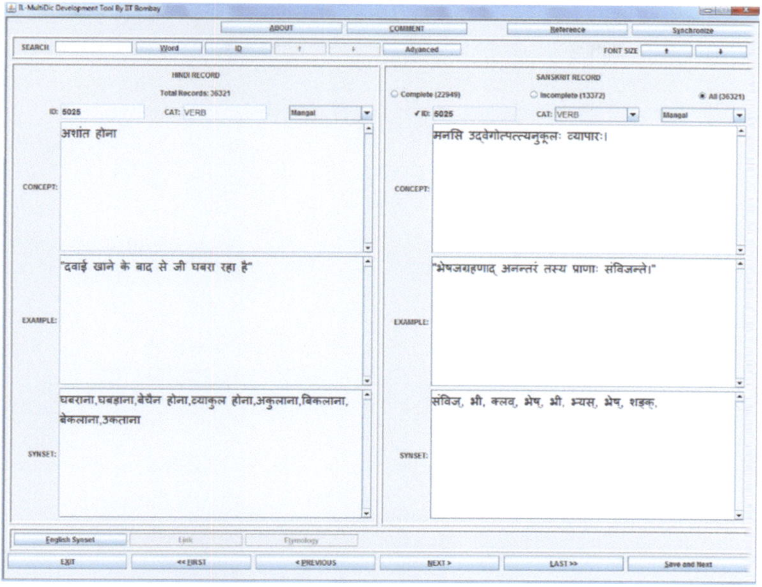

Fig. 14.4 Gloss of a verb in Sanskrit WordNet

14.5.2 Gloss

The gloss of verbs in Sanskrit WordNet is unique and is composed following the theory of verbal semantics advocated by the Paninian tradition which says that each and every action has two inherent parts, namely the process and the fruition/end/result. This practice can help us to link this resource for other NLP purposes such as parsing. For details, see Kulkarni et al. 2010 (Fig. 14.4).

14.5.3 Additional Information in Examples

Generally, examples associated with Hindi synsets are translated only if they *read* sensible when translated into Sanskrit. In some cases, quotations from the Sanskrit texts are included in the example field. A special field has been created to record the source of the quotations. This citation field is incorporated in the lexicographer's interface: The example with the citation is inserted in this format: (5) *shashi-divAkarayorgrahapIDanaM [bhartR 2.91]* (the eclipse of Sun and Moon). Here, *bhartR 2.91* indicates the place of the quotation in the original Sanskrit text authored by Bhartrhari (Fig. 14.5).

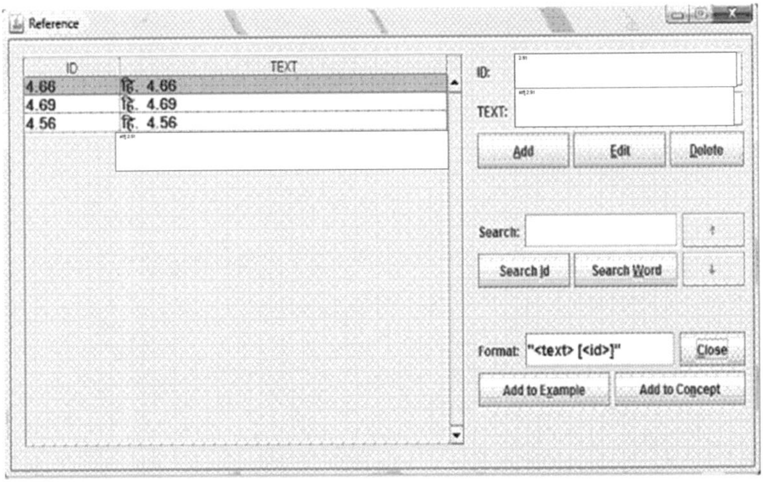

Fig. 14.5 Interface for entering additional information to an example

14.5.4 Semi-automatic Population

We also tried to populate the synsets of the Sanskrit WordNet using the currently available Sanskrit e-lexicon and its mappings with the English WordNet. This has not happened to any other Indian Language WordNet so far. Earlier, our procedure was as shown below:

Now, when we followed this procedure, we could also link directly to English WordNet (Princeton WordNet = PWN) (Fig. 14.6).

Our method can be described in the flow chart as shown below (Fig. 14.7):

Once the automatic population takes place, the lexicographer's job of validation starts and for that we created following interface (Fig. 14.8):

Fig. 14.6 Semi-automatic population of Sanskrit WordNet

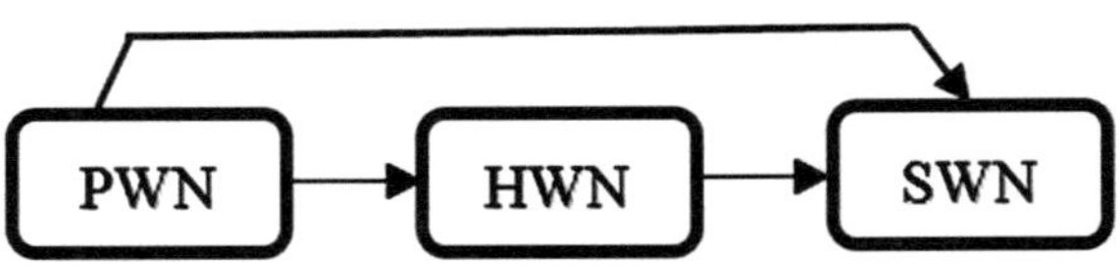

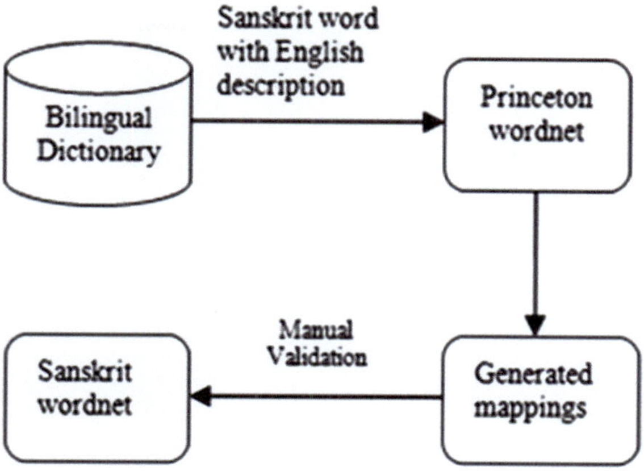

Fig. 14.7 Semi-automatic population of Sanskrit WordNet : Architecture diagram

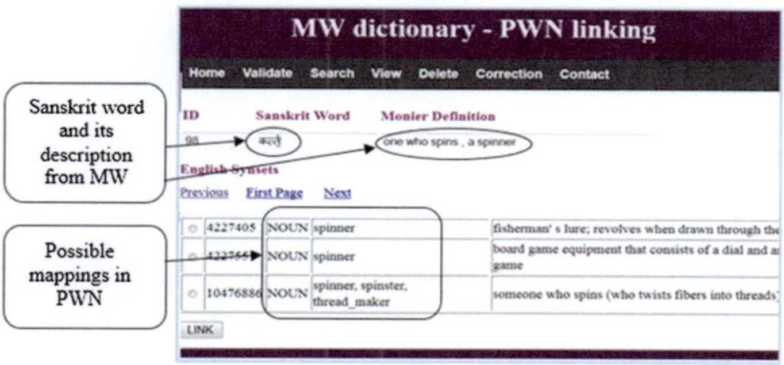

Fig. 14.8 Interface for validating multiple possible mappings (Bhingardive et al. 2014)

14.5.5 Compound Generation

The recent contribution of Sanskrit WordNet is creation of a tool called Compound word producer. This tool maps the concepts in Hindi to Sanskrit and by compounding the members of the synsets expressing two concepts produces synset members which express that compounded concept (Redkar et al. 2016). This tool will help populate the WordNet faster and is also believed to serve useful for the resources of modern Indian languages to incorporate words to express new ideas and concepts, thereby fulfilling the constitutional provision mentioned earlier. Compound is a very productive phenomenon in Indian languages. Compounding of Tatsama words is also a very much productive phenomenon amongst the Indian languages. It is believed that this tool will help to capture this important feature of Indian languages (Fig. 14.9).

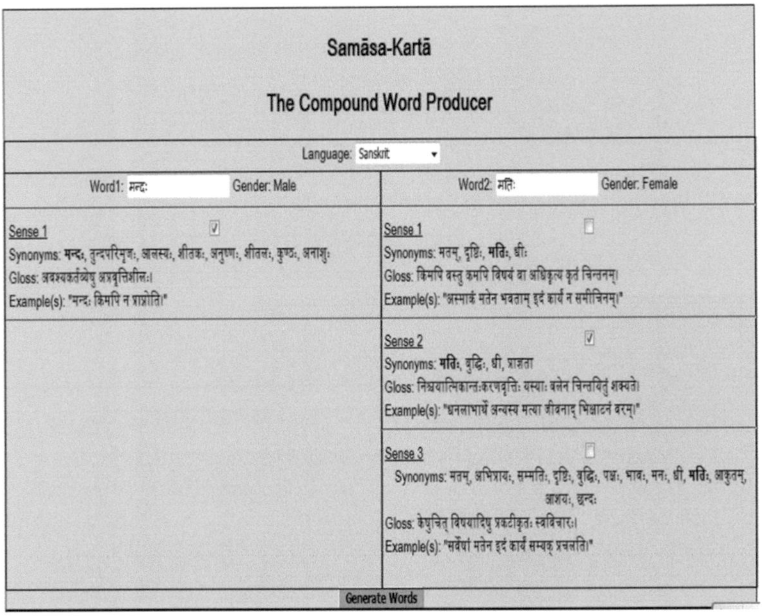

Fig. 14.9 Compound word producer tool

14.6 Future Challenges

Ontology based on the insights available in Sanskrit texts: Various philosophical schools have written their treatises in Sanskrit. Some of these treatises and philosophies have tried to mention categories of objects in the world. The team of Sanskrit WordNet is working to find out which ontological system can be best adopted for the purpose of building a resource like Sanskrit WordNet.

Bring it to match English WordNet: Currently, English WordNet built at Princeton University, USA, is considered to be the biggest WordNet with more than 1,19,000 synset entries. Hindi WordNet has approximately 39,000 synset entries. The aim of Sanskrit WordNet is to map all the English WordNet entries in Sanskrit WordNet and bring it on par with it.

References

Ajotikar, T., Kulkarni, M., & Bhattacharyya, P. (2012).In C. Fellbaum & P. Vossen (Eds.), *Verbal roots in Sanskrit WordNet, 6th Global WordNet conference, Matsue, Japan.*

Bhingardive, S., Ajotikar, T., Kulkarni, I.,Kulkarni, M., & Bhattacharyya, P. (2014). In H.Orav, C. Fellbaum & P. Vossen (Eds.), *Semi-automatic extension of Sanskrit WordNet using Bilingual Dictionary, GWC 2014, Estonia, Tartu.*

Constitution of India (As modified up to the 1st December, 2007). Government of India, Ministry of Law and Justice

Kulkarni, M., Dangarikar,C., Kulkarni, I., Nanda, A., & Bhattacharyya, P. (2010). In P. Bhattacharyya, C. Fellbaum & P Vossen (Eds.), *Introducing Sanskrit WordNet,* 5th *Global WordNet Conference, Mumbai.*

Kulkarni, M., Kulkarni, I., Dangarikar, D., & Bhattacharyya, P. (2010). *Gloss in Sanskrit WordNet.* In G. N. Jha (Ed.), *Proceedings of the 4th International Sanskrit Computational Linguistics Symposium.* LNCS, Springer.

Mohanty, S., & Das Adhikari, K. P. (2012). *Ontology of Sanskrit WordNet: nouns and verbs.* In C.Fellbaum & P. Vossen (Eds.), *Proceedings of the 6th Global WordNet Conference, Matsue, Japan.*

Naravane, Vishwanath. (1961). *Bharatiya Vyavahaara Kosha.* Mumbai: Triveni Sangam.

Redkar, H., Joshi, N., Singh, S., Kulkarni, I., Kulkarni, M, & Bhattacharyya, P. (2016). *Samasa-Karta: An online tool for producing compound words using IndoWordNet.* In V. MItitelu, C. Forascu & P. Vossen (Eds.), *Proceedings of the 8th Global WordNet Conference, Bucharest Romania.*

Chapter 15
Word Sense Disambiguation Using IndoWordNet

Sudha Bhingardive and Pushpak Bhattacharyya

Abstract Word sense disambiguation (WSD) is considered as one of the toughest problems in the field of natural language processing. IndoWordNet is a linked structure of WordNets of major Indian languages. Recently, several IndoWordNet-based WSD approaches have been proposed and implemented for Indian languages. In this chapter, we present the usage of various other features of IndoWordNet in performing WSD. Here, we have used features such as linked WordNets and lexico-semantic relations. We have followed two unsupervised approaches, viz. (1) use of IndoWordNet in bilingual WSD for finding the sense distribution with the help of expectation maximization algorithm and (2) use of IndoWordNet in WSD for finding the most frequent sense using word and sense embeddings. Both these approaches justify the importance of IndoWordNet for word sense disambiguation for Indian languages, as the results are found to be promising and can beat the baselines.

Keywords IndoWordNet · WordNet · Word sense disambiguation · WSD · Bilingual WSD · Unsupervised WSD · Most frequent sense · MFS

S. Bhingardive (✉) · P. Bhattacharyya
Department of Computer Science and Engineering,
Indian Institute of Technology-Bombay, Powai, Mumbai, India
e-mail: sudha@cse.iitb.ac.in

P. Bhattacharyya
e-mail: pb@cse.iitb.ac.in

N.S. Dash et al. (eds.), *The WordNet in Indian Languages*,
DOI 10.1007/978-981-10-1909-8_15

15.1 Introduction

15.1.1 What is Word Sense Disambiguation?

Word sense disambiguation (WSD) is the task of identifying the correct meaning of a word in a given context. The necessary condition for a word to be disambiguated is that it should have multiple senses. Generally, in order to disambiguate a given word, we should have a context in which the word has been used and knowledge about the word; otherwise, it becomes difficult to get the exact meaning of a word. Also, if the concept of a sense is not well defined, then it becomes very elusive task for WSD. The senses of a word differ from dictionary to dictionary. Some of them are coarse, while others provide a fine-grained distinction between possible senses. This may be the reason why there does not exist any WSD classifier which can give an accuracy of 100 %, not even human experts can agree on the sense of some words during manual disambiguation tasks. The following is the example in Hindi which explains the WSD.

S_1: *raam ne bagiiche ke paudhon ko kaataa*
(Ram cuts plants of the garden)
S_2: *kutte ne billi ko kaataa* (dog bites a cat)

Here, the word *kaataa* has two different senses. In sentence S_1, the correct sense of *kaataa* is 'to cut' as it appears with the context words *baagiichaa* (garden) and *paudhaa* (plant). However, in sentence S_2, the correct sense of *kaataa* is 'to bite' as it appears with the context word *kutta* (dog).

15.1.2 Variants of Word Sense Disambiguation

The word sense disambiguation task is broadly categorized into two types:

- **Target Word WSD**:
  The target WSD system disambiguates a restricted set of target words, usually one per sentence. Here, supervised approaches are generally used for this purpose where a tagged corpus is used to train the model. This trained model is then used to disambiguate the words in the target document.
- **All-Word WSD**:
  The all-word WSD system disambiguates all open-class words in the target document. Here, knowledge-based or unsupervised methods are usually used for this setting. This is because the supervised approach faces the problem of data sparseness. In supervised settings, it is not always possible to have a large tagged corpus for training in order to improve the coverage. Hence, unsupervised methods are preferred in the case of all-word WSD.

In this chapter, we will first describe various WSD approaches and how IndoWordNet is helpful for WSD in Indian languages. Then, the glimpse of existing WSD approaches which use IndoWordNet is given. Further, we will discuss our unsupervised approaches for WSD. These approaches make use of IndoWordNet (a) for context-based bilingual WSD and (b) for detecting the most frequent sense of a word.

15.2 Approaches for Word Sense Disambiguation

Over the years, many WSD approaches have been proposed. These are often classified according to the main source of knowledge used in sense differentiation. (a) Approaches that make use of annotated corpora for the training purpose or as seed data in a bootstrapping process are termed as *supervised* and *semi-supervised*, (b) approaches that rely completely on external information and are usually performed directly on raw corpora are termed as *unsupervised*, and (c) approaches that rely primarily on dictionaries, thesauri, and lexical knowledge bases, without using any corpus evidence, are termed as *dictionary-based* or *knowledge-based*.

15.2.1 Supervised WSD Approaches

Supervised methods (Lee et al. 2004; Ng and Lee 1996; Agirre and de Lacalle 2009; Giuliano et al. 2009) formulate WSD as a classification problem: The senses of a word represent classes, and a classifier assigns a class to each new instance of a word. Accordingly, almost any classifier from the machine learning literature can be applied. In addition to a dictionary, these algorithms need at least one annotated corpus, where each appearance of a word is tagged with the correct sense.

15.2.2 Unsupervised WSD Approaches

Creating annotated corpus for all language-domain pairs is impracticable looking at the amount of time and money required. Hence, unsupervised WSD approaches attract most of the researchers (Dagan et al. 1991; Schütze 1998; Diab and Resnik 2002; Hiroyuki and Morimoto 2002; Véronis 2004; Specia et al. 2005; Lefever and Hoste 2010; Khapra et al. 2011). Unsupervised methods have the potential to overcome the knowledge acquisition bottleneck and have achieved good results. These methods are able to induce word senses from training text by clustering word occurrences and then classifying new occurrences into the induced clusters/senses.

15.2.3 Knowledge-Based WSD Approaches

WSD heavily depends on knowledge. This knowledge must be in the machine-readable format. There are various structures designed for this purpose, and they are known as lexical resources. Lexical resources are of diverse types, for example, tagged and untagged corpora, machine-readable dictionaries, thesauri, glossaries, wordnets and ontologies. The main use of lexical resources in WSD is to associate senses with words. Here, selectional restrictions, overlap of definition text, and semantic similarity measures are used for knowledge-based WSD (Lesk 1986; Mihalcea 2006; Banerjee and Pedersen 2003; Jimeno-Yepes and Aronson 2010).

15.3 IndoWordNet for Word Sense Disambiguation

IndoWordNet (Bhattacharyya 2010) is a linked lexical knowledge base of wordnets of major Indian languages. It consists of synsets, semantic and lexical relations, ontological details, etc. It is mainly developed for the purpose of word sense disambiguation in Indian languages. However, it can be used for various other natural language processing applications such as machine translation, information retrieval, sentiment analysis, and text entailment.

15.3.1 IndoWordNet as Sense Repository for WSD

IndoWordNet is mainly used as a sense repository for Indian languages. Here, for each word, senses are provided according to its part-of-speech (POS) categories, viz. nouns, verbs, adjectives, and adverbs. The senses of words are chosen from this sense repository for creating the gold standard sense-annotated corpus. A sense-annotated corpus is created by human experts by manually annotating each occurrence of the target word or all content words in a text. This sense-annotated corpus is generally used for supervised WSD approaches.

15.3.2 IndoWordNet as Input Features for WSD

Various IndoWordNet-based features can be used for WSD, and they are described below:

- **Semantic Relations**:
  Semantic relations exist between synsets. These relations are very helpful for disambiguating a target word in a given context. Some of these relations are stated below:

- **Hypernymy and Hyponymy**: This relation captures *is-a-kind-of* relationship between synsets.
  Example: *aama* (mango) is a kind of *phala* (fruit). So, *aama* (mango) is the hyponymy of *phala* (fruit), and *phala* (fruit) is the hypernymy of *aama* (mango).
- **Meronymy and Holonymy**: This relation expresses *a-part-of* relationship and its inverse.
  Example: *pattaa* (leaf) is the meronym of *peda* (tree), and *peda* (tree) is the holonym of *pattaa* (leaf).
- **Entailment**: It is a semantic relationship between two verbs. A verb *X* entails a verb *Y*, if the meaning of *Y* follows logically and is strictly included in the meaning of *X*. This relation is unidirectional.
  Example: *kharrate maaranaa (*snoring) entails *sonaa* (sleeping), but *sonaa* (sleeping) does not entail *kharrate maarana* (snoring).
- **Troponymy**: It is a semantic relation between two verbs when one is a specific 'manner' elaboration of another.
  Example: *dahaadanaa* (to roar) is the troponym of *bolanaa* (to speak).

• **Lexical Relations**: Lexical relations exist between words. These relations are also helpful for disambiguating a target word in a particular context. Some of these relations are stated below.
  - **Synonymy**: This is the relationship between words in a synset. This relation is symmetric, reflexive, and transitive.
    Example: In synset {*haatha, hasta, kara, paaNi*} (hand), words *haatha, hasta, kara,* and *paaNi* are related through synonymy relation.
  - **Antonymy**: It is a lexical relation indicating 'opposites.'
    Example: *patalaa* (thin) is an antonym of *motaa* (fat) and vice versa.

• **Linked structure**: IndoWordNet being a linked structure of Indian language wordnets, its cross-linkages across wordnets are helpful for bilingual WSD.

15.3.3 Existing IndoWordNet-Based Approaches

Earlier, several WSD approaches by Sinha et al. (2006), Khapra et al. (2008), Mishra et al. (2009), Khapra et al. (2011), Singh and Siddiqui (2012) Singh et al. (2013), and Jain and Lobiyal (2015) have been proposed which make use of IndoWordNet as a lexical resource.

15.4 Our IndoWordNet-Based WSD Approaches

15.4.1 Unsupervised Context-Based Bilingual WSD

Recently, we, Bhingardive et al. (2013) published a paper on the usage of IndoWordNet for unsupervised context-based bilingual WSD approach. This uses expectation maximization (EM) algorithm for estimating sense distributions. It builds on the framework of Khapra et al. (2011). So, let us first understand the basic EM-based approach by Khapra et al. (2011).

15.4.1.1 Basic EM-Based WSD Approach

This approach relies on the key idea that, within a domain, the co-occurrence count of (word, sense) in one language can be used to estimate the sense distribution of their translations in another language. For example, the word *maan* in Marathi with sense 'neck' is translated to Hindi as *galaa* or *gardan* and with sense 'respect' as *aadar* or *izzat*. Hence, the probability of different senses of *maan* can be estimated by the counts of {*galaa*, *gardan*} and {*aadar*, *izzat*}. But in Hindi, the word *galaa* has two meanings, viz. 'neck' and 'voice'. Because the word *galaa* is itself ambiguous, the raw count of *galaa* cannot directly help in estimating the sense distribution of *maan*.

The approach needs in-domain corpora from two languages as opposed to supervised approaches which need annotated corpora. It uses EM algorithm for estimating sense distributions in comparable corpora. Every polysemous word is disambiguated using the raw counts of its translations in different senses. This approach uses a synset-aligned multilingual dictionary (Mohanty et al. 2008) for finding the translations. This dictionary links synsets from different languages with respect to sense. All the synsets with the same sense are aligned in the same row against its sense. In this dictionary, synsets are linked, and after that, the words inside the synsets are also linked. For example, for the concept of 'boy,' Hindi synset {*ladakaa, balak, bachhaa*} and Marathi synset {*mulagaa, poragaa, por*} are linked as shown in Fig. 15.1. The Marathi word '*mulagaa'* is linked to the Hindi word '*ladakaa*' which is its exact lexical substitution.

Algorithm:

Suppose words *u* in language L_1 and *v* in language L_2 are translations of each other and their senses are required. The EM-based formulation is as follows:

E-Step:

$$p(S^{L_1} \mid u) = \frac{\sum_v p\left(\pi_{L_2}(S^{L_1} \mid v\right).\#(v)}{\sum_{S_i^{L1}} \sum_x p\left(\pi_{L_2}(S_i^{L_1} \mid x\right).\#(x)}$$

Fig. 15.1 Synset-aligned multilingual dictionary

Concepts	L1 (English)	L2 (Hindi)	L3 (Marathi)
04321: a youthful male person	{malechild, boy}	{लड़का (*ladkaa*), बालक (*baalak*), बच्चा (*bachchaa*)}	{मुलगा (*mulgaa*), पोरगा (*porgaa*), पोर (*por*)}

where

$S_i^{L_1} \in synsets_{L_1}(u)$
$v \in crosslinks_{L_2}\left(u, S^{L_1}\right)$
$x \in crosslinks_{L_2}\left(u, S_i^{L_1}\right)$

M-Step:

$$\left(S^{L_2} \mid v\right) = \frac{\sum_u p\left(\pi_{L_1}(S^{L_2} \mid u\right).\#(u)}{\sum_{S_i^{L_2}} \sum_y p\left(\pi_{L_1}(S_i^{L_2} \mid y\right).\#(y)}$$

where

$S_i^{L_2} \in synsets_{L_2}(v)$
$u \in crosslinks_{L_1}\left(v, S^{L_2}\right)$
$y \in crosslinks_{L_1}\left(v, S_i^{L_2}\right)$

Here,

- '#' indicates the raw count
- $crosslinks_{L_1}\left(u, S^{L_2}\right)$ is the set of possible translations of the word u from language L_1 to L_2 in the sense S^{L_2}
- $\pi_{L_2}(S^{L_1})$ means the linked synset of the sense S^{L_1} in L_2

E and M steps are symmetric except for the change in language. In both the steps, they estimate sense distribution in one language using raw counts of translations in another language.

But this approach has the following limitations:

- **Poor performance on verbs**: This approach gives poor performance on verbs (25–38 %).
- **Same sense throughout the corpus**: Every occurrence of a word is tagged with the single sense found by the algorithm, throughout the corpus.
- **Closed loop of translations**: This formulation does not work for some common words which have the same translations in all senses. For example, the verb *karanaa* in Hindi has two different senses in the corpus, viz. '*to do*' (S_1) and '*to make*' (S_2). In both these senses, it gets translated as *karane* in Marathi. The word *karane* also back-translates to *karanaa* in Hindi through both its senses. In this case, the formulation works out as follows:
  The probabilities are initialized uniformly. Hence, $p(S_1 \mid karanaa) = p(S_2 \mid karanaa) = 0.5$. Now, in the first iteration, the sense of *karane* will be estimated as follows (E-step):

$$p(S_1 \mid karane) = \frac{p(S_1 \mid karanaa) * \#(karanaa)}{\#(karanaa)} = 0.5$$

$$p(S_2 \mid karane) = \frac{p(S_2 \mid karanaa) * \#(karanaa)}{\#(karanaa)} = 0.5$$

Similarly, in M-step, we will get $p(S_1 \mid karanaa) = p(S_2 \mid karanaa) = 0.5$. Eventually, it will end up with initial probabilities and no strong decision can be made.

To address these problems, we introduced contextual clues in their formulation by using semantic relatedness. Our modified approach overcomes all the mentioned limitations.

15.4.1.2 Modified Bilingual EM Approach Using WordNet Similarity

We, Bhingardive et al. (2013), introduced the context in the basic EM formulation stated earlier and treat the context as a bag of words. We assume that each word in the context influences the sense of the target word independently. Hence,

$$p(S \mid w, C) = \prod_{c_i \in C} p(S \mid w, c_i)$$

where w is the target word, S is one of the candidate synsets of w, C is the set of words in the context (sentence in our case), and C_i is one of the context words.

Suppose we would have sense-tagged data, $p(S \mid w, c)$ could have been computed as:

$$p(S \mid w, c) = \frac{\#(S, w, c)}{\#(w, c)}$$

But since the sense-tagged corpus is not available, we cannot find $\#(S, w, c)$ from the corpus directly. However, we can estimate it using the comparable corpus in other language. Here, we assume that given a word and its context word in language L_1, the sense distribution in L_1 will be the same as that in L_2 given the translation of a word and the translation of its context word in L_2. But these translations can be ambiguous; hence, we can use expectation maximization approach similar to Khapra et al. (2011) as follows:

E-Step:

$$p\left(S^{L_1} \mid u, a\right) = \frac{\sum_{v,b} p\left(\pi_{L_2}(S^{L_1} \mid v, b\right).\sigma(v, b)}{\sum_{S_i^{L_1}} \sum_{x,b} p\left(\pi_{L_2}(S_i^{L_1} \mid x, b\right).\sigma(x, b)}$$

where

$\mathrm{S_i^{L_1}} \in \mathrm{synsets_{L_1}(u)}$
$\mathrm{a} \in \mathrm{context(u)}$
$v \in crosslinks_{L_2}(u, S^{L_1})$
$\mathrm{b} \in \mathrm{crosslinks_{L_2}(a)}$
$x \in crosslinks_{L_2}(u, S_i^{L_1})$

$crosslinks_{L_1}(a, S^{L_2})$ is the set of all possible translations of the word a from L_1 to L_2 in all its senses. $\sigma(\mathrm{v}, \mathrm{b})$ is the semantic relatedness between the senses of v and senses of b. Since, v and b go over all possible translations of u and a respectively,

$\sigma(\mathrm{v}, \mathrm{b})$ has the effect of indirectly capturing the semantic similarity between the senses of u and a. A symmetric formulation in the M-step below takes the computation back from language L_2 to language L_1. The semantic relatedness comes as an additional weighing factor, capturing context, in the probabilistic score.

M-Step:

$$p\left(S^{L_2} \mid v, b\right) = \frac{\sum_{u,a} p\left(\pi_{L_1}(S^{L_2} \mid u, a\right).\sigma(u, a)}{\sum_{S_i^{L_2}} \sum_{y,a} p\left(\pi_{L_1}(S_i^{L_2} \mid y, a\right).\sigma(y, a)}$$

where

$\mathrm{S}_{\mathrm{i}}^{\mathrm{L}_2} \in \mathrm{synsets}_{\mathrm{L}_2}(\mathrm{v})$
$b \in \mathrm{context}(\mathrm{v})$
$u \in crosslinks_{L_2}(v, S^{L_2})$
$\mathrm{a} \in \mathrm{crosslinks}_{\mathrm{L}_1}(\mathrm{b})$
$y \in crosslinks_{L_1}(v, S_i^{L_2})$

$\sigma(\mathrm{u}, \mathrm{a})$ is the semantic relatedness between the senses of u and senses of a and contributes to the score like $\sigma(\mathrm{v}, \mathrm{b})$. Note how the computation moves back and forth between L_1 and L_2 considering translations of both target words and their context words.

In the above formulation, we could have considered the term $\#(word, context_{word})$ (i.e., the co-occurrence count of the translations of the word and the context word) instead of $\sigma(\mathrm{word}, \mathrm{context}_{\mathrm{word}})$ but it is very unlikely that every translation of a word will co-occur with every translation of its context word considerable number of times. This term may make sense only if we have arbitrarily large comparable corpus in the other language.

The semantic relatedness is computed by taking the inverse of the length of the shortest path among two senses in the WordNet graph Pedersen et al. (2005). All the semantic relations (including cross-part-of-speech links), viz. *hypernymy*, *hyponymy*, *meronymy*, *entailment*, and *attribute*, are used for computing the semantic relatedness. Sense scores thus obtained are used to disambiguate all words in the corpus. We consider all the content words from the context for disambiguation of a word. The winner sense is the one with the highest probability.

Experiments and Results

We used freely available in-domain comparable corpora[1] in Hindi and Marathi languages. These corpora are available for health and tourism domains. The dataset is the same as that used in Khapra et al. (2011) in order to compare the performance.

Tables 15.1 and 15.2 compare the performance of the following two approaches:

- EM-C (EM with context): Our modified approach
- EM: Basic EM-based approach by Khapra et al. (2011)

[1]http://www.cfilt.iitb.ac.in/wsd/annotated_corpus/

Table 15.1 Comparison (F-score) of EM-C and EM for health domain

Algorithm	Hin-health					Mar-health				
	Noun	Adv	Adj	Verb	Overall	Noun	Adv	Adj	Verb	Overall
EM-C	59.82	67.80	56.66	**60.38**	59.63	62.90	62.54	53.63	**52.49**	59.77
EM	60.68	67.48	55.54	**25.29**	58.16	63.88	58.88	55.71	**35.60**	58.03
WFS	53.49	73.24	55.16	**38.64**	54.46	59.35	67.32	38.12	**34.91**	52.57
RB	32.52	45.08	35.42	**17.93**	33.31	33.83	38.76	37.68	**18.49**	32.45

Table 15.2 Comparison (F-score) of EM-C and EM for tourism domain

Algorithm	Hin-tourism					Mar-tourism				
	Noun	Adv	Adj	Verb	Overall	Noun	Adv	Adj	Verb	Overall
EM-C	62.78	65.10	54.67	**55.24**	60.70	59.08	63.66	58.02	**55.23**	58.67
EM	61 16	62.31	56.02	**31.85**	57.92	59.66	62.15	58.42	**38.33**	56.90
WFS	63.98	75.94	52.72	**36.29**	60.22	61.95	62.39	48.29	**46.56**	57.47
RB	32.46	42.56	36.35	**18.29**	32.68	33.93	39.30	37.49	**15.99**	32.65

- WFS: WordNet first sense baseline.
- RB: Random baseline.

Results clearly show that EM-C outperforms EM especially in case of verbs in all language-domain pairs. In health domain, verb accuracy is increased by 35 % for Hindi and 17 % for Marathi, while in tourism domain, it is increased by 23 % for Hindi and 17 % for Marathi. The overall accuracy is increased by (1.8–2.8 %) for health domain and (1.5–1.7 %) for tourism domain. Since there are a less number of verbs, the improved accuracy is not directly reflected in the overall performance.

Error Analysis and Phenomena Study

Our approach tags most of the instances of a word depending on its context as opposed to basic EM approach. For example, consider the following sentence from the tourism domain:

- *vaha patte khel rahe the (They were playing cards/leaves)*

Here, the word *patte* (plural form of *pattaa*) has two senses, viz. *leaf* and *playing_card*. In tourism domain, the *leaf* sense is more dominant. Hence, basic EM will tag *pattaa* with *leaf* sense. But its true sense is *playing_card*. The true sense is captured only if the context is considered. Here, the word *khelanaa* (to play) (root form of *khel*) endorses the *playing_card* sense of the word *khelanaa*. This phenomenon is captured by our approach through semantic relatedness. But there are certain cases where our algorithm fails. For example, consider the following sentence:

- *vaha peda ke niche patte khel rahe the (They were playing cards/leaves below the tree)*

Here, two strong context words *peda* (tree) and *khelanaa* (play) are influencing the sense of the word *pattaa*. Semantic relatedness between *peda* (tree) and *pattaa* (leaf) is more than that of *khelanaa* (play) and *pattaa* (playing_card). Hence, the *leaf* sense is assigned to *pattaa*. This problem occurred because we considered the context as a bag of words. This problem can be solved by considering the semantic structure of the sentence. In this example, the word *pattaa* (leaf/playing_card) is the subject of the verb *khelanaa* (to play), while *peda* (tree) is not even in the same clause with *pattaa* (leaf/playing_card). Thus, we could consider *khelanaa* (to play) as the stronger clue for its disambiguation.

Our formulation solves the problems of 'inhibited progress due to lack of translation diversity' and 'uniform sense assignment irrespective of context' that the previous EM-based formulation of Khapra et al. suffers from. More importantly, our accuracy on verbs is much higher and more than the state of the art, to the best of our knowledge.

Here, we saw how the cross-linked structure of IndoWordNet is helpful for finding the translations in bilingual WSD. Let us see our another approach which uses various semantic relations from IndoWordNet for creating the sense embeddings and then used for finding the most frequent sense of a word.

15.4.2 Unsupervised MFS Detection for WSD

This approach proposed by Bhingardive et al. (2015) needs only untagged corpora. Here, features from Hindi WordNet (which is a part of IndoWordNet) are used for detecting the most frequent sense (MFS) of a word. Using a large amount of untagged corpora, we first train word embeddings. Then, sense embeddings are created using various semantic features from the IndoWordNet. We compare word embeddings of a word with sense embeddings to get the most frequent sense. Approach can be easily ported to various domains and across languages.

15.4.2.1 Most Frequent Sense (MFS)

The MFS baseline is often hard to beat for any WSD system, and it is considered as the strongest baseline in WSD (Agirre and Edmonds 2007). It has been observed that supervised WSD approaches generally outperform the MFS baseline, whereas unsupervised WSD approaches fail to beat this baseline. The MFS baseline can be easily created if we have a large amount of sense-annotated corpora. The frequencies of word senses are obtained from the available sense-annotated corpora. Creating such a costly resource for all languages is infeasible, looking at the amount of time and money required. Hence, unsupervised approaches have received widespread attention as they do not use any sense-annotated corpora.

McCarthy et al. (2007) proposed an unsupervised approach for finding the predominant sense using an automatic thesaurus. They used WordNet similarity for identifying the predominant sense. Their approach outperforms the SemCor baseline for words with SemCor frequency below five. Buitelaar and Sacaleanu (2001) presented the knowledge-based approach for ranking GermaNet synsets on specific domains. Lapata and Brew (2004) worked on detecting the predominant sense of verbs where verb senses are taken from the Levin classes. Our approach is similar to that of McCarthy et al. (2007) as we are also learning predominant senses from the untagged text. Our approach is also unsupervised for detecting the most frequent sense for Hindi language.

15.4.2.2 Word Embeddings

Word embeddings have recently gained popularity among natural language processing community (Bengio et al. 2003; Collobert et al. 2011). They are based on distributional hypothesis which works under the assumption that similar words occur in similar contexts (Harris 1968). Word embeddings represent each word with a low-dimensional real-valued vector with similar words occurring closer in that space.

In our approach, we use the word embedding of a given word and compare it with all its sense embeddings to find the most frequent sense of that word. Sense embeddings are created using the IndoWordNet-based features in light of the extended Lesk algorithm (Banerjee and Pedersen 2003).

15.4.2.3 Training of Word Embeddings

Word embeddings for Hindi have been trained using *word2vec*[2] tool (Mikolov et al. 2013). This tool provides two broad techniques for creating word embeddings: continuous bag of words (CBOW) and Skip-gram model. The CBOW model predicts the current word based on the surrounding context, whereas the Skip-gram model tries to maximize the probability of a word based on the other words in the same sentence (Mikolov et al. 2013). Word embeddings for Hindi have been trained on Bojar et al. (2014) corpus. This corpus contains 44 million sentences. Here, the Skip-gram model is used for obtaining word embeddings. The dimensions are set as 200 and the window size as 7 (i.e., $w = 7$). We used the test of similarity to establish the correctness of these word embeddings. We observed that given a word and its embedding, the list of words ranked by similarity score had at the top of the list those words which were actually similar to the given word.

[2]https://code.google.com/p/word2vec/

15.4.2.4 Sense Embedding Creation

Sense embeddings are similar to word embeddings which are low-dimensional real-valued vectors. Sense embeddings are obtained by taking the average of word embeddings of each word in the sense bag (Chen et al. 2014). The sense bag for each sense of a word is obtained by extracting the context words from the Hindi WordNet (a part of IndoWordNet) such as synset members (S), content words in the gloss (G), content words in the example sentence (E), synset members of the hypernymy–hyponymy synsets (HS), content words in the gloss of the hypernymy–hyponymy synsets (HG), and content words in the example sentence of the hypernymy–hyponymy synsets (HE). We consider word embeddings of all words in the sense bag as a cluster of points and choose the sense embedding as the centroid of this cluster.

Consider a word w with k senses $\mathrm{ws}_{S_1}, \mathrm{ws}_{S_2}, \ldots, \mathrm{ws}_{S_k}$ taken from the Hindi WordNet. Sense embeddings are created using the following formula:

$$vec(w_{S_i}) = \frac{\sum_{x \in SB(w_{S_i})} vec(x)}{N}$$

where N is the number of words present in the sense bag $SB(w_{S_i})$ and $SB(w_{S_i})$ is the sense bag for the sense w_{S_i} which is given as,

$$SB(w_{S_i} = \{x \mid x \in Features\,(w_{S_i})\}$$

where Features (w_{S_i}) includes the Hindi WordNet-based features for w_{S_i} which are mentioned earlier in this section.

As shown in Fig. 15.2, consider the sense bag created for the senses of a word *kaatanaa*. Here, the word *kaatanaa* has three senses: S_1: *to bite*, S_2: *to cut,* and S_3: *to spend or to pass time.* The corresponding word embeddings of all words in the sense bag will act as a cluster as shown in the figure. Here, there are three clusters with centroids C_1, C_2, C_3 which correspond to the three sense embeddings of the word *kaatanaa*.

15.4.2.5 Most Frequent Sense Identification

For a given word w, we obtain its word embeddings and sense embeddings as discussed earlier. We treat the most frequent sense identification problem as finding the closest cluster centroid (i.e., sense embedding) with respect to a given word. We use the cosine similarity as the similarity measure. The most frequent sense is obtained by using the following formulation:

$$MFS_w = argmax_{w_{S_i}} cos(vec\,(w),\, vec\,(w_{S_i}))$$

where $vec\,(w)$ is the word embedding for word w, w_{S_i} is the ith sense for word w, and $vec\,(w_{S_i})$ is the sense embedding for w_{S_i}. As shown in Fig. 15.2, the word embedding

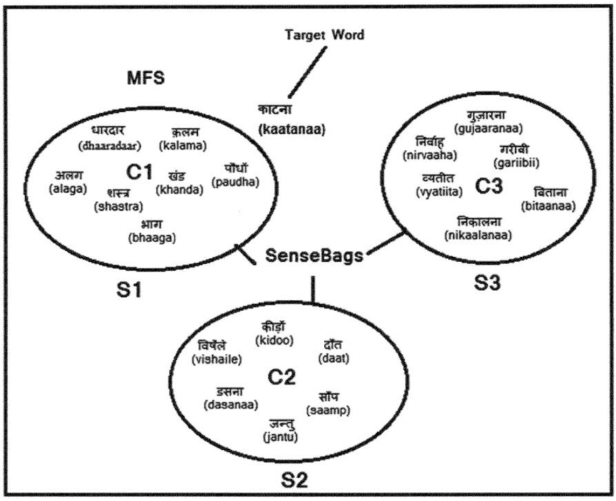

Fig. 15.2 Most frequent sense (MFS) detection using word embeddings and sense embeddings

of the word *kaatanaa* is closer to the centroid C1 as compared to the centroids C_2 and C_3. Therefore, the MFS of the word *kaatanaa* is chosen as S1:*to cut*.

15.4.2.6 Experiments

We performed several experiments to compare the accuracy of UMFS-WE for Hindi WSD. The experiments are restricted to only polysemous nouns. A sense-tagged newspaper dataset of around 80,000 polysemous noun entries was used. This is an in-house data. To compare the performance of UMFS-WE approach, we used the WFS baseline. In the WFS baseline, the first sense in the wordnet is used for WSD. For Hindi, the WFS is manually determined by a lexicographer based on his/her intuition. Results on the newspaper dataset are given in Table 15.3. The UMFS-WE approach achieves F-1 of 62 % for the newspaper dataset.

We have performed several tests using various combinations of wordnet-based features for Hindi WSD, as shown in Table 15.4. We study its impact on the performance of the system for WSD and present a detailed analysis below.

Our approach, UMFS-WE, achieves better performance for Hindi WSD as compared to the WFS baseline. We used various Hindi WordNet-based features for comparing results. It is observed that synset members alone are not sufficient for identifying the most frequent sense. This is because some of synsets have a very small number of synset members. Synset members along with gloss members improve results as gloss members are more direct in defining the sense. The

Table 15.3 Results of Hindi WSD on the newspaper dataset

System	P	R	F-score
UMFS-WE	62.43	61.58	**62.00**
WFS	61.73	59.31	60.49

Table 15.4 UMFS-WE accuracy on Hindi WSD with various WordNet features

WordNet features	P	R	F-score
S	51.73	38.13	43.89
S+G	53.31	52.39	52.85
S+G+E	56.61	55.84	56.22
S+C+E+HS	59.53	58.72	59.12
S+G+E+HG	60.57	59.75	60.16
S+G+E+HE	60.12	59.3	59.71
S+G+E+HS+HG	57.59	56.81	57.19
S+G+E+HS+HE	58.93	58.13	58.52
S+C+E+HG+HE	**62.43**	**61.58**	**62.00**
S+G+E+HS+HG+HE	58.56	57.76	58.16

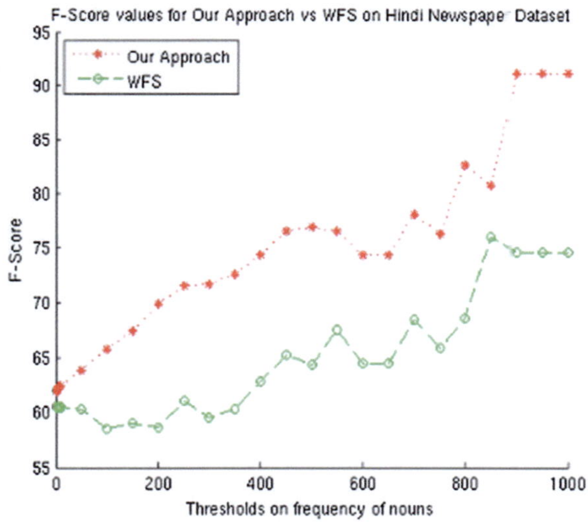

Fig. 15.3 UMFS-WE accuracy on Hindi WSD for words with various frequency thresholds in newspaper dataset

other reason is to bring down the impact of topic drift which may have occurred because of polysemous synset members. Similarly, it is observed that adding hypernym–hyponym gloss members gives better performance compared to hypernym–hyponym synset members. Example sentence members also provide additional information in determining the MFS of a word, which further improves the results. On the whole, we achieve the best performance when S, G, E, HG, and HE features are used together. This is shown in Table 15.4.

Also, we have calculated the F-1 score for increasing thresholds on the frequency of nouns appearing in the corpus. This is depicted in Fig. 15.3. Here, in the plot, it is clearly shown that as the frequency of nouns in the corpus increases, our approach outperforms baselines.

As opposed to baselines, our approach gives a feasible way to extract predominant senses in an unsupervised setup. Our approach is domain independent so that it can be very easily adapted to a domain-specific corpus. To get the domain-specific word embeddings, we simply have to run the *word2vec* program on the domain-specific corpus. The domain-specific word embeddings can be used to get the MFS for the domain of interest. Our approach is language independent.

15.5 Summary

In this chapter, we have highlighted the role of IndoWordNet for performing word sense disambiguation for Indian languages. IndoWordNet is used as a sense repository which consists of unique concepts, its semantic relations, lexical relations between words, etc. We have presented two major unsupervised approaches for WSD which use IndoWordNet sense repository.

In the first approach, a context-based bilingual WSD is used where two languages help each other in performing WSD. This is done using the linked properties of IndoWordNet. This approach relies on a key idea that, within a domain, a sense distribution and co-occurrence sense distribution remain the same across languages. Here, we have used EM-based algorithm for finding the sense distribution using the linked WordNets. This approach outperformed the basic bilingual EM-based WSD, especially for verbs.

In the second approach, the most frequent sense is detected by exploiting the usage of word embeddings and sense embeddings. The sense embeddings are created using various semantic features of wordnet, viz. gloss, example sentences, synonyms, hyponyms and hypernyms. This approach compares word embeddings with sense embeddings to obtain the most frequent sense. We have tested this approach on Hindi WSD, and the results are found to be very impressive. This proves that the word embeddings capture the most frequent sense of words.

Hence, we can say that the unsupervised approaches are better alternatives than supervised approaches as they do not require any sense-annotated corpora whose creation needs lots of manual efforts. The two approaches that are described above are found to be very useful invention for the NLP researches and can be used or extended further for their research purpose, in future.

References

Agirre, E., & Edmonds, P. (2007). *Word sense disambiguation: Algorithms and applications.* (Vol. 33). Springer Science and Business Media.

Agirre, E., & de Lacalle, O. L. (2009). Supervised domain adaption for wsd. *Proceedings of the 12th Conference of the European Chapter of the Association for Computational Linguistics* (pp. 42–50). Association for Computational Linguistics.

Banerjee, S., & Pedersen, T. (2003). Extended gloss overlaps as a measure of semantic relatedness. *In IJCAI,* (Vol. 3, pp. 805–810).

Bengio, Y., Ducharme, R., Vincent, P., & Janvin, C. (2003). A neural probabilistic language model. *The Journal of Machine Learning Research,* (pp. 1137–1155).

Bhattacharyya, P. (2010). *IndoWordNet.* Lexical Resources Engineering Conference (LREC). Malta, May.

Bhingardive, S., Shaikh, S., & Bhattacharyya, P. (2013). *Neighbors Help: Bilingual unsupervised WSD using context.* Sofia, Bulgaria: Association for Computational Linguistics.

Bhingardive, S., Singh, D., Rudramurty, V., Redkar, H. H., & Bhattacharyya, P. (2015). *Unsupervised Most Frequent Sense Detection using Word Embeddings.* Denver, Colorado: NAACL.

Bojar, O., Diatka, V., Rychlý, P., Straňák, P., Suchomel, V., Tamchyna, A., & Zeman, D. (2014). HindEnCorp-Hindi-English and Hindi-only corpus for machine translation. *Proceedings of the Ninth International Conference on Language Resources and Evaluation (LREC'14).*

Buitelaar, P., & Sacaleanu, B. (2001). Ranking and selecting synsets by domain relevance. *Proceedings of WordNet and Other Lexical Resources: Applications, Extensions and Customizations,* NAACL 2001 Workshop.

Chen, X., Liu, Z., & Sun, M. (2014). A unified model for word sense representation and disambiguation. *In EMNLP.*

Collobert, R., Weston, J., Bottou, L., Karlen, M., Kavukcuoglu, K., & Kuksa, P. (2011). *Natural language processing (almost) from Scratch.* CoRR, http://arxiv.org/abs/1103.0398.

Dagan, I., Itai, A., & Schwall, U. (1991). Two languages are more informative than one. *In Proceedings of the 29th Annual Meeting on Association for Computational Linguistics, ACL* (pp. 130–137).

Diab, M., & Resnik, P. (2002). An unsupervised method for word sense tagging using parallel corpora. *Proceedings of the 40th Annual Meeting on Association for Computational Linguistics, ACL'02* (pp. 255–262). Morristown, NJ, USA.

Giuliano, C., Gliozzo, A. M., & Strapparava, C. (2009). Kernel methods for minimally supervised wsd. *Computational Linguistics, 35*(4), 513–528.

Harris, Z. (1968). *Mathematical structures of language.* New York: Wiley.

Hiroyuki, K., & Morimoto, Y., (2002). Unsupervised word sense disambiguation using bilingual comparable Corpora. *Proceedings of the 19th International Conference on Computational Linguistics—Volume 1, COLING '02* (pp. 1–7). Stroudsburg, PA, USA: Association for Computational Linguistics.

Jain, A., & Lobiyal, D. K., (2015). *Unsupervised Hindi word sense disambiguation based on network agglomeration.* In Computing for Sustainable Global Development (INDIACom), 2015 2nd International Conference., pp. 195–200. IEEE.

Jimeno-Yepes, A. J., & Aronson, A. R. (2010). Knowledge-based biomedical word sense disambiguation: comparison of approaches. *BMC Bioinformatics, 11*(1).

Khapra, M., Bhattacharyya, P., Chauhan, S., Nair, S., & Sharma, A. (2008). Domain specific iterative word sense disambiguation in a multilingual setting. *Proceedings of International Conference on NLP (ICON 2008),* Pune, India.

Khapra, M., Joshi, S., & Bhattacharyya, P. (2011). It takes two to tango: A bilingual unsupervised approach for estimating sense distributions using expectation maximization. *Proceedings of 5th International Joint Conference on Natural Language Processing* (pp. 695–704), Chiang Mai, Thailand, November. Asian Federation of Natural Language Processing.

Lapata, M., & Brew, C. (2004). Verb class disambiguation using informative priors. *Computational Linguistics, 30*(1), 45–73.

Lee, Y. K., Ng, H. T., & Chia, T. K. (2004). Supervised word sense disambiguation with support vector machines and multiple knowledge sources. *Proceedings of Senseval-3: Third International Workshop on the Evaluation of Systems for the Semantic Analysis of Text* (pp. 137–140).

Lefever, E., & Hoste. V. (2010). Semeval-2010 task 3: cross-lingual word sense disambiguation. In: K. Erk & C. Strapparava (Eds.), *SemEval 2010: 5th International Workshop on Semantic Evaluation: Proceedings of the Workshop* (pp. 15–20). Association for Computational Linguistics (ACL).

Lesk, M. (1986). Automated sense disambiguation using machine-readable dictionaries: How to tell a pine cone from an ice cream cone. *Proceedings of the 1986 ACM SIGDOC Conference*, Toronto, Canada (pp. 24–26).

McCarthy, D., Koeling, R., Weeds, J., & Carroll, J. (2007). Unsupervised acquisition of predominant word senses. *Computational Linguistics, 33*(4), 553–590.

Mihalcea, R., (2006). *Knowledge-based methods for WSD*. Word Sense Disambiguation: Algorithms and Applications (pp. 107–131).

Mikolov, T., Chen, K., Corrado, G., & Dean, J. (2013). *Efficient estimation of word representations in vector space*. arXiv preprint arXiv:1301.3781.

Mishra, N., Yadav, S., & Siddiqui, T. J. (2009). An unsupervised approach to Hindi word sense disambiguation. *Proceedings of the First International Conference on Intelligent Human Computer Interaction* (pp. 327–335). India: Springer.

Mohanty, R., Bhattacharyya, P., Pande, P., Kalele, S., Khapra, M., & Sharma, A. (2008). Synset based multilingual dictionary: Insights, applications and challenges. *In Global Wordnet Conference*.

Ng, H. T., & Lee, H. B. (1996). Integrating multiple knowledge sources to disambiguate word sense: An exemplar-based approach. *Proceedings of the 34th annual meeting on Association for Computational Linguistics* (pp. 40–47). Morristown, NJ, USA: Association for Computational Linguistics.

Pedersen, T., Banerjee, S., & Patwardhan, S. (2005). *Maximizing Semantic Relatedness to Perform Word Sense Disambiguation.* Research Report UMSI 2005/25, University of Minnesota Supercomputing Institute, March.

Schütze, H. (1998). Automatic word sense discrimination. *Computational Linguistics, 24*(1), 97–123.

Singh, S., & Siddiqui, T. J. (2012). Evaluating effect of context window size, stemming and stop word removal on Hindi word sense disambiguation. *In International Conference on Information Retrieval and Knowledge Management (CAMP)* (pp. 1–5). IEEE.

Singh, S., Singh, V. K., & Siddiqui, T. J. (2013). Hindi Word Sense Disambiguation Using Semantic Relatedness Measure. *Multi-disciplinary Trends in Artificial Intelligence* (pp. 247–256). Berlin Heidelberg: Springer.

Sinha, M., Reddy, M., & Bhattacharyya, P. (2006). An approach towards construction and application of multilingual indo-wordnet. *3rd Global Wordnet Conference (GWC 06)*, Jeju Island, Korea.

Specia, L., Nunes, M. G., & Stevenson, M. (2005). Exploiting parallel texts to produce a multilingual sense tagged corpus for word sense disambiguation. *Proceedings of RANLP-05*, Borovets (pp. 525–531).

Véronis, J. (2004). Hyperlex: Lexical cartography for information retrieval. *Computer Speech and Language, 18*(3), 223–252.

Appendix
The Team of IndoWordNet

Team members	Affiliation
Aadil Amin Kak	Department of Linguistics University of Kashmir, Srinagar Jammu & Kashmir, India Email: aadil.kak@gmail.com Email: aadilaminkak@yahoo.com
Bhimasena Bhol	Centre for Applied Linguistics & Translation Studies, University of Hyderabad, India
Brijesh S. Bhatt	Department of Computer Engineering, Faculty of Technology, Dharmsinh Desai University, Nadiad, Gujarat, India Email: brij.s.bhatt@gmail.com Email: brij_bhatt@hotmail.com
C.K. Bhensdadia	Department of Computer Engineering, Faculty of Technology, Dharmsinh Desai University, Nadiad, Gujarat, India Email: ckbhensdadia@yahoo.co.in
Dinesh Chauhan	Department of Computer Engineering, Faculty of Technology, Dharmsinh Desai University, Nadiad, Gujarat, India
Farooq Ahmad	Department of Linguistics University of Kashmir, Srinagar Jammu & Kashmir, India
Jyoti D. Pawar	Department of Computer Science & Technology Goa University, Taleigao Plateau, Taleigao, Goa, India. Email: jdp@unigoa.ac.in Email: jyotidpawar@gmail.com

(continued)

N.S. Dash et al. (eds.), *The WordNet in Indian Languages*,
DOI 10.1007/978-981-10-1909-8

(continued)

Team members	Affiliation
K.P. Soman	Department of Computational Engineering and Networking, Amrita Vishwa Vidyapeetham, Ettimadai, Coimbatore 641105, Coimbatore, Tamil Nadu, India
Kirit Patel	Department of Computer Engineering, Faculty of Technology, Dharmsinh Desai University, Nadiad, Gujarat, India
Lata Popale	Department of Computer Science and Engineering Indian Institute of Technology-Bombay, Powai, Mumbai, India Email: popale.lata@gmail.com
Laxmi Kashyap	Department of Computer Science and Engineering, Indian Institute of Technology-Bombay, Powai, Mumbai, India Email: yupu@cse.iitb.ac.in
M.C. Kesava Murty	Department of Dravidian & Computational Linguistics Dravidian University, Kuppam - 517426 Email: kesavamurty.mc@gmail.com
Malhar Kulkarni	Department of Humanities and Social Sciences Indian Institute of Technology-Bombay, Powai, Mumbai, India Email: malhar@iitb.ac.in
Mansoor Farooq	Department of Linguistics University of Kashmir, Srinagar Jammu & Kashmir, India
Mazhar Mehdi Hussain	Centre of Indian Languages Jawaharlal Nehru University New Delhi, India Email: mazhar.jnu@gmail.com
Muneera Hakim	Department of Linguistics University of Kashmir, Srinagar Jammu & Kashmir, India
Nazima Mehdi	Department of Linguistics University of Kashmir, Srinagar Jammu & Kashmir, India Email: nazimamehdi@gmail.com
Niladri Sekhar Dash	Linguistic Research Unit Indian Statistical Institute 203, B.T. Road, Baranagar, Kolkata-700108, WB, India Email: ns_dash@yahoo.com

(continued)

(continued)

Team members	Affiliation
Panchanan Mohanty	Centre for Applied Linguistics & Translation Studies University of Hyderabad, Hyderabad-500046, Telangana, India Email: panchananmohanty@gmail.com
Parteek Kumar Bhatia	Department of Computer Science and Engineering Thapar University, Patiala Punjab, India Email: parteek.bhatia@thapar.edu
Pushpak Bhattacharyya	Department of Computer Science and Engineering Indian Institute of Technology-Bombay, Powai, Mumbai, India Email: pb@cse.iitb.ac.in
R.K. Sharma	School of Mathematics and Computer Applications Thapar University, Patiala. Mobile: 098722-02705 Email: rksharma@thapar.edu
Ramdas N. Karmali	Department of Computer Science & Technology Goa University, Taleigao Plateau, Taleigao, Goa, India. Email: rnk@unigoa.ac.in
Ramesh C. Malik	Centre for Applied Linguistics & Translation Studies University of Hyderabad, Hyderabad-500046, Telangana, India
Rizwanur Rahman	Centre for Arabic and African Studies Jawaharlal Nehru University New Delhi, India Email: rrahmanjnu@gmail.com
S. Rajendran	Department of Computational Engineering and Networking, Amrita Vishwa Vidyapeetham, Ettimadai, Coimbatore 641105, Coimbatore, Tamil Nadu, India Email: raj_ushush@yahoo.com
Salil Rajeev Joshi	Department of Computer Science and Engineering Indian Institute of Technology-Bombay Powai, Mumbai, India Email: salilj@cse.iitb.ac.in
Selvaraj Arulmozi	Centre for Applied Linguistics & Translation Studies University of Hyderabad, Hyderabad-500046, Telangana, India Email: arulmozi@uohyd.ac.in
Shantaram W. Walawalikar	Department of Computer Science & Technology Goa University, Taleigao Plateau, Taleigao, Goa, India

(continued)

(continued)

Team members	Affiliation
Shilpa N. Desai	Department of Computer Science & Technology Goa University, Taleigao Plateau, Taleigao, Goa, India
Sudha Bhingardive	Department of Computer Science and Engineering, Indian Institute of Technology-Bombay, Powai, Mumbai, India. Email: sudha@cse.iitb.ac.in
Languages	Institution
Bangla	Indian Statistical Institute, Kolkata
Gujarati	Dharmsinh Desai University, Nadiad
Hindi	Indian Institute of Technology-Bombay
Kashmiri	University of Kashmir, Srinagar
Konkani	Goa University, Goa
Malayalam	Amrita Vishwa Vidyapeetham, Coimbatore
Marathi	Indian Institute of Technology-Bombay
Odia	University of Hyderabad, Hyderabad
Punjabi	Thapar University, Patiala
Sanskrit	Indian Institute of Technology-Bombay
Telugu	Dravidian University, Kuppam
Urdu	Jawaharlal Nehru University, New Delhi

MIX
Papier aus verantwortungsvollen Quellen
Paper from responsible sources
FSC® C105338
FSC
www.fsc.org

If you have any concerns about our products,
you can contact us on
ProductSafety@springernature.com

In case Publisher is established outside the EU,
the EU authorized representative is:
Springer Nature Customer Service Center GmbH
Europaplatz 3, 69115 Heidelberg, Germany

Printed by Libri Plureos GmbH
in Hamburg, Germany